WISH AND WISDOM

BY JOSEPH JASTROW

Fact and Fable in Psychology

The Subconscious

Character and Temperament

The Qualities of Men

The Psychology of Conviction

Keeping Mentally Fit

Piloting Your Life

Managing Your Mind

The House That Freud Built

Wish and Wisdom

WISH AND WISDOM

EPISODES IN THE VAGARIES OF BELIEF

BY

JOSEPH JASTROW

D. APPLETON-CENTURY COMPANY

INCORPORATED

NEW YORK   LONDON

1935

TO

B. S. L.

SHARING MY CARES
A SHARE IN MY LABORS

FOREWORD

A PROLOGUE may serve to indicate how the author came to write his book and to what end. I have long been impressed with the possibilities of a wholly distinctive approach and treatment of the data of psychology. For intelligible reasons psychologists concentrate upon the exploration and ordering of the mental *processes*—how the mind, particularly our kind of mind, works. Anthropologists incline to the other emphasis—what minds, of all sorts and under all conditions, have turned out. The richest trail of mind is found in the mind-prints of beliefs that men have evolved and cherished and lived by. Long realizing that the story of mind could be told in dramatic episodes, I collected material for the project. Under a growing conviction of its value, I have carried it through to the present issue.

The standard order of thinking, such as leads to science, renders but a partial and far too favorable account of the mind's employment. A more adequate survey of the intellectual ventures appeals to the catholic psychologist and to the layman, to whom, in the familiar phrase, nothing human is alien. It must be conducted with not too close a regard for value. Its aim is to restore the natural perspective of the thinking *psyche,* which is the same that feels and acts. In that total aspect of mental behavior, misleads, futilities, and vagaries, great and small, come to the fore.

In appearance an excursion into erratic beliefs, the analysis of the believing mind remains the central theme of the survey. The psychological diagnosis is legible in the

continuity of the sections; they center about the typical
deflections that bend wisdom to wish and lead the thinker
astray. Embodied in episodes, they stand forth as charac-
ter-types in the composite picture of wayward beliefs. The
moral of the tale thus adorned points to the direction of
thinking to truthful and useful ends. Episodes and argument developed together; the collection grew out of an
interest, and in turn suggested an analysis.

The leading inclinations set the plots. First is *credulity,*
the will to believe—to believe not wisely but too well.
Second is the thrill of *marvel,* which is bound up with
magic. Magic is the primitive explanation of how things
happen; it is the child's favorite fiat, for there is no need
for a deeper philosophy. Against this *Weltanschauung,*
which begins in the nursery and continues by right of
primogeniture, the recognition of the true order of nature had to make its way. Close of kin is *transcendence,* the
crediting and claim of supernatural powers; and everywhere, once committed by whatever route, the *pre-*
possessed mind finds what it looks for. The beliefs chosen
among the many called owe their preferment to *congenial-*
ity of conclusion. One and another individual solution,
when pursued with fanatical singleness of mind, becomes
a *vagary;* while in all the higher reaches of thought there
is an appeal to evidence, a form of attempted *rationaliza-*
tion, which is the pride of intellect. Neither deadly sins
nor desirable practices, the *seven inclinations* form devia-
tions from the path of wisdom by yielding to wish.

Such are the ways of belief, and such are the belief-
products of the mind, presented by way of an expedition
arranged with a planned purpose. By mutual support of
episodes and argument, the design and furnishing of the
house of wishful wisdom came into being.

If reason be the staff of the mental life, it is even truer
than of the bodily one that man does not live by bread

alone. When human interests enter, pure reason is a figment of an abstracting philosopher. Large areas of the mental domain owe their cultivations to the proper use of the imagination, always dependent on a rich emotional soil; in others, reason must be subordinated to and congenialized with the deeper claims of a rich psyche.

My position as a naturalistic psychologist emphasizes that what nature has joined together, man, even though a psychologist, shall not put asunder. It is not Freud alone who recognizes that the genetic layers underlying the level at which reason usually works are fundamental to a wholesome personality. Rich feeling, sensitive æsthetic taste, a flair for the refinements of social intercourse, an appreciation of the complement of sex to sex give value to the sublimated *élan* of which they are the civilized issue. The cerebral man is not the whole of him, in many relations not the best of him. Fortunately, in our day the priority and potential dignity of the emotional life has come to its own, not always in a fortunate expression.

My theme concerns the life of reason, and the emotional encroachments, intrusions, distortions, and perversions that illustrate its course and endanger its sanity. Among the older emotionalisms that still survive is the interpretation of events for their personal significance, which William James, sympathetic with all varieties of human experience, called an abomination; and so it is. The inclinations around which I have gathered my sheaf of stories are of the same family, variously delinquent. An exposure of the emotionalisms that detract from the soundness and the wholeness of the intellectual life is entirely compatible with the highest regard for emotional man at his best. To that optimum of expression a loyalty to reason contributes notably. To the ancient ideal of a sound mind incorporated in a sound body may be added the ideal of sound emotions coördinated with sound reasoning.

The all-inclusive thesis is that wish diverts wisdom. There are included incidents of all ages and periods, focusing mainly upon forms of thinking that still influence our ways of belief. The evolution of the art of thinking and the contrasts of early and late mental habits will appear to every discerning reader. The essay aims to complete the psychology of "mind in the making" and its course, by which the mental stature has been increased and the world transformed. This hitherto neglected story of mind will, I trust, find its place in the "proper study of mankind," in that it reveals the liabilities attending our efforts to live a life of reason.

To supply so far as may be the scenery of beliefs, I have assembled pictorial mementoes of ideas, scenes, constructions, and of personages associated with them, which both validate the episodes and aid the reader to image the story. In some instances the data themselves were pictorial as well as picturesque, and in others the tale is more graphically rendered by the aid of illustrations. In assembling them I have borrowed freely from various sources and delved diligently in less commonly visited nooks of library stacks. My acknowledgments are indicated. I am indebted particularly to the courtesies of officials of the New York Public Library, including Miss Italia Lanz, who aided me in the preparation of illustrations. In form and content and in the vital matter of selection and presentation, the work owes much to the critical coöperation of Miss Elsie Junghans, who has been associated with all my writings of recent years.

JOSEPH JASTROW

CONTENTS

xi

ILLUSTRATIONS

WISH AND WISDOM

As the book consists of an argument illustrated by episodes and the episodes make the content, the reader will more readily follow the introductory chapter, "The Ways of Belief," if it is read after the tales than before, even though it serves as a sketch-map of the course. Each section is prefaced with a statement of the failing or fallacy of thought dominantly figuring in the episodes that follow. Tale and moral, doctrine and critique, will thus be associated in the reader's mind.

WISH AND WISDOM

CHAPTER I

THE WAYS OF BELIEF

Wisdom came to earth and could find no dwelling place.
—ENOCH.

Strange mixed harvests of thinking and guesswork go into
the making of civilization.—ISAIAH BOWMAN.

We always move on two feet—the two poles of knowledge and
desire.—ELIE FAURE.

IN THE BEGINNING was *Wish and Wisdom*—the
tree of knowledge and the tempting fruit. The successive sons of Adam and daughters of Eve sought both
the illumination and the consolation of belief. Beliefs arose
from age to age in companionate alliance of yearning and
learning. Knowledge and desire kept house together in the
same tenement of clay. From the beginning conflict was
inevitable in satisfying longings while heeding the increasing lessons of experience. The struggle for a life of reason
continued amid the clamoring demands of a many-sided
urge-driven nature.

Men believe with heart as well as head; they must believe concretely, eagerly, to carry on. The needs of com-
pleter living have the prior claim; men practise with what
knowledge they have, with such guesses of the meaning of
the whole as they can conceive. Ways of belief at every
age and stage of growth mark the course of mind in the
making. Primitive thinking is saturated with emotional
trends; yet it constantly reaches toward rules that seem to
prove and solutions that seem to explain. The supreme

1

human endowment is the capacity and the will to believe, no less unique because employed in strange as well as fair uses. The momentous story of man is that of the framer of beliefs.

WISH AND WISDOM

The historical drama of *Wish and Wisdom* portrays the belief-behavior of Man the Thinker, following his natural bent, corrected by experience, much of it of his own devising. The plot turns upon the mind's frailties in the quest of wisdom, ever spurred—even when confused—by wish. The record of the triumphs of mind appears in the discovery of the secrets of matter, in the progression of invention, in laws disclosed and rules applied to the enrichment and convenience of life. Practice is supported by theory, which is the racial intelligence quotient, the tests advancing from age to age. The movement is slow, halting, irregular; deflected by false leads, requiring constant corrections and revisions. One age spends its best energies in off-setting and outgrowing the errors of another.

The interests of psychology extend to all the products of mind in the entire panorama of belief. The clearing of the jungle is as expressive of mind-ways as the cultivation of the garden. Blossoms once cherished come to be neglected and rejected; the weeding is incessant. The unselected story of thinking is riddled with fantasies, follies, and errors. Yet it all belongs in the great epic of belief, whose plot is living—not by bread alone—and learning—before and beyond the three R's—with a romantic use of the imagination. Belief is vital, as much as is loving or constructing; reflections of the love-life and of the inventive flair direct the believing mind. In the ancestry of *our* ways of belief stands the long and tortuous route—the rough roads of mind—that beliefs have traveled before they became the well-paved highways and charted maps of our orderly and extensive knowledge. The story of belief is as glorious a tale as that of action and conquest, and vitally determines their course.

Man's mind is born as naked as his body. His beliefs— his mental clothing—are draped, like his costumes, to the human frame, serving its needs and covering its nakedness. How the mind shall be clothed is as far removed from an innate dispensation as are the changing dictates of fashion. With all the freedom of convention and the wide play of circumstance, there is a primal biological stress favoring wits, as climate and protection determine dress, with a place for inclination and conformity in both orders of invention. Nature places a premium on mind; it sets man the alternative, *Think or perish!* Weak in physique, lacking fangs, claws, horns, jaws, or limbs to compete on equal terms with his rivals of the jungle, poor in attack and escape, his biological capital is his wits; rightly and wrongly he has ever lived by them.

Outside the range of immediate needs, man has been free to believe according to his lights and inclinations; and the habit of belief thus inaugurated affected his entire mental world. Man the hunter and trapper became wise in the natural ways of animals; true to his own nature, he developed a mystic and mythical animal-lore of a wholly different, supernatural order. To insure the success of his hunting, he devised rituals derived from his beliefs. The human mind serves two masters: the stress of practice and the craving for a larger wisdom; ways of belief reflect both dominions.

Adventures in thinking are vital quests for guidance in action and for insight into order and destiny. How men lived outwardly when mind was young has been lavishly reconstructed for our privileged days in the show-cases of our great ethnological museums. To portray the inner life which directed and accompanied it would require an equally extensive Museum of Beliefs, less demonstrable but no less vital. The exhibits would illustrate not only what men believed, but what the inclinations that led to their devising and acceptance, what the sources of satisfaction, what the appeal of the solutions. Despite the zigzag and irregular course, there is a spiral procession of mind upward to an enlarging scope and command. Crude schemes, largely dominated by equally crude wish, give way to more critical interpretations, seeking increasing sanctions of evidence. Amid the débris of futile structures, enduring landmarks and monuments may be mapped in the eternal city of mind. Doctrines, systems, cults, institutions, and folk-ways no less, are deposits of racial wisdom, embodiments of once vital, still influential beliefs. The logical march of time is a profoundly significant record of man's psychology.

We stand at the end of the procession. We can no more divest ourselves of our sophisticated beliefs—the slow deposits of successive cumulations of thinking—than of our systems of communication and the paraphernalia and regalia of our ways of living. Battle-ax and ox-cart become extinct; machine-gun and automobile retain no vestige of their remote predecessors. But the older trends of belief survive, or are renewed in other guise. The sway of primitive belief holds on; it rules by the prior claim of original nature. The primitive jungle, never completely cleared, grows up again; the entanglements of mind in its quest for wisdom encounter the persistent solutions directed by wish. We are the heirs both of ancestral wish and of traditional wisdom.

THE CEREBRAL URGE

The Atlas that supports the world of thought is the cerebral urge. In that mysterious trend of protoplasm lies the germ of the mental life—the force that makes the mental world go round, go right or go wrong. There is a native push from within that leads the man-cub to observe and explore, in due course to imagine and explain, as well as to create and reflect. Only recently have thinkers felt the need of a name for the obvious urge to life: to Bergson an *élan vital*, to Freud a *libido*. There is a parallel urge to cerebrate. Eventually civilization erects homes to shelter and shrines to honor the cerebral urge: libraries, laboratories, universities, and institutions for shaping the instruments of social control through beliefs. To see the urge toward the mental life steadily and to see it whole, the focus of vision must not move too far from the common inclinations of the common man. What and how he believes determines the representative products of the cerebral urge. The study of beliefs has been too narrowly in the hands of philosophers, disposed to interpret the human scene by their own rationalizing patterns of thought. The resulting picture of the mind's occupations bears the stamp of the academic studio. The commoner harvests of folk-thinking have been too much neglected.

The cerebral urge with all its triumphs is not an unalloyed blessing. Professor Carveth Read, considering how much cerebration has been of the primitive order of magic and superstition, asks whether, with all its gain, this bigger brain of ours has been worth its cost; whether, in a cosmic mood, we may not envy our anthropoid ancestors, with brains enough to meet their realistic needs, untroubled by complexes, incapable of inventing either totems or taboos. For the dominance of the cerebral urge is represented anatomically in the overgrowth of the big brain, three times as large proportionately as that of our nearest of anthropoid kin. Sir Arthur Keith questions whether, in this heroic venture, nature has not overshot the mark. It is, however, millions of years too late to regret the incident which made possible at once the achievements of science and the follies and errors of human history. The direction of the cerebral urge is the persistent problem of education.

TWO ORDERS OF THINKING

Wish and Wisdom expresses the thesis that thinking has a double allegiance. An independent recognition of this fundamental principle is Freud's distinction of the "two orders of thinking"—*thinking* representing the entire mental movement. The mind has more than one gait. The primary and congenial order Freud describes as thinking by the "pleasure principle," allied to wish; the other is thinking by "the reality principle" in adjusting belief to fact. Thinking pleasurably is thinking wishfully, joy-riding with the mind. It is the mental movement of dreaming, revery, fantasy, with its undertone of desire. It does not have free rein, being held in check by prudence, convention, and the demands of rugged reality, which Freud in moral vein personifies as the "censor."

We are so primed to think of ourselves as rational that we forget the vast areas of emotional and imaginative thinking to which we are prone. *Rêverie*—which is French for dreamery—says the author of *The Mind in the Making*, "is at all times a potent and in many cases an omnipotent rival to every other kind of thinking"; practical issues interrupt it, require it to be "laboriously controlled and directed." It inevitably circles about the beloved Ego and its affairs. "We learn politely and generously to overlook this truth, but if we dare to think of it, it blazes forth like the noontide sun." It dominates unreservedly in early stages of the mental life. It appears in the child-pattern of mind-play, disposed to a primitive faith in magic; but even the child cannot linger there uninterruptedly. Strenuous and rigid thinking reality-wise shapes duty and work; increasing doses of logic are required to set and hold a course.

With every release from chores and errands, the mind strolls and wanders. Relaxed or off-guard, it reverts to the simpler, easier gait of revery. Without intent, and while on business bent, serious thinking admits the wishful, dream-toned themes of the agreeable conclusion. Much of what passes for thinking, alike in work and play, is a blend of the two orders, with *rêverie* dominant in the fusion. This confusing mixture, Henshaw Ward's *thobbing*, is defined as "*TH*inking out an *O*pinion that pleases us, and *B*elieving it." Unrestrained thobbing is exceptional; thob-tainted thinking most common. Following the trail of thought as long as the path is logically clear, the thinker thobs on in the underbrush.

The second order of the mental movement, which bears the sterling trade-mark of science and the visé of common sense, is thinking effectively. So far as we follow it, we lead a life of reason. Its central criterion is consistency and proof, not agreeableness. Though we ask the age-old question, What is truth? we approach it with a disciplined experience, as logicians, and as psychologists with an interest in the mind's frailties that invite the acceptance of dross for gold. We know well that truth or error is not a matter of black or white; its color-scheme is indefinitely complex. Error in many of its moods is a parody of truth. Logic has to tread as straight and narrow a path as virtue; The crooked ways of thought are as seductive as vice. Science stands as the monument of reality-tested thinking. It represents the heights to which the cerebral urge, rationally directed, can attain. It has come about by the "wise acceptance of evidence."

SUBJECTIVISM

The path that leads from the primary, imaginative mental movement broadens into *subjectivism*, which is a formal name for a familiar product. It results from the tendency to project one's imaginings upon the world. To distinguish the subjective—which is what the mind puts into the picture—from the objective—which is what is there offered for its contemplation—is one of the older tests of sanity. If applied too rigidly, it would decimate the ranks of the sane. There are degrees and varieties of subjectivism, as of prejudices and prepossessions, delusions and hallucinations, distortions, and imaginings—subjectivisms all, even to the paranoid system which for the patient becomes his view of life. Extreme subjectivisms are readily recognized; when slight, vague, insidious, they escape our notice. The question is fanciful but suggestive whether a spider endowed with consciousness would know that the splendid and convenient web serving as his habitat is his own construction. If so, he would be more knowing than many a theorist who himself spins a web that he accepts as a discovery. Dr. Bleuler, psychiatrist, calls this type of self-spun thinking *autistic,* and does not limit it to asylum products of schemes and delusions. Many prepossessions—and vagaries particularly—that form the episodes of erratic psychology are markedly autistic; they reveal no sense of distinction between what is constructed and what is found. When Dr. Bleuler calls the same subjective products *dereistic,* he names them for their departure from reality. Objective and subjective are like Caesar and God; the problem is to render unto each what to each belongs.

Subjectivism in its varied moods and tenses affects ways of belief from fantasy to philosophy, from delusion to pseudo-science. It forms one of the great distortions of conclusions. Rooted in the one order of thinking—alias dreaming—it is grafted upon the other—serious, objective thinking—to its undoing so far as meeting the criteria of truth. There is an autistic spider in many if not every mind, often an ambitious one, converting an attempt at higher wisdom into higher folly.

JUNGLE MAGIC

In its belief-habits the human mind has emerged from jungle magic. Primitive explanations proceed upon the basis of a hidden virtue or *mana,* which assumes an over-world from which it derives. Sorceries, incantations, mystic ceremonies, magic prescriptions, totems, and taboos express the primitive supernatural; and it is all *psychic* in its pattern of operation. This is what is meant by animism —that the primitive world is a soul-world. Mana is sought and avoided; like good and evil fate, it is dispensed as reward and punishment. It extends to all the world, animate and inanimate, for all nature is conceived as animated by an indwelling spirit.

As applied to healing, mana is "the mighty medicine," a term which Giddings uses for the entire range of magic influences. "It is a child of fear. It was born in the jungle and reared in the bush.... It is vouched for by doctors of magic, heirs and assigns of the medicine-man." It survives as superstition, at times as crude as that of the jungle, more commonly reduced to a misty faith in another order of cause and effect than directs the usual course of nature.

However real our kinship with a remote mental past, our habit of mind, when prone to accept wishful solutions, is no longer that of voodoo and fetish. This manner of belief has passed through many crucibles in the long stages of "our credulous heritage." It survives as a lingering inclination to recognize exceptional varieties of relation in an otherwise natural world; to reserve an area of belief for a lost Paradise. But it contributes no less, for all its refinement, to error and confusion. The sponsors of the anti-natural have profited by the advances of natural knowledge; they are as sophisticated as scientific thinkers; their name is legion, and they are found in many camps. They may be allied with ignorance in perpetuating cults of character-reading and fortune-telling; they may be devotees of transcendence, believing in clairvoyance, thought-forms and psychometry; they may be rationalistic advocates of ectoplasm and psychic structures; they may be modern occultists, presenting new varieties of ancient fantasies. In its conflict with science, superstition, it has been said, loses every battle, but wins the war.

THE STREAM OF BELIEF

The material of *Wish and Wisdom* is carried in the stream of belief. In it two main currents may be detected—*folklore*, as handed down by tradition, and the systematized body of *doctrine*. Folk belief forms an authentic product of the psyche at work. It has its own way of interpreting experience, shapes its own traditions, and develops its own criteria of evidence. It has a formidable power of imagination and a tenacious hold. Its logic embodies the ways of wish-wisdom. The folk-mind produces werewolves and witches, haunted houses and ghosts, premonitions and prophecies, blessings and blights, the evil eye and the protecting charm, mascots and hoodoos, emblems and magic words, customs innumerable and superstitions inexhaustible, contributing richly to the dramatic wealth of beliefdom.

It proceeds by the logic of analogy, resemblance, hidden connection, congenial conclusion. It appears in the "Adirondack" mind of a guide who "trolled" for the body of a drowned man by means of a floating cork, which "by the power of the human brain" would be drawn downward when passing over the corpse. The folk-mind, though it works largely by recipes, considered tried and true, also devises doctrine—a principle to go by—which may be as assumptive as "the power of the human brain." Adepts in folk-wisdom acquire prestige and authority; though the belief-habits travel mainly on their own credentials. They find allies in ignorance and credulity; their assurance is that of an observed and credited order of event. The "Adirondack" habit extends from the backwoods to the sophisticated haunts of men.

The doctrinal mind retains the impress of jungle magic. Primitive doctrines follow folklore clues; they deal with common hopes and fears and the desire for understanding. The adept mind, at whatever level of culture, makes a profession of pondering, explaining, advising, systematizing. Mind-lore grows as do rite and custom, by elaboration. Astrology is a product of the doctrinal mind; the horoscope is quite beyond the range of invention of the folkmind, which reads the future as assuredly in simpler signs. It is through the contributions of the adept doctrinal mind, strongly affected by jungle magic, that new jungles arise, and older pseudo-sciences reappear, claiming the prestige of science in our tutored days. The complications and authority of learning conceal the weak analogies and veiled assumptions.

Both folk-mind and doctrinal mind are impressed with the power of words. Sesames, incantations, words tabooed and words sacred, are stepping-stones to mystic formulae and momentous occult concepts of an "astral" plane. Because so articulate, the doctrinal mind crowds the pages of futile cerebration. The story of belief is replete with verbal magic.

Prominent in the stream of belief is the dogma of vested interest, which—so largely a clash of scientific and theological opinion—falls outside the frame of my project. Dogma blocks inquiry, delays and misleads. It enlists the instituted powers to enforce opinion or give prestige to doctrine, to the further confusion of solutions. Central in importance to the historian of belief, its course interests the psychologist for the motives by which it prevails. Earlier cosmologists made the earth central as the dwelling place of man, and made man the lord of creation. Astronomy reduced the earth to a minor planet, and geology minimized human generations; in due course evolution established relations of men and apes. These were shocks to human dignity, decentralizing the place of man. Dogmatic intrusion, moral intrusion, occult intrusion, glorified, prettified, and falsified the order of nature. The rationalistic falsification is most germane to the stream of belief; it appears repeatedly in the sheaf of episodes of strange doctrines and weird wisdoms.

MIND IN THE MAKING

James Harvey Robinson finds "four historical layers underlying the minds of civilized men—the animal mind, the child mind, the savage mind and the [early] traditional civilized mind." These heritages are predominantly of ways of belief. Our minds as we use them are animalic, as are the features of our bodies, in general structure; our minds remain childish and child-like in a hundred ways, primitive in a thousand; to which organic heritage we add the load of early stages of reflection and the lag of tradition.

If we could assemble and gage the total mass of thinking that has gone on through the ages, shaping belief and behavior, hopes and fears, institutions and ways of living, by far the greater volume of it would be the product of the feebly-tutored, strongly traditioned folk-mind with its predilection for guess and fantasy and faith. At each stage and increasingly, it is markedly modified by the several instruments of schooling which civilization has brought into being for the purpose of rationalizing life. Yet the thinking of all the racial yesterdays and even of today still reflects the folk-mind level. It is strongly tinctured with the early phases of human interest and the simpler sets of mind.

Thinking is a fine art, the "wise acceptance of evidence,"

a difficult ideal. Only a minority have rigidly schooled, critically cultivated minds emancipated from these several survivals; for the variation in capacity to lead a life of reason is as conspicuous and notable a feature of the human species as the gift of reason itself. Most of us who succeed reasonably in guiding living by thinking, are, however, not grossly under the influence of the "historical layers" of our minds; we are indeed subject to their subtle sway, and under stress of emotion revert to them. So far we may go in the pride of our modern age but not much farther; we cannot deny our poor relations. Mind is still in the making as an instrument of social control. We still fail dismally and in every phase of human endeavor to live the life of reason within the reach of our privileged capacities. The lesson of wishful wisdom needs to be enforced in and for the modern temper.

PART I
CREDULITY
THE URGE TO BELIEVE

Delight in deceiving and aptness to be deceived, imposture and credulity, although they appear to be of a diverse nature, yet certainly they do for the most part concur.—BACON.

> At credulity's booth are all things sold;
> Each ounce of dross costs its ounce of gold.
> —LOWELL

Populus vult decipi: People want to be deceived.—ROMAN SAYING.

Civilization could scarcely have had a beginning if the law of demonstration had always held sway. What was first needed was a rough-hewn scheme and a faith-yielding people.—ISAIAH BOWMAN.

ARGUMENT

CREDULITY *is too ready faith-yielding. The uncritical habit makes the human race eternally gullible. Deception is too encyclopedic a theme for the psychologist's canvas. The technique of the deceiver is a matter by itself; he makes capital of the wide prevalence of credulity. Dupes are sought and easily found in matters financial, where the love of profit bends judgment to wish. Hoaxes and fakes are prompted by ready credulity in matters scientific; they may have no other reward to the believers than the thrill of crediting them, to the hoaxer, of showing his power to impose. As it costs less, men invest even more recklessly in the stock of beliefs than in "securities" stock—both often proving insecure. The psychology of credulity concerns the "aptness to be deceived" rather than the "delight in deceiving." Since Bacon's time their "concurrence" has developed the arts of exploiting and racketeering, far beyond the knaveries of his intrigue-filled days.*

The habit of faith-yielding has its large uses; credulity is only its hazard. Life would be intolerable if we had constantly to mistrust and distrust our fellow-men; we are dependent upon the right knowledge as well as upon the good faith of authorities. Caution, prudence, a critical care in the disposal of our trust, is a practical requirement. We gage the growing intelligence of children by what they no longer believe, when told in jest or earnest. In the battle of wits we build our defenses against imposition even as we yield our faith. As laymen we are dependent upon experts, and derive most of our beliefs by acceptance, not by personal proof or critical test. Credulity comes to refer to a loosely or grossly uncritical judgment of the conclusions offered and a rash acceptance of the arguments in their support. Standards of belief move upward

17

with increase of knowledge; the credulities of one age seem incredible to later ones.

Credulity combines with other failings, with prepossession particularly; the will to believe extends beyond faith-yielding. Matured by experience, with lessons costly and repeated, we arrive; we come to operate in the crowded world of beliefs—as stock-brokers operate in the market—with a total knowledge of the investment field, and some knowledge of the rules and hazards of the game. The sincerity, questioned in the stock exchange, is assumed in the laboratory. So credulity in matters of explanation, as exemplified in Wish and Wisdom, *comes to be a matter of intellectual standards and of the general mental background and system of habits in which the believing tendencies operate.*

Credulities readily dramatize into episodes. Private and minor credulities have a limited interest. It is when the tale is widely accepted, and the plot thickens, that it acquires the scale of "news" value and by that route, its place in psychological annals; they must be in the statistical sense popular delusions, vulgar errors. We may appropriately enter upon the comédie humaine *of the foibles of belief—comedies often with a tragic note and issue—by way of a selection of incidents showing credulity variously at work in very different stage-settings. With a common plot, the episodes vary widely in content, as do case-histories sharing a similar diagnosis.*

CHAPTER II

AN ANCIENT MIRACLE-MONGER: LUCIAN'S ALEXANDER

THE TEMPTATION to deceive is as old as the human race, and so is the inclination to succumb to deception, which is credulity. There is an instance of it, classical in every sense, which, written eighteen hundred years ago, reads like a modern exposé, even to the details of ways and means. This sprightly tale we owe to Lucian of Samosata, a Græco-Roman satirist of the foibles of his day.

It concerns Alexander, the miracle-monger of Abonoteichous, a town in Asia Minor. It is set down in Greek in the form of a letter to his friend Celsus, in the year 180 A.D.—ten years after Alexander's death. Lucian's opinion of Alexander is concise:

He was an out and out rascal, a man who does not deserve to have genteel people read about him. Tall, handsome, god-like, with fair skin and long locks partly natural, partly artificial, with fine eyes and a pleasing voice, he was also shrewd and talented, . . . but made poor use of his endowments. He was a soul-blend of lying and trickery, masqueraded as kindly and respectable, with a quality of magnificence.

Alexander started his exploiting career early. Apprenticed in boyhood to a quack, selling enchantments, he formed a partnership with Coconnas, a young man of like tastes, and found a rich Macedonian woman, "charming but no longer young," to finance them. Thus launched as itinerant sorcerers, they "trimmed the fat-heads."

19

These two consummate rascals, greatly daring, duly prepared for mischief, put their heads together, and readily dis-
cerned that human nature is swayed by two great tyrants—
hope and fear; and that a man who could use both of these
to advantage, would speedily enrich himself.

In due course they set up a prophetic shrine and oracle,
such being the "psychic" profession of the day. They
opened their season in Alexander's home town, diverting
their attentions to the superstitious and wealthy. In those
far-off days—not so different from our own—any one who
professed to tell fortunes attracted the crowd. Coconnas
died; Alexander continued, contrary to the proverb, to
flourish as a prophet in his own land. On occasion, he
feigned madness; epilepsy was then regarded as a visitation
from the gods, conferring the power of prophecy. He produced foam at the mouth—perhaps this was the original
"ectoplasm"—by chewing soapwort such as was used
by dyers.

Alexander's reputation was established by a great miracle. He went at night to a temple still under construction.
In a pool of water formed by the excavations he hid a
goose-egg which he had previously blown and into which
he had inserted a tiny snake. Next day, clad in loin cloth,
with hair and beard flying, he announced in the market-
place that the god would appear in person at the temple
site. Followed by the crowd, he approached the altar
chanting, and besought Æsculapius and Apollo to give
evidence of their presence. Taking a libation saucer, he
deftly slipped the egg under it, covered with mud. At the
proper moment, he produced the snake. The crowd beheld
the miracle and shouted! A serpent coiled around a staff
was the symbol of Æsculapius, the god of healing, also associated with the offices of Apollo; so the miraculous
appearance of the snake was a sign of grace from the gods
of healing.

Alexander remained in seclusion for several days to allow the report of the miracle to spread. He then appeared lying on a couch with a snake coiled at his feet, its head concealed under his arm. This tame snake he had bought of a snake charmer as a property for his show. Using it as a model, he fashioned a masterpiece, a large snake's head made of linen, with a painted human face. The head of the real snake he concealed, and made the humanized linen head take its place. By means of horsehair, the snake opened and closed its mouth and protruded a forked black tongue. Here was a second miracle! Lucian reports the séance:

Please imagine a little room not very bright and not admitting any too much daylight; also a crowd of heterogeneous humanity, excited, wonderstruck in advance, agog with hopes. The thing of course seemed to them a miracle—that the formerly tiny snake, within a few days, had turned into so great a serpent, with a human face moreover, and tame.

Anticipating Barnum, who disposed of the crowd by putting up a sign: "This way to the Egress!" Alexander's accomplices hurried the crowd to the exit before they could look too closely. The show had a long run. The performance was repeated upon request, especially when rich patrons were present. Tokens struck in honor of the cult of Alexander are still in existence to confirm Lucian's tale.

The great serpent Alexander called Glycon. He opened the séance with the announcement, spoken through the serpent's mouth: *"Glycon am I, the grandson of Zeus! Bright beacon to mortals!"* The god would prophesy at the rate of two obols per prediction. The questions were written by the clients on a scroll, tied and sealed with wax. The prophet then retired to his sanctuary—the original "cabinet"—and returned with the seals intact and an answer from the god. "You," writes Lucian to his friend, "like myself, will see through it all as obvious; but to those driveling idiots it was miraculous and almost as good as incredible."

Lucian tells how the trick was done. You heat a needle, melt off the wax seal, read the scroll, warm the wax, and put the seal back. Or you make an impression in hard plaster, break the seal, and make a new one. That was the conjuring part of the performance. It required psychology to frame the answers. Alexander's methods were those of all mediums since: "At times his responses were obscure, ambiguous and downright unintelligible, in the oracular manner. 'It shall all come about when I will, and when Alexander my prophet asks it of me and prays for it.'" For the rest, he depended on his own shrewdness and the credulity of his customers; and when nonplussed, put off the answer to another day.

Alexander played the health game. Then as now, health-seekers patronized fortune-tellers. So he prescribed remedies. He had an ointment which he called "cymides" that would cure all complaints and was charged for accordingly, though it was little more than bear's grease. The most expensive oracles were the "autophones" spoken directly through the wondrous snake's head. Actually an accomplice spoke in a mysterious voice through a tube made by joining cranes' windpipes. The autophones—veritable voice of the god himself—were reserved for the rich and noble. The great oracle-showman did a big business— 70,000 drachmas a year, probably worth as much in dollars. His overhead, including publicity, was large: assistants, scouts to get private information, traveling salesmen to advertise the show. These spread the news that Alexander had "recovered fugitive slaves, detected thieves and robbers, found hidden treasure, healed the sick, and even raised the dead."

After successfully touring the provinces, Alexander moved on to Rome and played for high stakes, seeking the favor of officials and the aristocracy. Rutilinus, a man of means and position, sent his servants to meet Alexander "and they inflamed the poor old man and made him almost crazy." The oracle advised Rutilinus to take Alexander's daughter to wife, claiming that she was the daughter of Selene. This the old man did, and propitiated his mother-in-law, the Moon, with whole hecatombs.

At the same time the plaguey scoundrel devised a trick which was really clever and which one would not expect from the ordinary swindler. In opening and reading the forwarded scrolls, if he came upon damaging information, he would keep it to himself, and not send it back. You understand what questions are likely to be put by questioners who are rich and very powerful; so he used to derive much gain from those who knew he had them in his power.

Thus he added blackmail to his other professions.

Like the other Alexander, sighing for new worlds to conquer, he spread rumors of approaching plagues, conflagrations, and earthquakes. He arranged penitential processions, himself appearing on the floats. He "had winning ways with women," and husbands were proud when he kissed their wives. He organized a group of the young girls called "Those within the Kiss," none to be over eighteen years of age.

"The crowd," writes Lucian, "with brogans on their feet and breath that reeked of garlic, cried 'Hail Glycon!' 'Hail Alexander!'" Alexander even exhibited, as a sign of his deity, a golden thigh which was actually gilded leather; and "there was once a discussion between two of our learned idiots whether he had the soul of Pythagoras on account of the golden thigh, or some other akin to it."

For the final exposé of Alexander, Lucian set a trap. He sent a question by his servant, telling him it was a request for a prescription for a pain in the side. The question in the scroll was actually the old one, "Where was Homer born?" Lucian obtained his prescription; so he knew that his servant had been "pumped." To the question, "When will Alexander be caught cheating?" there was no reply.

At length Lucian bearded the lion in his den. In approaching, he was supposed to kiss the great prophet's hand; instead, he bit it severely. Lucian nearly lost his life by Alexander's desire for revenge. But Alexander's game was up; his power began to wane. False prophecies proved to be damaging. A young man traveling in dangerous regions was reported lost by the oracle. Unexpectedly he turned up in Rome, safe and sound; and the mob was prepared to stone him for proving the great Alexander false. Rumors began to float about of graft and scandal. Eventually men "recovered from their profound intoxication." The tale ends with the departure of Lucian by ship, arranged as a compromise by Alexander, though with secret instructions to the captain to throw his passengers overboard during the voyage; and with the captain's refusal, whereby a remarkable tale was preserved for the benefit of posterity.

Lucian was far more than an exposer of false prophets. He is entitled to remembrance as one of the first students of the strange beliefs of men. He questioned the conclusions of the philosophers; he denounced superstitions and the credulity that gave circulation to tall "travelers' tales"; he wrote an essay on lying and asked why the habit was so universal. He was associated with the Epicureans, the sophisticated skeptics of the day. As such he held it his business to expose humbugs and scoff at credulity. He had listened to many wonder tales, such as that of the Flying Stranger:

"What! You saw this Hyperborean actually flying and walking on water?" "I did; he wore brogues as Hyperboreans
usually do.... He would make people fall in love, call up
spirits, resuscitate corpses, bring down the moon!... I was an
unbeliever once, worse than you, but..."

We need only change the character of the miracles to
imagine ourselves listening to a "psychic" protagonist of
today. Both will insist that seeing is believing; and
Lucian's successor may have no better chance than had
Lucian of bringing home the lesson that in many instances believing is the source of seeing.

Lucian when on imagination bent could invent as
plausibly as the adepts in fabrication. He was a forerunner
of a combined Gulliver and Jules Verne; for he wrote
of an imaginary trip to the moon, reaching there by some
sort of projectile, and described the gigantic proportions
and weird ways of the inhabitants. Concerning the ways
of wish passing for wisdom, Lucian summarized a caution
for all time:

"To defend one's mind against these follies, a man must
have an adamantine faith, so that, even if he is not able
to detect the precise trick by which the illusion is produced, he at any rate retains his conviction that the whole
thing is a lie and an impossibility."

For that sentence alone Lucian deserves a place among
the rationalists of all ages.

Chapter III

A MODERN EXPLOITER:
"LEO TAXIL"

A SPAN of seventeen centuries changes the scenario but not the psychology of the miracle-monger and of his victims. The name of "Leo Taxil" is presumably as unknown as that of his distant predecessor, Lucian's Alexander. Like Alexander, he was a sensational celebrity of his day. He suggests a combination of the Lucian satire with Alexander's deviltry.

The first impression in reading the exploits of "Leo Taxil" is that of an unscrupulous scoundrel who "put over" fantastic fabulations and slanderous fictions, to his own glory and profit. A second judgment gives him a place among the great hoaxers, with a farceur's glee in carrying a joke to the limit, regardless of consequences, and a philosopher's interest in exploiting credulity to demonstrate the extent of human gullibility.

The story deals with violent and bitter religious feuds, which the world in its tolerant mood prefers to forget. But the tale is indispensable to the presentation of credulity as the ally of prejudice, which makes men ready to believe anything and the worst of those in the opposite camp. It could be dramatized with the title, "What price prejudice!"

"Leo Taxil" was Gabriel Jogand-Pagés, born in Marseilles in 1854. His chief talent seems to have been a lively imagination and the inclination to use it to stir up trouble. His first hoax was the report of sharks in the harbor of Marseilles. There was great excitement; no such thing had occurred in the memory of man. The police closed the bath-houses; parties went out in boats, armed with all sorts of weapons; but they found no sharks. They disappeared as mysteriously as they came. Some years later he announced the discovery of a buried city at the bottom of Lake Leman. Several historians swallowed the tale; they gave learned explanations of how the city came to be submerged and discussed whether it was of Lake Dwelling or of Roman origin. These successful escapades may have set Taxil to plan his "great mystification." He could hardly have anticipated the dramatic sequel that awaited his *magnum opus*.

In the stage of his career which we may call Taxil I, he was a rabid anti-clerical. Reared as a Catholic, he reacted violently against religion and became a radical freethinker. He founded an anti-clerical society; he published a series of tracts and books, accusing the clergy of greed and lust and tyranny and usury and all the sins carnal and spiritual. To say that these volumes of writings were pure or rather impure fabrications, sacrilegious, lewd, grotesque, and extravagant, is an understatement. Taxil employed an artist who entered into the spirit of the enterprise. A typical drawing presents a priest and a maid, their heads alone appearing above the screen of a huge fig-leaf. "The Flight into Egypt" pictures Joseph and Mary in scant robes, both mounted on one high-wheel bicycle, trailing in leash a small basket on wheels, containing the Infant. Read a half century later, we see the daredevil touch in it. In their day these tracts were highly incendiary. The boldest of the libels was a pamphlet, *The Secret Amours of Pius IX,* the Pope's head surrounded by a halo of a bevy of women. For this glaring offense, Taxil and his publisher were fined 65,000 francs and sentenced

to imprisonment; but they managed to have the indictment quashed.

Such is the story of Leo Taxil I! He played the diabolical part for ten years; but it was more a mocking than
a malicious Mephistopheles. As he tells the story, he was
reconverted by an act of grace. "I was suddenly shaken
by strange convulsions. Convulsed with fearful agitations,
I burst into sobs! 'Pardon me, oh God,' I cried in a voice
choked with tears." He spent the night in prayer. In his
autobiography he mentions also that he was moved by
the sacrifice of an aunt, who was also his godmother, who
disposed of her worldly possessions and entered a convent
in order to expiate her nephew's grievous sin; likewise
that Joan of Arc came to him in a vision, which sign of
grace completed his conversion.

The first step of the reformed Taxil was to call a
meeting of the Anti-clerical League and Freethinkers Society of which he was the founder, to resign and to return
to his orthodox faith. The Anti-clericals promptly denounced him as an infamous scoundrel. But he was received by the Papal Nuncio of Paris. Absolved from his
sins, he entered upon his major and exciting career.

The instigation of the change of heart was the Encyclical
of Leo XIII (cited as *Humanus Genus,* August 21, 1884)
dividing the human race into two classes: those for and
those against the Church, and naming well-known fraternal
orders as "synagogues of Satan." This seems to have given
Taxil the idea of an extensive and intensive campaign
against the Masons. Four volumes appeared in quick succession. Hundreds of thousands of copies were sold by
promotion schemes. The books were translated into English, German, Italian, and Spanish. There were elaborate
editions for the wealthy and popular ones for the masses.
The receipts were abundant. The volumes recount in
lurid detail imaginary revelations concerning the sacri-

legious orgies and devil-worship of the Masonic mysteries. They describe the terror of the initiatory rites. From a cabinet fitted with mirrors there speaks a voice: "Tremble, Profane One! You will see the head of a brother who has violated the oath of secrecy"; whereupon there appears in the mirror a severed human head on a bloody cloth.

The appeal of the contents may be gathered from the fact that the German version omitted the volume on the *Masonic Sisters* in order not to outrage the moral sense of Teutonic countries by recounting the "filthiness of the hellish crew." Even so they carried the game too far. The accusation by name of a German lady who was supposed to have stolen a consecrated wafer for the Satanic rites resulted in a suit against the *Moniteur de Rome* and the payment of a heavy fine.

Taxil found collaborators in Italy and Germany. A kindred soul was Dr. Karl Hacks, who wrote *Devil Worshippers in the XIXth Century*. He brought into the story a fictitious person, Sophia Walder, heralded as the future grandmother of the antichrist. He relates that he saw a gigantic tree bow before Sophia and present her with a bouquet. Her real father was the devil Bitru; and here is the devil's signature signing the contract:

THE DEVIL'S SIGNATURE

This fantastic signature, with its pitchfork, cock, and strange symbols, is derived from the devil-lore of earlier days.

This grotesque composition should have excited suspicion; but it seems to have been accepted as genuine.

Dr. Hacks, or Bataille, as he called himself, outdid Taxil, and like Taxil, exulted later in describing his deceptions:

Sometimes I fabricated the most incredible stories as that of the serpent inditing prophecies on the back of Sophia Walder, or that of a demon who in order to marry a Freemason transformed himself into a young lady and played the piano nights in the form of a crocodile. My colleagues were aghast and exclaimed: "You'll spoil the whole joke with your nonsense." But I replied: "Let me have my way and you will see!"

There was circulated a tale of the discovery of devils residing in the caves under the cliffs of Gibraltar; that Dr. Hacks was there received by Tubal Cain, who addressed him in French and gave him a vial that would spread cholera, in case he needed such a weapon. It appears that the conspirators had a correspondent in the United States; for the highly spiced narrative included stories concerning the Grand Master of the Freemasons at Charleston, mentioning him by name, Charles Pike. "One day Satan took Pike gently in his arms and made a trip with him to Sirius, traversing the whole distance in a few minutes. After exploring the fixed star, he was brought back safe and sound to his room in Washington." The Masonic Grand Master was pictured as a Satanic Pope, using a telephone, invented and operated by devils, whereby he put a girdle around the earth in forty seconds; he also possessed a magic bracelet by which he summoned Lucifer at his pleasure.

In the closing years of the nineteenth century Taxil and Co. actually succeeded in gaining believers aplenty for tales which match those of the credulous Dark Ages. But the mauve decade is of our times. There were doubtless skeptics abundant and emphatic protests. Bishop Northrup of Charleston journeyed to Rome expressly to warn His Holiness that Taxil was an unscrupulous rascal, that the effect of these slanders was disastrous to the interests of the Church. Furthermore, the Bishop explained that the Masons of Charleston were respected citizens, that he had been invited to visit the Masonic Temple and found no evidence of the unholy rituals imputed to them. He was rebuked for his zeal and admonished to be silent. The Apostolic Nuncio of Gibraltar brought to Rome the denial of the absurd "Tubal Cain" myth, but met with the same reception.

Taxil's ready imagination and extraordinary fertility in invention filled his volumes with readable and plausible slanders for readers inclined to believe in them. But his most adroit creation was "Diana Vaughan," at first a myth, whom later he dared to materialize in person. It was given out that she was a descendant of Thomas Vaughan, an English mystic of the seventeenth century; that she had a document signed by said ancestor, stating that while he was living among the American Indians, the goddess Astarte visited him, and later gave birth to his child. Diana was accordingly of Luciferian origin. The wild tales of adventure and miracle invented by Taxil to enhance the mystery of Diana had to compete with those of Dr. Hacks concerning her fictitious rival Sophia:

Her Luciferian origin and principles were shown by her horror of all religious observances, by the devils who attended her and through whose aid she made excursions to Mars, where she rode on Schiaparelli's canals, sailed on the Sea of the Sirens, and strolled among the gigantic inhabitants of the planet.

Many remarkable incidents of her curious personality are retailed for the benefit of believers; while poetic justice is appeased by her final conversion to the Church through the instrumentality of the spirit of Joan of Arc. We shall meet Diana as leading lady in the final act and scene.

The sequence of the tale requires that we follow Taxil II in his greatest triumph to a Congress held in Trent on September 26, 1896. Here he was received as an illustrious champion of the faith. The Pope's message expressed the wish that, as eight centuries before they had proceeded against Islam, they would now suppress the enemies of Rome in the Western World.

Taxil had been received (1887) by His Holiness. Conscious of the blasting record of his youth, he prostrated himself before the Papal throne. When asked what was his dearest wish, he had the impertinence to declare that it would be to perish at this supreme moment of his pardon. The Pope gave him his blessing and assured him that he had still to serve the faith on earth. A letter written by a high dignitary expresses the same sentiment: "Your pen and your piety are predestined to demolish the foes of mankind." At Trent Taxil had the pleasure of seeing his own portrait displayed along with those of the saints. When he spoke, despite the occasional irony which he could not repress, he was greeted with shouts of "Eviva Taxil!"

But there were also protests and rumblings of dissent. These centered about Diana Vaughan. Was there any such person? It was true that she had written a book revealing the diabolic proceedings of the Masonic orders. The books had been approved by two eminent cardinals, and there was a letter from the private secretary of the Pope himself. Indeed the Holy Father had pointed out to Taxil the latter's books on the papal shelves. But were the revelations genuine? A commission was appointed to investigate. They reported four months later that there was no decisive evidence for or against the reality of Diana Vaughan. Clearly the skies were lowering; the end was nearing. Taxil continued to play his part boldly. His finale was brilliant; though it may be the dénouement was precipitated by Dr. Hack's intention to give away the plot.

So far as there was any "Diana Vaughan" through all these years of a profitable campaign, she was a bright American girl, employed in a typing establishment, who served as secretary for Taxil's vast correspondence. There was also a legendary "Diana Vaughan," who was reported to have entered a convent and to have there written her memoirs, which "were worth their weight in gold." Taxil fathered this tale:

A priest of the Holy Sacrament, Father de la Porte, had often declared that he would gladly give his life for the conversion of Diana Vaughan. She attended mass in the cloister for the first time on Corpus Christi Day, and left her sacred retreat on the following Saturday. On the very day of her departure, Father de la Porte died. And yet there are persons who doubt the existence of Miss Vaughan!

Finally, when challenged to produce the mystic maiden, Taxil induced his secretary to play the part. A few prelates were invited to breakfast with Diana at a hotel in Paris. At this function she declined chartreuse in her coffee, as that liqueur was made in a monastery—an "Adonaic" liqueur, she called it; she accepted brandy. The interview was promptly reported to baffle the skeptics.

We reach Taxil III, the exposer of Taxil I and Taxil II. The time is April 19, 1897; the place is the auditorium of the Geographical Society of Paris, crowded with three hundred guests; the heroine is Diana Vaughan. She was announced to appear on the stage to an expectant audience. The program was arranged with a showman's skill. It began with the lottery of an American typewriter, which was won by a Turkish reporter who regretted that it could not write Turkish. The printed program stated that after Diana's appearance there would be shown lantern slides presenting scenes from her life and that of Sophia Walder, their encounters with the agencies of Satan, their conversion, and finally, scenes of Taxil with the Encyclical of Pope Leo XIII.

That trouble was expected was indicated by the request that canes and umbrellas be checked at the door. When the moment arrived, Taxil stepped forward and said simply: "Reverend Sirs, Ladies and Gentlemen. You wish to see Diana Vaughan. Look at me! I myself am that lady!" Then followed an explicit account of the twelve years of imposture, and an impudent expression of thanks to the clergy for their unwitting aid in his magnificent hoax; a forced retreat to a neighboring café to escape the vengeance of the crowd; a momentary furore, some discussion pro and con; and then the story ends and the world wagged on. Needless to say, the lantern slides were never shown.

My hesitation to revive the story of Leo Taxil and include this "diabolical" double-edged plot of duplicity, lest it might be unacceptable to the affiliations involved, is removed by its citation under official auspices by Father C. M. de Heredia (1922). He concludes that this "brilliant gigantic fraud...has taught Catholics a lesson." He regards Taxil as a hoaxer for the relish of the sport and its remuneration. Presumably M. Jogand was neither a fiend nor a paranoid fanatic. He was, indeed, daringly clever in romantic fabrication. The career of Taxil could not be repeated today, not only because we are less credulous, but because we are more tolerant. In the annals of credulity the story of Leo Taxil has an enduring place.

CHAPTER IV

"THE ENIGMA OF HIS TIME":
KASPAR HAUSER

THE YEAR 1932 marks the centenary of the death of an unknown notable. Kaspar Hauser, though he lived but twenty-one years, became in his brief day, and far more so after it, a sensational mystery of Europe. A hundred years later, belief in his importance survives to the extent of arranging a celebration in his honor: memorial addresses, an exhibition of his personal effects, a collection of the immense literature—the Kaspar Hauser bibliography contains over a thousand entries—that has accumulated to prove one theory or another regarding his origin. With the Teutonic thoroughness that is expended indiscriminately upon important issues and those far less so, there has arisen a specialty called *Hauser-Forschung*—research in the history of "the orphan of Nuremberg." Learned professors deliver lectures upon the topic, and even suggest it as a proper subject for a semester's course. On the tomb of the obscure celebrity appears in Latin the inscription:

> Here lies Kaspar Hauser, the enigma of his time.
> His birth unknown, his death a mystery.

Kaspar came into public notice as a "child of nature." This engaging but gratuitous notion had been made current by Rousseau's dubious thesis of the "noble savage," posing him as a superior being, with civilization responsible for the present decline of the human estate. There

35

was also the theological doctrine of the state of innocence before the fall. On a slight clue in the letter which the lad presented when he appeared on the streets of Nuremberg on May 26, 1828, the burghers transformed him into an exemplar of the original virtues of unspoiled man. The idealizing artist pictures him after he had been made somewhat presentable. In all essentials the legend of the boy's origin was fashioned by the credulity of the naïve citizens, who little thought that they had started a tale that would travel around the world and be remembered a century later. The legendary Kaspar Hauser belongs to the memorabilia of credulity.

The story over which generations of sentimental readers have been moved to pity is that of the cruel confinement of a lad from early infancy until his sixteenth year. He is pictured as squatting in a small dark cell, without room to walk or stand, shut off from all the world, hearing no voice but that of the keeper who brought him his crusts and water, and with no companions but two wooden horses. Then, suddenly, for no well-defined reason, his jailer takes him at night from this living death and deserts the boy at the gates of Nuremberg. There fortune favored him; he became at once the object of kindly curiosity when the burgomaster published the pitiful and strange history. Crowds flocked to see the "wild boy of nature" confined in the tower; the best citizens paid their respects; learned men studied him as a rare phenomenon. As the show piece of Nuremberg, the city fathers voted funds from the public treasury for Kaspar's support. The burgomaster's spark of credulity had started a conflagration. Kaspar was a psychological freak and a drawing card for the provincial curiosity.

The official record is commonplace enough. It states that the lad was detained as a vagrant; that he presented a letter addressed to "the captain of the Fourth Squadron

KASPAR HAUSER, "THE ENIGMA OF HIS TIME"

An artist's version upon his arrival at Nuremberg.
From a lithograph of 1828.

of the Schmolischer regiment"; that he spoke with a marked dialect, wrote his name, said that he had gone to school, and showed a strong liking for horses. The letter was designed to block inquiry; it set forth that no one knew of the boy's existence, that he had no money, that his name was Kaspar, that he wanted to become a trooper as his father had been before him. In this letter was enclosed another (presumably by the same hand, disguised), purporting to have been written fifteen years earlier by the mother when she abandoned the infant under circumstances unknown.

On that slender and suspicious basis the burgomaster elaborated the story, which traveled far and wide. He was aided by the like-minded medical examiner, Dr. Preu, who pronounced the lad "neither crazy nor idiotic, but evidently violently estranged in the most shameful manner from all human and social culture. He is like a half-wild man brought up in the woods." Thus was official sanction given to popular credulity.

The marvel of Kaspar's education exceeded that of his deprivation. At first he could blurt only simple words and had to be talked to like a baby. In three days he picked out tones on a spinnet, soon afterwards knitted a stocking, and five weeks later told the tale—absorbing much of it from the comments of his throngs of visitors— that made him and Nuremberg famous. Under the tutelage of Professor Daumer, in a month or more Kaspar was carrying on polite conversation, playing chess and checkers, and still innocent as a babe: "a being of angelic purity, displaying the most delicate moral feelings, and a perfect love of truth"—an opinion which he later changed to the very opposite.

With every month the wonder grew. In Kaspar credulous minds found the embodiment of current belief. As an unspoiled child of nature, he was a "sensitive." He could see a gnat in a spider's web in the dark; he could tell apple, pear, and plum trees by smelling their leaves; he was overcome by the odors of a graveyard. He could recognize metals by their attraction for his fingers, could detect a needle at the bottom of a pile of papers, and would shudder in passing a hardware shop. To avoid the unpleasant contact with metals, kindly Professor Daumer had Kaspar eat his meals with a wooden spoon. In other hands Kaspar proved the truth of homeopathy, reacting to the minutest dilutions of drugs. Kaspar had only to play a passive part; the atmosphere of credulity did the rest.

But chiefly he was a moral, psychological wonder, a forgiving soul who had been cruelly wronged. The influential sponsor of that legend was the distinguished jurist, Professor Anselm von Feuerbach, in whose account judicial habits of mind are strangely absent. He became Kaspar's biographer in *The History of a Crime Against a Human Soul,* a crime which he discussed with all the obfuscation of legal jargon. The book was promptly translated into several languages and spread the highly colored story over the civilized world.

Von Feuerbach speaks of Kaspar as "gentle, mild, free from evil inclinations, unmoved by passion, and innocent of all deceit. His quiet even temper is like a calm lake in a moonlight night." Despite having before him an abundance of detailed evidence to the contrary, the credulous jurist reports:

Kaspar Hauser showed such an utter deficiency of words and ideas, such perfect ignorance of the commonest things and appearances of nature, such horror of all the customs, conveniences and necessities of civilized life, and with all this such peculiarities in his social, mental and physical disposition that one might have felt one's self driven to the alternative of believing him to be a citizen of another planet transferred

by some miracle to our own, or else the man described by
Plato, who was born and brought up under the earth and
only emerged to the light of day when he had attained the
age of manhood.

Freiherr von Tucher, who later became Kaspar's guardian,
indulges in the same sickly sentimentality. To him Kaspar
is "a being such as we may imagine in Paradise before
the Fall, a precious, unique, ever-to-be-remembered embodiment, which shone like a ray of heaven's own light
upon this impure, degraded world of sinners."

This engaging legend held the stage; but it did not
deceive everybody. In due course the Superior Court returned the burgomaster's report with the comment that
"in the official records there was not a trace" of the child-
of-nature myth; that "the whole story was full of improb-
able circumstances as well as inexplicable contradictions";
which meant that it was all concocted by the burgomaster,
prompting or prompted by Kaspar. This judicial statement came too late; the legend had been started, and
Kaspar's star was in the ascendant.

When suspicion grew and interest was beginning to
wane, the excitement was renewed by the report (October
7, 1828) that an attack had been made on Kaspar's life.
He was the sole witness. The cut on his forehead, he
claimed, had been made by a knife in the hands of a man
wearing a black handkerchief across his face. No such
man was found; but Kaspar was given a bodyguard of
two *polizei*. On the very day of the attack, his tutor had
detected the boy in a glaring falsehood; there had been
a scene. Professor Daumer had to conclude that between
May and October, the boy's "nature had lost much of its
original purity, and that a highly regrettable tendency
to untruthfulness and dissimulation had manifested itself."
His doubts were grave, and he asked to be relieved of
his charge.

The same disillusionment was in store for the successive custodians of the "ward of Nuremberg." Each discovered the boy's propensity for lying, for neglecting his studies and drifting into the rôle of a pampered favorite. There was also a second attempt at his life which was lamely explained as the accidental discharge of a pistol, when the police rushed in so promptly that there was no time to frame an alibi. One cannot tell the story consecutively, as during the three eventful years, the speculations concerning Kaspar veered from a "noble savage" to a "noble scion." We approach the second phase of the Kaspar Hauser legend.

The keen interest in social and political intrigue in high circles is responsible for the formidable dimensions of the literature on Kaspar Hauser. Von Feuerbach—of whom a friend said that perhaps he was writing a romance in his old age—certainly preferred the romantic to the judicial interpretation of the evidence. He seems to have become convinced rather early that the abandonment of the child was a criminal plot; from then on his mind was closed to the fairly obvious facts of the case. The "child of nature" interest died down, as Kaspar's education proceeded; it now seemed a more provocative question to ask—whose child was he? Why these attempts upon his life, if not to prevent an ugly secret from coming to light?

The speculations concerning Kaspar Hauser's origin involved the complications of post-Napoleonic Europe; they show a different order of credulity and the usual prepossessions that prevail when feuds and factions arise. The cross currents of controversy that kept the tale alive fall outside the psychological interest in the case.

The dominant figure in the narrative is the Earl of Stanhope, a member of a distinguished English family, conversant with the Europe of his day. In his travels in

Germany he had heard much of the "wonder lad of Nuremberg," and was in touch with von Feuerbach. He did not meet Kaspar until 1831, and was then much impressed by the boy's proficiency in the polite arts after but three years' acquaintance with the ways of civilization. Stanhope was strongly influenced by von Feuerbach's theories, and took a practical step to solve the problem; he offered a reward of five hundred gulden for proof of the boy's origin. Nothing came of it—only more speculation.

One supposition made Kaspar an Hungarian, apparently because it was reported that some Hungarian words spoken in his presence induced convulsions. That was enough to send Kaspar, accompanied by his guardian von Tucher and his tutor Major Hinkel, to Hungary at Stanhope's expense. This was all very agreeable to Kaspar, who fell into the part by recognizing as a face familiar to his childhood a portrait in the Art Gallery in Vienna, the date of which unfortunately proved to be 1628! It was all a wild-goose chase, but did not prevent Major Hinkel from making a second journey on the professed recognition by Kaspar of an Hungarian countess as his mother, much to the annoyance of the Magyar family concerned.

We reach the fatal year 1832. In May von Feuerbach died. Stanhope agreed to become responsible for the lad's expenses. He was to be apprenticed to a bookbinder, or made a clerk, neither occupation acceptable to the boy's aspirations, which apparently were set upon going to England with the munificent milord. Kaspar was faced with a new situation. He was removed to Anspach in the care of a Dr. Meyer, who had the usual experience with his troublesome charge; he neglected his work, he lied, he evaded. There was a stormy scene on December 9th. Five days later Kaspar burst into the room highly agitated, displaying a wound in his breast. He reported that a man with a knife had given him a bag, and then stabbed him;

the bag they would find in the Hofgarten. It was found
to contain a misleading note written in mirror-script. The
wound proved to be more serious than was at first supposed. Three days later Kaspar died. After a judicial inquiry lasting nine months, the verdict was rendered that
Kaspar was *not* murdered. There were no footprints other
than Kaspar's in the snow at the spot where the bag was
found and near which today stands his tombstone.

With the death of the two principals, the responsibility
of restoring a rational view of the *affaire* Kaspar Hauser
fell upon the Earl of Stanhope. In 1836, to offset von
Feuerbach's fantastic account, he published both in German and in English a simple "Tract," now a rare document, confessing that he had been completely deceived in
regard to the boy, whom he now supposed—a fair guess
at the truth—was nothing more than a simple-minded
tailor's or glover's traveling apprentice, whose home may
have been on the Austrian side of the Bavarian frontier.
He specifies scores of discrepancies between the von Feuerbach account and the actual incidents. He recalled a remark
of von Feuerbach's to the effect that from the Nuremberg records one might infer that Kaspar Hauser was an
impostor, and that "they should be destroyed." He suggested that there was just one hour in Kaspar's life that
contained the truth—the protocol of his first appearance,
before the myth was evolved which the credulity of the
day so avidly swallowed. Stanhope makes the laconic comment that he may be the only author who ever wrote a
book to prove himself in the wrong.

A generation passed; and still, or again, the case found
sponsors for one version or another. In 1859 Professor
Daumer, now elderly, forgetting how he had been duped
right and left by Kaspar's fabrications, evolved a new
theory. He made Kaspar an heir to an English estate,

implied that his cruel relatives for no good purpose had sent the child to Hungary; that Stanhope adopted Kaspar in order to get him under his control, that he had poisoned von Feuerbach and had plotted the murder of Kaspar. Pious Professor Daumer was hardly the person to invent these terrific charges. An industrious inquirer traces them to a Countess Alberdorf, an Englishwoman, who seems to have had a grudge against Stanhope. Her charges led to an inquiry, the commissioners finding her "an extremely loquacious, foolish and confused witness," thriving on gossip which she circulated as fact. As the Earl of Stanhope had died in 1885, his daughter, then Countess of Cleveland, wrote a sober and restrained reply to all these slanders, reminding the public that her father had admitted that he had been grossly deceived, but had never adopted Kaspar.

The most persistent rumors foisted Kaspar on the House of Baden, apparently because in 1812 an heir was born to Grand Duke Karl and the Duchess Stephanie, the child dying in infancy. The tale that this infant had been otherwise disposed of spread in court circles. Gossips found a resemblance between Kaspar's features and the Duchess Stephanie. It came to the attention of Emperor William, who saw fit to issue a denial of Kaspar's ducal birth. This tale, extravagantly embellished, was circulated as late as 1892 in the "true story" written by Elizabeth Evans, who speaks of Kaspar throughout as the "Hereditary Prince of Baden," and makes Stanhope a despicable adventurer. Apparently the source of these venomous tales is the Countess Hochberg, morganatic wife of Grand Duke Karl. A still more diabolical account of surreptitious exchange of infants in the royal bedchamber is given by Lockhart, based on the same spicy gossip.

M. Edmond Bapot as recently as 1930 gives a more sedate account, with elaborate documents based on the supposition that Kaspar was an important personage. In addition to the historical, there were also dramatic and fictional versions of the story of Kaspar Hauser, the last to cause a stir being the novel by Jacob Wassermann (1926). Discarding all critical sense and indulging in sentimental embroidery, Herr Wassermann credits all the legends and offers his story as a belated tribute to a greatly wronged person. The scholarly work, which exploded the most prolific legend of modern times, is that of Antonius van der Linde (1887). It definitely protocols the case.

In these social-historical speculations the boy Kaspar falls into a secondary place; the sponsors of the myth form the major characters in the hundred-year episode of credulity. Had Kaspar fallen into critical hands, the entire literature of a thousand entries would never have appeared. Had there been any practical knowledge of psychology a hundred years ago, the utter preposterousness of Kaspar's rapid acquisitions after fifteen years of extreme neglect would have been apparent. Such miracles do not occur.

Credulity alone might have produced the initial furore and the fatal error. But Teutonic pedantry has much to answer for. A small group of German scholars lost their heads on the topic; men of letters contributed to the confusion. It would all be ridiculous—a tempest in a teapot—had it not been so serious, had not so many persons of influence been involved in the storm. A spark of credulity may under favoring circumstances set going a legend even in modern enlightened times. To the inscription on Kaspar's tomb might well be added: "A monument to human credulity."

Can we at this late day reconstruct the actual Kaspar Hauser, and how should we classify him? Stated with impolite brevity, he was a psychopathic liar with a shrewdness that occasionally accompanies an otherwise low-grade mentality. Had he turned up in present day Boston instead of a century ago in provincial Nuremberg, he might have been referred to Dr. William Healy, who has described a group of similar cases, no two alike, except in the chronic tendency to fabricate, sometimes to lie plausibly. Attempted suicide to secure attention also occurs as a symptom in these psychopathic personalities. Many are vain, self-centered, unstable vagrants looking for excitement and inventing fantastic tales to make themselves more interesting.

The ready fabrication appears in Kaspar's career from the beginning to the end. The letters which he presented upon his appearance were obviously concocted. They were wholly inconsistent with the "child of nature" myth, which of course was not in Kaspar's mind. They contain statements that the boy can read and write, and—a characteristic bit of vanity—"if he had parents (which he has not) he would have been a scholar; only show him a thing and he can do it." Kaspar Hauser's unusual fate was that of a mythomaniac whose fabrications were for a time credited, and in whose behalf other myths reinforcing his own were invented. Under the "detective" facilities and the psychological resources of 1928, the mystery of a hundred years earlier would have been solved in short order, and the world deprived of a valuable example of several varieties of human credulity.

CHAPTER V

SERMONS IN STONES:
THE FOSSILS OF PROFESSOR BERINGER

THE ABUNDANT supply of credulity makes its exploitation tempting, even when not profitable. The inclination is strong to prove your own wisdom by way of another's credulity. To "fool" the other fellow is a gratifying demonstration of your superior wisdom. The first of April is not the only day dedicated to the demonstration of human folly. When the deception is carried out on a large scale, or the folly becomes public, the hoax becomes a candidate for the Hall of Fame of Error.

The famous hoaxes of history may be said to belong to the story of credulity; so do the "bubbles" of wild financial speculation. They show that when wish runs high, wisdom runs low. But to include them would expand unduly this chapter in wishful unwisdom. I shall limit it to one extraordinary instance.

It is the story of a hoax perpetrated on one victim, who under the intense wish to establish by visible proof a belief deeply cherished as a faith, gave the hoaxed evidence publicity, to the undoing of his reputation. It is a tale to excite one's pity even as one wonders how a man of scientific training could fall for so gross a deception. The episode concerns the amazing fossils of Würzburg, excavated under unusual circumstances in the years preceding 1726.

To understand how a mind of that period might go about considering the origin of fossils, we must recall the

46

agelong and violent conflict between religious doctrine and science to decide such matters as the origin of the earth and of the creatures dwelling thereon. We must remember that the truth of the Biblical account of creation was a basic article of faith. The impression is common that the religious opposition to scientific explanations belongs to a remote past. It is in fact only a few generations away. The fundamentalism that still survives is near of kin. Even later than the fossil hoax I am about to relate, was the opposition to the great naturalist Linnæus, who named man *homo sapiens.* He described more than four thousand animal forms, thus making doubtful whether Noah had assembled and named all of them in the Ark. He was called to account for his heretical views, and as well for his explanation of a reported reddening of water as due to minute insects; for the theologians regarded the phenomenon as the miracle of water turned to blood. The Linnæan explanation was held to be impious, and referred to the wiles of Satan. Later in the same eighteenth century—a period of enlightenment—another great naturalist, Buffon, had stated simple geological facts as to the age of the earth. For questioning whether all the animals were created in six days just as they now exist, he was forced by the Theological Society of Paris to recant: "I abandon everything in my book respecting the formation of the earth, and generally all which may be contrary to the narrative of Moses." So recent is the emancipation from dogma.

With this in mind, it will seem less strange that in 1726 a doctor of philosophy and of medicine, holding a chair of "natural philosophy," a contributor to botanical knowledge, should hold that fossils were made by God when He was trying out forms of animal life; that they were hidden in the earth for His own pleasure, or to test human faith, or for reasons past finding out. Theological zoölogy was in the saddle. There was an earlier explanation, that fossils were formed by "lapidific juice"; which lucid accounting, though free from religious bias, was hardly illuminating. When fossil sea-shells were found in mountainous regions of Europe, Voltaire, lest this fact be used to strengthen the Mosaic account of the Flood, suggested that the fossil shells were accidentally dropped by returning Crusaders. In citing Voltaire, one is never quite sure whether he is ridiculing opinion or illustrating it. At all events explanations were not very discerning in the best of minds. The influence of theology was too powerful, the voice of science too weak.

Not fossils alone were theologically explained. There were other puzzling finds, such as the stone axes and spears and arrow-heads that now fill the cases of our ethnological museums. We know them as specimens of the craft of primitive man many thousands of years before the age assigned to the earth by the interpreters of *Genesis*. To many generations, they were known as "thunder-stones"; they were regarded as the missiles of gods or demigods hurled in anger or sport. Reasoning and believing according to our standards of credibility is a rather recent possession.

When Professor Beringer at the University of Würzburg, lecturing on zoölogy, became enthusiastic concerning his theory of fossils as the work of a sportive or experimental Creator, there were skeptical minds and practical jokers in his class who decided to put the professor's faith to test. They thought they could do as well as the Creator; so they buried clay specimens in the professor's favorite digging places and awaited the result. Dr. Beringer in due course found them, and published them for the greater glory of God and his own theory.

The students began modestly with simplified spiders and scorpions hardly anatomically perfect; but they grew bolder as the good doctor took the bait. In the order of creation, they followed the insects with fossils of birds

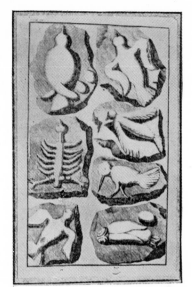

THE FOSSILS OF PROFESSOR BERINGER

Insects; birds; comets, stars, crescent moon, and sun; finally, the climax of the hoaxers' art, the "fossil" inscriptions in Hebrew with the signature of Jehovah.

equally quaint, some even shown along with their eggs; then appeared fishes and even a fish with a bird's head; and later shells with stars and crescents and trailing comets, such as were never seen on sea or land or sky.

But the climax was still to come. To enable Dr. Beringer to dumbfound his critics and clinch the thesis that God was the authentic author of these "insectiform stones," the students devised stones, some in forms of shells, containing Hebrew and Syriac inscriptions, and even the autographic name of Jehovah plainly lettered. It became known among the professors of Würzburg that Herr Professor Doktor Beringer was busy preparing for publication an account of his revolutionary discoveries. His colleagues tried to convince him that he had been the victim of a questionable joke. But he took their approaches as an attempt to deprive him of the great honor attaching to a profound scientific revelation.

The book with its elaborate illustrations was dedicated with a pompous eulogy to the Prince Bishop of Würzburg. Promptly Beringer found himself famous; but it was not the fame he had expected. Credulity has its limits; the book became the joke of the day, and Beringer the laughing-stock. The students confessed. Poor Beringer spent all his savings in buying up the books and hoped that all would be forgotten. He never recovered from the blow. The clay fossils of Würzburg became famous; they find a unique place in the museum of credulity.

To proclaim a fundamentalist faith from pulpit or platform was one thing; actually to dig up proof and in such crude and startling form was quite another. Reconciling religion and science by dialectic was a noble service; but presenting absurdities in clay was a fool's project. Checking up on the Creator's tryouts was a dubious intrusion. Beringer was ridiculed for having the courage of his convictions. He is one of the few martyrs of logic.

Even the grave did not close the incident. A bookseller of Hamburg, more enterprising than scrupulous, bought up the plates and reissued the volume. He profited by the venture, so curious was the public to read how one poor scholar had been victimized, ruined by credulity in a blind zeal to establish a favorite theory—one who had believed, not wisely but too well.

CHAPTER VI

THE RETURN OF THE FAIRIES, VIA SIR ARTHUR CONAN DOYLE

CREDULITY comes to be a matter of standards. By our mature and critical standards, children are credulous and earlier generations decidedly so. When there is a sharp contrast between the status of the belief and that of the believing mind, such as that of the belief in fairies and the mind of Sir Arthur Conan Doyle, we meet another type of credulity. Should two well-educated children report to their families actual encounters with living fairies in the woods, the incident would not raise a commotion, though it might suggest the need of discipline. When a man with the training and reputation of Sir Arthur Conan Doyle publishes a book on the reality of fairies with photographs as witnesses, it *is* news; indeed an incredible item. The "fairy-tale" is the typical myth of childhood; yet in the year of grace and enlightenment 1923, a sound mind sets forth that fairies may be hunted with a camera like any wild game, if only the fairies give one the gift to see them, and one can entice them to pose.

The intimates of the fairies were Elsie, aged sixteen, and her cousin Frances, aged ten. They borrowed a camera, went off alone to a sheltered glen and bagged the pictures, expressing surprise when the fairy forms appeared on the developed plates. Thus returned the fairies; but we should never have heard of them but for their endorsement by a distinguished sponsor. The "case" of Elsie and Frances is a minor consideration. The "case" in point is that of Sir

Arthur, student of medicine, novelist, psychic researcher, who looked upon his contributions to the reality of the "beyond" as the crowning achievement of his memorable life.

The reader should be informed that Sir Arthur believed in the genuineness of spirit photographs, in which "extra" faces appear "in a cloud of ectoplasm." He founded the S.S.S.P.—Society for the Study of Supernormal Photographs. That all spirit photographs are fraudulently produced has been abundantly demonstrated. Dr. W. F. Prince, Research Officer for the American Society for Psychical Research, so declares them and proves to the hilt the detailed methods of their manipulation. All this evidence Sir Arthur ignored. His correspondence with Houdini illustrates his credulity in the presence of the most evident trickery, when spirits are concerned. With this predilection, it becomes more intelligible that he should admit fairies to the crew of the actualized supernormal, made visible in the "flesh."

Sir Arthur does not absolutely and unreservedly declare that the photographs are "genuine" proof that fairies exist; but his hospitality to the belief is so close to complete credulity that the line between them disappears. He examines the photographs with a high-power lens as objectively as "Sherlock Holmes," the creation of his imagination, inspects the ash of a cigar or a fingerprint in running down the clue of a crime.

One fact of interest is this presence of a double pipe—the very sort which the ancients associated with fauns and naiads —in each picture. But if pipes, why not everything else? Does it not suggest a complete range of utensils and instruments for their own life? Their clothing is substantial enough.... It seems to me that with fuller knowledge and with fresh means of vision, these people are destined to become just as solid and real as the Eskimos.... And what joy is in the complete abandon of their little graceful figures as they let

FAIRY PHOTOGRAPHS

On the left, Frances with a whole troupe of fairy dancers; on the right, a fairy offering a posy of harebells to Elsie.

themselves go in the dance! They may have their shadows and
trials as we have, but at least there is a great gladness manifest in this demonstration of their life.

A second general observation is that the elves are a compound of the human and the butterfly, while the gnome has
more of the moth. This may be merely the result of under-
exposure of the negative and dullness of the weather. Perhaps
the little gnome is really of the same tribe, but represents an
elderly male, while the elves are romping young women.
Most observers of fairy life have reported, however, that there
are separate species, varying very much in size, appearance
and locality.

Four years after the first fairy pictures were taken, the
two girls were brought back to the glen and "a stereoscopic
camera and a cinema camera placed at their disposal" in
the hope of securing more information; for only Elsie and
Frances were supposed to have this rare power of seeing
fairies. We are then told that "the fates were most un-
kind"; there were no results. It rained incessantly.

A small seam of coal had been found in the Fairy Glen and
it had been greatly polluted by human magnetism. These conditions might perhaps have been overcome; but the chief im-
pediment of all was the change in the girls, the one through
womanhood and the other through board-school education.

Apart from the obvious moral that credulity unbridled
may lead the rider to destruction, there is an instructive
lesson in the analysis of the resulting perversions of logic
and flimsy defenses; they make the belief in fairies the
minor credulity.

To believe in fairies one must (1) dismiss the explanation of fraud; otherwise the episode is just the story of a
mischievous prank and not the thesis of a serious book.
As is customary when miracles are concerned, the children
and all connected with the story are vouched for as honest.
A strong desire to accept a super-world closes the door to
deception as an explanation. This brings with it a train

of suppositions, each more credit-straining than the one
before. One must believe (2) that the ability to see fairies
is a special gift of peculiarly endowed natures, which may
be extended to cameras in their hands; (3) that Fairyland,
which is a lost paradise to most of us, when regained, can
alas, again be lost! And by what? By (4) "pollution, by
human magnetism," by (5) "womanhood," by (6) "board-
school education!" We land in a series of assumptions as
crass as those of a medieval belief, saturated with credulity,
riddled with superstitions. If fairies, why not centaurs,
mermaids, and dragons?

The next logical lapse (7) is of a different order: that
the veridity of all the details is supported by the confirmation of ancient (imaginative) representations such as *the
double pipe of Pan!* The fallacy accepts imitation as convincing confirmation. By the same logic in reverse, it is
held (8) that fairies must be real or they could not be
photographed! (In the same vein we may argue that as the
fairies' clothes look as though made in Paris or Hollywood
—real places on the map—the fairies must be as real as their
clothes and these cities.)

But the climax of perversity is (9) the setting of the
argument in the garb of scientific research. *"Fuller knowledge and fresh means of vision may make fairies as real as
Eskimos."* The implied fallacy of analogy would read:
"Since by such inquiry we have learned more about
microbes and meteors, why not about fairies also?" In
further yielding to that order of thinking, we come to (10)
the same fallacy twice compounded: the conclusion that
there are or may be composites of humans and butterflies,
with further speculations about gnomes and moths, tribes,
species, and sexes! (Again, why not the biology of mermaids and centaurs?)

Thus simple credulity invites complex rationalization.
But the reasoning is so deteriorated that the mental ma-

chinery seems to have become completely disordered. Without this extreme if pitiable example of credulity, its dire possibilities—sporadic and exceptional, unquestionably— would remain unrealized.

In that the infection of credulity spreads from belief to proof, it makes for irrationality; it rots the mind. Such degenerations are, however, local infections confined to a limited area, the area determined by prepossession. Thus arise complexes, fixed ideas, and cherished conclusions; hence logic-tight compartments of belief. A mind sound and mature in other employments and versed in the technique of proof, continues to use the accredited forms of argument, but through the infection of credulity, uses them foolishly, perversely, absurdly. The belief in fairies has not come as a lapse to primitive thinking. The return is by the misuse of science; and that is the paradox. As most of us have no tendency to admit fairies to the workaday world of which cameras are a product, we look upon the photographs not as evidence of the return of the fairies but as an exceptional instance of the return of credulity.

A selection of reels from the panorama of credulity is likely to leave the impression that men have used their minds to slight advantage. The selections are dramatic examples and in so far exceptional. The world would not have progressed, nor sanity have been retained, had the ways of credulity been the prevalent modes of thinking generally. These are striking footprints in the sands of credulity; their contemplation will serve to further the appreciation of sound, critical thinking.

PART II

MAGIC AND MARVEL

THE APPEAL OF WONDER

It is easier to believe than to be scientifically instructed.—LOCKE.

Nothing persuades people of small understanding so much as that which they cannot understand.—CARDINAL RETZ.

Come and see my shining palace built upon the sand.—EDNA ST. VINCENT MILLAY.

ARGUMENT

THE PLACE *of wonder in human psychology is prominent in the life of the mind, though one would hardly gather this impression from its slight treatment in the texts of psychology. Like curiosity and surprise, it is an emotion arising in the exercise of intelligence—an intellectual emotion, and by that status, a sentiment. Its principle is simple: the unusual and exceptional impresses, and when on a grand scale, adds the giant wonder of size. The ancients listed the seven wonders of the world, partly fabled, partly actual. Wonder tales are universal. The mental appetite demands thrills along with information, requires spice as well as nutrition. The Latin preface to a remarkable tale was* mirabile dictu, *wonderful to relate; the modern version is* Believe it or Not! *The popularity of that caption is directed to freaks of nature or art and the miscellanies called curios—wayward expressions or exceptions in the order of things. Wonder, like all complex emotions, is expressed at many levels of intelligence; the evolution of wonder runs through the story of belief.*

Wonder makes alliance with fear, even with horror; it combines with the sense of awe and mystery, impressive as a power, weird, uncanny, menacing. But typically, wonder proceeds in the mood of admiration: that the world and we ourselves are fearfully and wonderfully made. Wonder is sought in that it provides an escape from the commonplace; the ego is stimulated by sharing in the thrill of bigger, stranger, more awesome things. The imagination craves and creates a realm of wonder, to put a "kick" into belief.

Marvel furnishes the plot; it verges upon philosophy, when it posits a scheme of forces by which the marvel is wrought. Presently the mind, moderately imaginative and also reflective, creates another world standing out above the ordinary natural series of events, in due course called supernatural.

The portal of marvel is magic. The primitive mind does not yet clearly distinguish natural and supernatural, accepts a world of magic as equally natural with the world of fact. How the world ruled by magic-marvel was transformed into a world ruled by natural law is the story of science. It was a creeping and laborious process, with the modern mind far off in the making. The transition shows a clinging to the magical explanation even as the allegiance is transferred to the natural. The realms go on side by side, interact, at times aware of their inconsistency, as commonly ignoring it.

Belief in marvel implies credulity. A glimpse of "Our Credulous Heritage" is the indispensable overture to the historical play of Magic and Marvel, transformed by no fairy's wand, but by endless, prosaic steps of hard-won gains in knowledge, into the natural marvels of science. The thrill of wonder, distilled from wish, exceeds in influence the calm pursuit of inquiry, which in comparison seems pallid and grubby.

I select two exhibits of our credulous heritage, the one the belief in wondrous animals; for the other, nothing less would be convincing than a cross-section of a few notable minds, progressive for their day, hopelessly credulous by our standards. To show its range from innocent white to deadly black, I must include the ghastly side of belief in marvel, which created so deadly a conglomerate of doctrine as demonology, which belief in turn created the horror of witchcraft manias. There is a sting and even a curse, as well as a thrill, in the exercise of the imagination. As a constructive tale with a happy ending, there is the cult of the magnet, a wonder-tale of science with a succession of dramatic turns. For the revival of marvel on a grand scale, there is the story of Theosophy, which turns upon the venture of an extraordinary woman. The record of her vital ventures and prodigious output is cramped in a chapter of any dimensions. Her magnificence in a variegated, flamboyant repertory is a marvel of quite other quality than that in which she regarded it. These eclectically selected tales, with no unity of ensemble, serve to give a realistic picture of the vicissitudes of belief as affected by the appeal of wonder.

CHAPTER VII

OUR CREDULOUS HERITAGE

THE COURSE of belief is set by inclinations and standards; inclinations cater to wish, standards wait upon wisdom. Primitive, childlike, and unschooled minds believe what they have "a mind to." Beliefs the mind must acquire to live at all; once started, they continue. Standards are derived from the test of experience; they mature with the slow growth of the ages. Until otherwise cultivated, the natural appetite of the mind is prone to accept the plausible, the congenial, the comforting, the thrilling, and is avid for the spice of wonder. In the early stages of thinking, there are vast regions of the ununderstood; any fact or explanation may be accepted, if it provides some measure of insight, some support to cling to, some satisfaction of the urge to wonder.

Belief is compliant. People believe what they are told; those in authority, by grace or prestige, become the doctrine makers. People believe, as they act, gregariously; their fellow-beings are fellow-believers. Tradition molds; each generation affects the next; cumulatively there arises a heritage of belief. Whether we turn back a few or many pages of our mental history, and whatever the pages, we come upon the many-sided, credulous heritage from which we have emerged. The emergence may be so complete that our reaction to the wonder tales which our ancestors believed is the wonder that they could have believed them. They seem to us to have dwelled in walled cities of belief, the walls constructed of tradition and prepossession. Much of what was vital to them is wholly indifferent to us; what to them was significant is to us meaningless, to them convincing and to us absurd.

A survey of our credulous heritage might readily extend to volumes, a cyclopedia of superstition, an epitome of error. Its temper appears in the character of the beliefs and in the temper of the believing mind. For the one I shall select some phase of credulous zoölogy, which is more truly fabulous; for the other some believing minds among the notable intellectuals of the seventeenth century—a period when older credulities continued beyond the dawn of a newer enlightenment.

FABULOUS ZOÖLOGY

Fabled beasts form an interesting relic of our mental heritage, a Noah's Ark of the imagination. In the medieval interpretation which persisted in and through the Renaissance, the forms of creation are both texts and zoölogical specimens. Speculation has the place of honor; observations play a minor part. The Biblical account of creation set a pattern for scholastic embellishment. Under theological sanction we read: "Before Adam's sin there was no death and therefore neither ferocity nor venom" (Wesley). Zoölogical peace reigned everywhere, with lions and lambs amiable. "None of these attempted to devour or in any wise hurt one another; the spider was as harmless as the fly, and did not lie in wait for blood." St. Augustine declared it so, and even that plants had no poison until the Fall. The Venerable Bede explains the evil in noxious creatures: "Thus fierce and poisonous animals were created for terrifying man (because God foresaw that he would sin), in order that he might be made aware of the final punishment of hell."

St. Augustine was troubled by mice and frogs and flies and worms, not as plagues but as zoö-theological perplexities. He confessed that he did not know why they were created. He classified animals as useful, hurtful, or superfluous; the hurtful to prevent too much cherishing and love of this life; the superfluous, although they are not necessary to our service, yet the whole design of the universe is thereby completed and finished. Luther was less complacent; to him the fly was not superfluous, but noxious, sent by the Devil to vex him while reading. Zoölogy, like many another phase of knowledge, had to fit in to a man-made scheme, though it was ascribed to the Creator. A theologian by name of Watson, a contemporary of John Wesley, sets forth that before the Fall all serpents stood erect, walked, and talked. "We have no reason at all to believe that the animal had a serpentine form in any mode or degree until its transformation; that he was then degraded to a reptile to go upon his belly imparts, on the contrary, an entire loss and alteration of the original form." The beliefs are never as quaint or as out of focus as the reasons for them.

A choice depository of fabulous zoölogy is contained in the *Bestiary,* a collection of marvels of nature relating to stones, plants, and animals, also called *Physiologus.* Their currency is due to their revival and embellishment in medieval and later times. The stories were believed and circulated widely; they were carved in stone, engraved in print, and told in popular lore. Partly allegory, partly presented as a dispensation of "nature," the fusion was acceptable as fact. The Bestiary begins with the king of the beasts.

The Lion has three amazing habits: he sleeps with his eyes open; when pursued he covers his tracks with his tail; and (in the medieval version) "the lioness giveth birth to cubs which remain three days without life. Then cometh the lion, breatheth upon them, and bringeth them to life. Thus it is that Jesus Christ during three days was deprived of life, but God the Father raised Him gloriously." The natural history of the Phœnix is likewise a Resurrection homily, circumstantially related. "The phœnix dwells in India and lives alone. After 500 years he begins to feel the effect of age and flees to the city of Leopolis, where the priests, awaiting his coming, have erected an altar upon which the phœnix lays himself as a sacrifice. He rises from the ashes."

THE FATHER LION BREATHING LIFE INTO THE CUB
From a Bestiary.

The Bestiary tales recount prodigies as eagerly as moralities. There is the Whale, which goes by the strange name of the Sea-turtle. He is a huge and sluggish beast, lying in the water stationary for years, with only his back visible. Bushes take root and grow upon it. Mariners, mistaking it for an island, land and build a fire. When the whale feels the heat, he plunges to the bottom, taking with him mariners and all.

The Ant-Lion tale is said to have arisen through a difficulty or error in translating a Hebrew text. It reads in *Physiologus*:

As to the ant-lion, his father hath the shape of a lion, his mother that of an ant; the father liveth upon flesh and the mother upon herbs; these bring forth the ant-lion, a compound of both and in part like to either; for his fore-part is like that of a lion and his hind part like that of an ant. Being thus composed, he is neither able to eat flesh like his father nor herbs like his mother; and so he perisheth.

Through similar sources we learn that the basilisk kills serpents by his breath and men by his glance, that the pelican nourishes her young with her own blood, that the salamander quenches fire, that the hyena talks with shepherds, that certain birds are born when a fruit of a certain tree falls upon the water; and that in Ethiopia are ants with horns of the size of dogs, while the ants of India dig up gold out of the sand with their feet and hoard it, which tales are turned to indicate the barking attacks of vicious heretics, who dig gold out of the Scriptures and put it to no use.

Credulous zoölogy is a subject of many chapters. The early attempts in factual natural history seem at our distance as fantastic as those in which imagination and moral value have full license. Albertus Magnus, the outstanding scholar of the thirteenth century, while discrediting older tales, such as were derived from Aristotle and Pliny, added many of his own, equally credulous. The contribution of Albertus is the combination of sea and land. Marine transformations of a snail, a hare, and a lion produce a snail-fish, a hare-fish, and a lion-fish, which he accepted, though relegating mermaids and centaurs to the land of myths. [1]

[1] The obstruction of dogma supported general credulity. Occasionally the Scriptural version sought confirmation in science. Since Eve was created from a rib of Adam, there should be one rib missing in every man; the fact that Vesalius could not find it was resented. The belief in an "incorruptible" bone led to the search for it when victims were burnt at the stake, but in vain.
So real was the spiritual world in the minds of men that a report could arise in the twelfth century that so long as the cross of Christ remained in possession of the infidel, children would have only twenty-two

Topsell, an English "naturalist" of the seventeenth century, favors scales; he depicts a Gorgon which no zoölogical garden has ever been able to capture; and his serpents are many and strange. Gessner, another popular-izer, shows a great sea serpent in the act of encircling a vessel and selecting the most tempting sailor for his repast; while Aldrovandus pictures snails such as never crawled on land or sea.

Natural history in the temper of wonder produces a fabulous zoölogy, covering appearance and habits. Pliny set the pattern for fabulous zoölogy; the Munchausen touch which we find in his tales was doubtless as acceptable to him as his verifiable observations. Pliny gave currency to the myth of the salamander "so extremely cold as to extinguish fire by its contact in the same way as ice doth."

It was with the extension of experience in the days of the pioneer travelers that the reporting of marvels became current. The *Voyages of Sir John Mandeville* brought accounts of men with such large lips that they covered their faces with them when asleep; of dwarfs in another "yle" with no mouths and but only a little round hole through which they "eat their meate with a pipe," and whistle as they have no tongue; of men in Ethiopia with only one foot, but that so swift that they travel at a marvelous pace, and so large that it protects them from sun or rain.

Fabulous zoölogy became a medley of ecclesiastic homilies, naturalistic errors, and superstitious folk-beliefs,

---

instead of thirty-two teeth. It was mainly by way of bringing observations into harmony with the Scriptures that the naturalist was lost in the theologian. The distribution of animals—even such a fact, when it became known, as that the kangaroo was found only in Australia—had to be reconciled with an original habitat in the Ark of Ararat; fossils were explained as tryouts of the Creator (see p. 47). The same habit of mind became traditional and is represented so late as 1736 by Bishop Butler's *Analogy of Religion, Natural and Revealed, to the Constitution and Course of Nature*, while the *Bridgewater Treatises*, though conceding the independence of the natural sciences, carry on the older argument.

FABULOUS ANIMALS

Upper left, the gorgon, from the title-page of Edward Topsell's *Historie of Four-footed Beastes*. Upper right, a lion-fish as described by Albertus. Middle left, the sea-serpent, from Konrad Gesner's *Historiae Animalium*. Middle right, a snail-fish as described by Albertus. Lower left, a unique snail, cochlea, from Aldrovandus' *De Animalibus*. Lower right, the boas, from the title-page of Edward Topsell's *Historie of Serpents*.

which may be sampled eclectically. There were the goose-barnacles, so called from their shape, hanging down in salt water, which were supposed to develop into actual geese, with the further implication that being thus of marine origin, they were admissible as Lenten diet. There was the precious horn of the rhinoceros, with the property of counteracting any poison that might be drunk from it when used as a cup. There was the tale of the gigantic crab that retired into his hole and caused the tides when he left it; there was the toad with the jewel in its head, which might be induced to give up the gem by making it snap at a bit of red flannel. There are beliefs that swallows winter at the bottom of ponds, that eels could be bred from horsehair dissolved in water, that birds were generated from seeds. There is the tale of the oven-bird of South America that plasters its nest but desisted from work on Sunday after the introduction of Christianity; there is the grasshopper, the praying mantis, so called from the resemblance of its position to that of devotion, which in the Arabian legend turns toward Mecca, and in the Hottentot version confers sainthood on any one on whom it alights.

By the same order of fable-making credulity, animals—crocodile, ibis, white elephant, bull, cat, scarab—become sacred. These beliefs form but a small section of the great animistic chapter of totems and taboos, which survive in the British Lion, the Russian Bear, the American Eagle, to say nothing of fraternal orders of Elks or Moose or the Wisconsin Badger and the Minnesota Wolverine.

Fabulous zoölogy, from Pegasus to the stork, left its impress on ways of belief, enriching myth and distorting fact. Its appeal to marvel prolonged its rule and post-poned to a modern day the study of animals in a strictly naturalistic temper. As knowledge advanced, credulity re-tired. But diverse other misconceptions prevailed similarly sponsored. The footsteps of credulity appear everywhere in the sands of time.

Another and more realistic picture of the credulous habit of our intellectual ancestors is reflected in the beliefs of scholarly minds who, as they ventured upon newer solutions, still held to the older ones. An illuminating record is that of Jerome Cardan, a pioneer in autobiography. The frank account of his life relates his achievements and opinions, his travels and practices, his equal devotion to science and to superstitions. He has been described as a genius and a child, a madman and a philosopher, with a touch of the charlatan, like his senior contemporary Paracelsus. In vanity, rebellion, and the spirit of venture, they have much in common; both must be reckoned as distinguished physicians given to grandiose theories. It has been said of Cardan, that for all for which his contemporaries thought him wise we should think him mad, and for all that they held him mad we should hold him wise.

Cardan was born in Pavia in 1501 and lived to be seventy-five years old, though his astrological forecast predicted his death at forty-five. He was the illegitimate child of a jurist, which stigma was cited thirty years later as cause for his exclusion from the medical guild. He knew poverty and illness, misfortune and disgrace, also prosperity and reputation. An inveterate gambler with dice and cards, he gambled with fortune in his career. Despite scant and irregular schooling, he became an eminent physician at a time when medical standards were dubious; he found no incompatibility between the principles of his profession and a hospitality to personal superstitions and occultisms.

He records the planetary indications at the hour of his birth:

The malefics were not within the angles; Mars was casting an evil influence on each luminary because of the incompatibility of their positions, and its aspect was square to the moon. Therefore I could easily have been a monster, except for the fact that the place of the preceding conjunction had been 29 degrees in Virgo, over which Mercury is the ruler, and indeed was so near it that I came forth literally torn from my mother's womb. Since the Sun, both malefics, and Venus and Mercury were in the human signs, I did not deviate from the human form.

Cardan describes himself as "prophetic, what Ptolemy called harpocratic," and would today be called "psychic." Like his father, he stammered, thus disclosing a nervous liability. He experienced premonitions, and believed in his own intuitions or "hunches," and in protecting portents. When released miraculously from his most threatening infirmity, he vowed his energies to medicine:

I had read in some notes collected by my father that if any one at eight o'clock in the morning of the first day of April should on bended knee, beseech the Holy Virgin, she might intercede for a legitimate petition, if he add as well the Lord's Prayer and the Ave Maria. I observed the day and the hour, and forthwith on Corpus Christi day in the same year I was freed from my trouble.

There are many "providential" adventures, such as that of the Garter. On October 7, 1562, on setting out for Bologna to deliver lectures, he found that the brass tip, binding "hose to doublet," was missing. Recalling that there were six sets of garters in his chest at home, he returned and found, not only the garters, but books and manuscripts that had been forgotten. Later the chest was broken into, and all its remaining contents stolen.

If it had not been for my garter I should not have been able to give my lectures. I should have lost my post and gone begging, so many memoires would have perished; I should have died ere long of grief. And all this depended on an insignificant instant! Alas, for the unhappy conditions of mankind!

He relates that as a lad of twenty he was induced to buy a copy of the tales of Apuleius, possibly attracted by the title, *The Golden Ass.*

I who for a truth had been only once up to this time in an elementary school, and had no understanding of the Latin language, yet had the folly to buy the book because of the gilded decoration, and on the following day found myself as proficient in Latin as I am this very day.

He records as of date 1531:

A dog of the neighborhood, ordinarily a well behaved beast, howled for hours without stopping; ravens sat on the ridge pole, croaking with unwonted persistence; when the house boy broke the kindling fagots, fiery sparks flew forth, and before I rightly knew what I was about, I found myself married. From that moment, all sorts of adversities were my constant companions.

What was to become the crowning disaster of his life was thus heralded: "The guardian angel foreseeing what was imminent in my affairs, sent me a palpitation of the heart after a manner peculiar to himself, so that it should assume the form of a tremor in the bedroom" and a violent shaking of the bed. On that very evening, his son had promised to wed Brandonia di Seroni, a girl "utterly without dowry," in the tactful French phrase, "with a regrettable education." Some years later his son was charged with poisoning his unfaithful wife.

By the merest chance, looking closely at my hands, I observed on the ring finger of the right one, at the root, the image of a bloody sword. Suddenly I felt afraid. What now? That evening came a messenger, saying my son had been arrested. For 53 days the sign gradually ascended from the base and on the last day reached the tip where it blazed a blood red flame. I did not know what had happened. At midnight, my son was beheaded, and in the morning the portent had almost disappeared; on the second day following, it had vanished.

Turning the autobiographical pages, one comes upon varied instances of his readily believing mind. He notes that enterprises undertaken before the full moon turn out successfully; that all his journeys up to the age of sixty occurred in February; that he was fond of river-crabs because while his mother carried him, she ate many of them; that he heard murmurs in the ear when he was being discussed elsewhere, in the right ear if the opinion was favorable, in the left if unfavorable. When he seemed to hear grunting on the street at night, he knew some one was about to die; in one instance, his neighbor was killed by lightning; when his mother died, he heard drops falling on the pavement, although it was not raining; when ill, his flesh gave off an odor of sulphur incense. From about 1534 on, he began to see in his dreams events shortly to come to pass; at times the church bells rang with no one ringing them; when a pet dog chewed up his lecture notes at the end of the year, he accepted it as an omen to abandon the project then in hand. "Only a man will rise to the top who understands the significance of all these influences and knows how to heed them in his business. Wherefore in any events whatsoever, things of apparently no significance ought to be duly observed."

With all his "inclinations," he had a keen wit, a shrewd observation, an independent bent, a critical view of the failings of others. He was a rebel against authority. "If his deductions seem wild," writes the translator of his autobiography, "we must realize how absurd were his premises." Such were the ways of belief of a savant of three centuries ago; for that he was: mathematician, physicist, naturalist, and physician, covering like other savants of the day the entire field of knowledge.[2] He was progressive, opposing the blind following of authority, and irregular, ready to prove the untried.

It was a lucky "cure" of a senator's daughter that started Cardan on a lucrative practice and led to the signal adventure of his life—his summons from Naples to Paris and thence to Aberdeen, to treat the Bishop, John Hamilton, illegitimate brother of the Regent. The distinguished prelate, ill for ten years, was under the care of a Franco-Spanish doctor, Cassanante. This doctor had been impressed by Cardan's writings, and set off for Lyons with a tempting purse to persuade him to make the formidable journey to Scotland. To the attending physicians Cardan appeared with the prestige of a magician. They were impressed by his deep insight when he completely reversed the treatment. He found the cause of the trouble, which seems to have been asthma, not in the excessive cold and moisture of the brain, but in its excess of heat. His dietary prescription was impressive: tortoise soup, distilled snails, barley water, and two to four pints of asses' milk; and his further treatment still more so: "The purging of the brain was a serious business and was compassed by anointing the coronal suture with an ointment made of Greek pitch, ship's tar, white mustard, euphisbium and honey of anathardus, and if needed, a blister fly." At all events, whether because of, despite, or irrespective of this treatment, the Bishop improved, and the great Doctor Cardan received a royal fee.

The expedition to Great Britain occupied ten months; his return through the Continent was a triumphal procession. In London he was asked to pronounce upon the condition of a royal patient, Edward VI. Assuming the prophetic vein, he predicted that in his fifty-sixth year the

---

[2] His most fantastic contribution is the *Metaposcopia*, reading character from wrinkles of the forehead. See p. 252.

"King would be troubled with divers illnesses." Edward died the following year, whereupon Cardan ascribed his favorable prophecy to his pity for the young king.

Cardan's declining years brought declining fortunes. His mind is said to have been affected by the tragedy of his son. His practices fell under suspicion. Though debarred from practising, he seems to have kept his standing with the Church and lived in Rome on a pension granted by the Pope. That such could be the career and the views of a famous physician documents our credulous heritage at a critical period of modern science.

Cardan's mind and his career find their parallel in other savants of his time. Equally typical, equally versatile, was Giovanni Baptista Porta. A prodigy he was, if it be true as he tells us that his book, *Natural Magick*,[3] was written when he was fifteen years old. The book became a popular and standard compendium of knowledge generations after. It was translated into several languages and reissued when Porta was fifty (1589).

It was a repository of information for the household as well as for the student, but above all a wonder-book. In this composite of the natural and the magical, Porta's mind was dominated far more by magic than by consideration of nature. His *Natural Magick*, for all its information, is a book of credulity.

Sir Thomas Browne (1605-1682) is another scholarly member of the credulous guild; he was physician, collector, traveler, savant in general. Commenting in the *Vulgar Errors* on the frailties of his time, he himself stands committed on that count, and by his confession: "I am, I confess, naturally inclined to that which misguided zeal terms superstition." He could rank Harvey's discovery of the

[3] Porta revived Aristotle's form of Physiognomy, as indicated in Chapter XX, "Signs and Lines of Head and Hand." Examples of his medical remedies are given in Chapter XIX, "Unwisdom about the Body."

circulation above the enterprise of Columbus, yet dabble in alchemy and the search for the philosopher's stone. He could believe that the age of 63—in that it is 7 times 9—is a climacteric year. "It is expected and entertained with fear and esteemed a favor of fate to pass it over." He could discuss why the Devil had a cloven foot and why Adam could not have had a navel. In his *Religio Medici,* he set high ideals for the physician; in practice, he gave testimony which condemned two women to a witch's death, holding that the Devil acted upon human bodies by stirring up the humors. Yet he "was often constrained to stand alone against the strength of opinion."

Robert Burton, author of *The Anatomy of Melancholy* (1621), is of the same company. Melancholia, he expounds, may result from natural and from supernatural causes—the latter mainly devils, of which there are many varieties in all lands, duly accredited. The Devil reigns in a thousand shapes and is the chief cause of melancholy. But Burton likewise anatomizes the humors, making the blood a hot, sweet, temperate red humor, prepared in the "meseraic" veins, and begetting spirits in the heart; and these also have their effect upon melancholy. It is also affected by diet; the Carthusian friars, whose chief diet is fish, are given to melancholy. Good air, good liquor, merry tales and pleasant jests, are sovereign remedies. One should not resort to magic, though amulets, without incantations, are permissible. His horoscope appears on his tombstone; the story goes that, to justify the correctness of his prediction of his death, he committed suicide on the designated day.

The older examples of outworn notions and discarded faiths present the more dramatic episodes. But the same order of credulity, the same clinging to feeble logic and wayward principles, appears in every province of the empire of belief. Modern credulities reflect the survival of our credulous heritage.

Chapter VIII

THE DEVIL IN HIS PRIME

BELIEVING in the unreal is a trick the mind has turned a hundred times, but never with so grave an issue as in devising devils. Demonology remains an exhibit of the mind's diabolical power to create a devastating fiction and live in it and by it. That there are no devils offers no hindrance to an inflamed imagination to compose circumstantial accounts of their appearance and their powers. A completely illusory dominion ruled when the Devil was in his prime; yet his kingdom was as full of circumstance and as rich in detail and ceremony and doctrine as though it were all discovery and not invention.

The fear world no less than the wish world is an achievement of human psychology; in the total perspective, fear may exceed hope in the mind's occupation. A like psychology created heavens and hells, with far more ingenuity and imagination spent upon the nether regions. The biography of the Devil extends over all chronology; his annals are no less authentic, for having lived only in the imagination of men. No other devil than fear created the state of mind of which demonology is the product. A chapter of erratic psychology must be devoted to the realm of fear, thereby giving the Devil his due.

WITCHCRAFT

How disastrously fear blocked the ways of wisdom, appears in the beliefs composing the great delusion of witchcraft—the most eventful episode in the Devil's career. Since witchcraft flourished, habits of mind have changed as radically as ways of living. Nothing is more remote from our schooled inclinations than to detect the Devil's work in our daily rounds. The demonological cult, which reached its climax in trials for witchcraft, is to us as alien as madness; we cannot reinstate that climate of opinion. We read the records, as we look upon exhibits of primitive culture in museums of anthropology, with a sense of the dire reality of false beliefs and of the great mental distance between ourselves and our fetich-bound or witch-hunting ancestors.

POSSESSION

A gate of entrance to the Devil's domain is *possession*. It was by that symptom that the doctor recognized the Devil, and through its scriptural sanction, the priest likewise. In the atmosphere thus created, it required only an unstable personality and a yielding faith to transform a sense of fear or unrest or guilt or compulsion into an invasion by demons. Possession was the Devil's hysteria; and exorcism the Church's cure. In 1588, Marthe Brossier, a country girl, was beset by convulsions. Screaming, contorting, and cursing, she begged the priest to exorcise the devils who were tormenting her. The Bishop, exceptionally wise, placed before her two bowls, one filled with spring water, the other with holy water, but so disposed them that Marthe accepted the spring water as holy; the spasms vanished. A passage of Virgil, intoned as an exorcism, worked as well as the orthodox formula. This demonstration, the monks declared, also was one of the Devil's tricks.

The effective possession was the fixed idea of the Devil's power and eternal vigilance. A typical case of collective hysteria, interpreted as possession, is that of the nuns of Loudun. In their ravings they mentioned the name of

Urban Grandier, an unpopular priest of the neighborhood. When the Archbishop of Bordeaux dismissed the
charges, finding so many contradictions in the testimony,
a second trial was held by decree of Cardinal Richelieu.
The devils, speaking out of the mouths of the nuns, accused Grandier. Though under torture, he refused to
confess; he was condemned "to pray pardon courteously
and bareheaded, and to have his body burned alive, together with the facts and magic characters now resting in
the office of the registrar." The evidence of traffic with the
powers of evil had been submitted: the pact, one page
signed by Grandier, the other by six devils, each with his
seal, and the attest of the Devil's secretary. The whole
was written in Latin in mirror-script, and admitted gross
immorality with the nuns.

In the course of the procedure, expert doctors of the
Sorbonne, questioning neither the document nor the possession, disputed whether the testimony of Satan, a notori-
ous liar, was reliable; they were met by the argument that
a properly exorcised devil could not help confessing the
truth. Such was the ideology of the tribunal of the Devil's
adversaries, with charges, evidence, and conviction all the
issue of one grievous state of mind.

Hysterical manifestations provided varied symptoms
which fell in with the universal "devil complex" that ruled
clerical and lay mind alike. Exorcism was a ministering
service of casting out devils from unfortunate victims.
Witchcraft focused upon the detection of imps and familiars as shrewd emissaries of the Devil. As demoniacs played
a decreasing part in the delusion, witchcraft became a
drama of Satan contending with God for the possession
of human souls. Every one, and not religious leaders alone,
from St. Anthony to Luther, gave thought in his daily
occupations to outwitting the Devil. Midwives were closely
watched lest they dedicate infants to Satan before the rites

of baptism could be administered. The folk beliefs laid the foundations; the learned professions did the awful rest. It was all the work of the Devil, but his instrument was the witch.

EVOCATION

The Devil was both feared and sought; belief in his power created a cult to command it; and there arose the Black Arts. To summon the Devil, learned minds could devise such a fantastically circumstantial ceremony as this:

THE NECROMANCER'S CIRCLE

Georg Conrad Horst, *Zauber-Bibliothek*, 1821.

Lay out a circle to protect all who take part in the rite from evil influence. Make it nine "shoes" (feet) in size. Inscribe on it the powerful words as indicated, each division separated by the sign of the Cross. The words must be written in blood taken from a pure white dove.

The necromancer must carry a wand of hazel, with the words cut in it: *Jesus of Nazareth, King of the Jews*; he must wear a cap and shoulder-piece made of "virgin" paper, mystically inscribed, and a long black coat. He must write the seal or signature or title of the spirit to be summoned with the blood of a coal-black raven on virgin paper which has been blackened, and hang it on the hazel stick, which is set up to receive it at the edge of the circle.

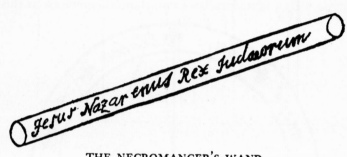

THE NECROMANCER'S WAND

This must all be done at the proper time as indicated in the astrological almanac, the final test on a Monday or Friday night, at the first or sixth hour after sunset. "Find a safe and lonely spot. If it is in a house, the bed must be turned toward the East, the door or one window must be open. It is better to make the test under an open sky."

A fire is then lighted to produce a smudge. The recipe for the powder to be burned includes black pepper and coriander.

When the solemn moment arrives, the Master, strong and fearless, speaks the "citation," while the apprentices keep silence. The conjuration is a series of prayers with a ritual specifying the purpose: to reveal a name or treasure, to inflict injury, or make a wish come true.

Should the spirit called upon not comply, let the Master take the paper that bears the spirit's name and seal, and shake it and beat it with the stick and bring it close to the fire and smoke, and gradually burn it, and the spirits thus threatened will instantly obey.

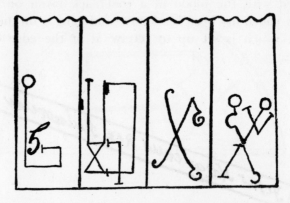

INSCRIPTION ON THE NECROMANCER'S CAP

"Then let the Master enter the circle and say: *Harim, Karis, Astacos, Enet, Miran, Baal, Alisa, Kappi, Megraret, Sagisia, Surat-bakar.*" The conjuration is complete, and the spirits are summoned to do their deadly work.

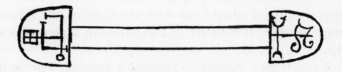

THE NECROMANCER'S SCAPULAR

The mystic necromantic art was a composite of all the motley superstitions of bigoted days. It was incorporated in a grandiose text called *The Key of Solomon*. Many a nobleman and many a physician in the seventeenth century had a copy among his private belongings and consulted it with the thrill of an initiate. The power to command the Devil's adjutants inspired fear and respect. One necromancer was accompanied by two fierce dogs wearing black-art devices on their collars, the dogs believed to be demons; another was condemned on the charge of

SEAL OF THE EVOKED DEVIL

keeping demons in a bottle; even a pope was accused of selling his soul to the Devil to attain his high office. Such were the ways of belief of the learned no less than of the ignorant, when the Devil was in his prime.

WITCH MANIAS

Beliefs reflect psychology; history moves by circumstance. But for papal intervention, the disposal of witches might have remained a phase in the regulation of sorcery, which was a common concern of the civil and ecclesiastical authorities. When all communities were subject to the Devil's dominion, sorcery was a constant menace; every one was subject to the casting of spells and to bewitchment by the evil eye. The practice of sorcery was always prohibited, but it continued in secret. Measures against it were at times severe and at times lenient; punished by death in one reign, it was subject only to the stocks, fine, or imprisonment in another.

**Mallens
maleficarum**

TITLE-PAGE OF "MALLEUS MALEFICARUM"
After the rare copy in the Harvard University Library.

The critical change in opinion, converting witchcraft from a sin to a heresy, was precipitated by the famous Bull of Pope Innocent VIII (1484), dividing the *humanum genus* into those who sought the kingdom of God and those who followed in the footsteps of evil. Two German zealots, Jacob Sprenger and Heinrich Krämer, achieved a dismal immortality when they obtained the Pope's sanction to direct the Inquisition against witches, and to that end wrote the *Malleus Maleficarum,* or *Witch Hammer* (1489). This gruesome tome brought torture and death to hundreds of thousands of wretched victims of the witch mania. It became the authoritative code for the conduct of witch trials. It is a compendium of authorized superstition. Recently available in English, in it may be read, in terrible detail, the frenzied ideology of the Devil, which for centuries blocked the progressive and humane thought of Europe.

The procedure at the witch trials projects the fanatical state of mind. The first question asked of the accused was "Do you believe in witches?" To answer "no" would imply that witches had been innocently burned. *Heresis est maxima opera maleficarum non credere,* the greatest heresy is not to believe in witchcraft. If the accused kept silent, that was *maleficium tacturnitatis,* the sin of silence, to be absolved by torture. He (or she) was then commanded to confess what acts of the Devil had been committed; refusal led to immediate and increasing torture. If the witch did not confess the first day, the torture might be "repeated" but not "continued," the subtle distinction lying between the use of the same instruments, or more brutal ones. The witch was commanded in the name of the Virgin to weep; if tears did not instantly flow, that was a sign of guilt. The judge was permitted to promise the witch immunity on confession, and then turn over the case to another judge for commitment. The judge was himself in danger of the malicious influence. For his protection he carried consecrated herbs and salt; he was not to look at the witch lest he lose his power to condemn; consequently the witches were carried backward into the court room.

The ordinary charges extended to every interference with the course of nature as it affected the concerns of men. A common ground for indictment was the bewitchment of cattle. The witch sticks an ax into the wall of the barn, takes a milk-pan between her knees, and calls out to the Devil to send her the milk of the cow that belongs to the person against whom the witch has a grudge. The Devil thereupon milks the cow and brings the milk to the witch, whence it appears to run out of the ax-handle. But the Devil deceives the witch as he has actually brought the milk through the air.

Such myths are but elaborations, with a doctrinal slant, of the many forms of the dread superstition that beset the medieval mind. A phase of mythology, which the cult of the witch adopted, is the power to assume animal form, particularly that of the "werewolf"—lycanthropy. In 1573 at Lyons a doctor of laws read the indictment that Gilles Garnier had seized and killed a girl of twelve, using his hands like wolf's paws; that he had dragged her bleeding body into the woods and devoured her; also that in the shape of a wolf he had devoured a boy of thirteen. There were many depositions to this effect. He confessed under torture, was burned at the stake, his ashes strewn to the winds; to add the legal touch, his estate was charged with the costs of the prosecution.

Though the primary charge of witchcraft was devotion to the Devil by renunciation of the grace of baptism, it came to be an ecclesiastical version of all the traditional bewitchments of the darker ages.[1]

---

[1] Historically versed students must overlook the detachment of selected phases and periods of the witch's activities in the interest of a concentration upon an outstanding psychological product—the witch mania. To suggest its extent, one may cite that "seven thousand are said to have been burned at Treves; six hundred by a single bishop in Bamberg (1622-1633), and nine hundred in the bishopric of Würzburg. In 1515 five hundred persons were executed in Geneva as Protestant witches. Four hundred died together in Toulouse in one day. It was the proud boast of a French

THE CREED

Demonological doctrine was shaped into a creed and cult of the witch, explaining the source of her powers. To begin with, it was set forth that witches were generally women because of their ready faith, their weakness, their treacherous tongues and prying curiosity, by which they taunt the Devil, and, going too far, fall into his clutches. The primary article of the creed was a compact with the Devil. It was his personal mark that produced the anesthetic spots on the skin—a common symptom in cases of hysteria—and thus was indicated the test of pricking to detect a witch.

By the same token the witch was empowered by the "prince of the power of the air" to ride to the Witches' Sabbath on so domestic an article as a broomstick. For this sacrament their naked bodies were rubbed with ointment composed of the blood of unbaptized children, and fetid ingredients.

The Black Mass was an orgy of profanation. Through witches, devils beget children to replenish their kind. Furthermore, they render men impotent and women sterile. They incite to sinful infatuation, and set snares for maidens against which the offices of the Church afford the only protection. The *Malleus Maleficarum* is minutely occupied with generative details. It sets forth how the Devil

judge that he had burned eight hundred women in sixteen years. In Como a thousand were executed in one year."

The witch had her prime in early civilizations. The pagan element strongly influenced the Christian doctrine. Græco-Roman mysteries—the Dianic cult—furnished a basis for the Sabbath on the Brocken. There actually were witches' "covens." Adventuring in the magical and forbidden has ever been a temptation; the Church parried with popular pictures in stone and print of the Devil's claim and torture of sinners, and with sermons threatening fire and brimstone. Outwitting the Devil as well as fearing the Devil belong equally to the Devil's biography. Carus, in *The History of the Devil* (1900), tells the story adequately and pictorially.

secures a human father for his child. The scholastic difficulty is that his is but a "virtual," not a "corporeal" contact; a chapter considers whether witches can produce a
"glamour" or "prestige" which induces in male victims the
delusion of loss (or the actual loss) of virility of the member in which "the Power of the Devil lies." Gynecological
examinations were made in witch trials, and are prescribed in the code.

The scholastic phase of the creed arrived at such dogmas
as that the Devil cannot truly speak, as he has no tongue
or lungs; that in the first stage of his formation the Devil
is air, then "inspissated air, partaking of some of the properties of earth"; that devils exercise their powers by con-
sent of God, so that witchcraft must be theologically
justified; that witches do not become rich, despite their
spells, because devils like to show their contempt for the
Creator by buying witches for the lowest possible price;
that princes and inquisitors are immune to witchcraft by
reason of serving the cause of justice, and enjoying the
protection of counteracting angels. Witchcraft is not an
isolated outbreak of a peculiarly fiendish character; it is
an issue of a complete mental attitude toward the nature
of man, and toward the powers in the spiritual and material realms that shape his welfare. The creed of the
witch is a portentous document in the psychology of fear
under the dominion of dogma. It is a complete picture
of mental slavery to a delusion.

The same scholastic ingenuity could invent the familiar
tale—circulated by St. Gregory—of the nun who forgot to
make the sign of the cross before partaking of her supper,
and who in consequence swallowed a demon concealed
among the leaves of lettuce; or it could calculate, as did
Weirus, by methods beyond our comprehension, that there
were just 7,405,926 devils divided into seventy-two com-
panies, each under a captain.

The composite shock of the *Witch Hammer* upon the modern mind arises from the inclusion within one pair of covers of abstruse theological doctrine, of "carnal" details usually reserved for medical confidence, of crass superstitions and fabled tales gathered among the ignorant but credited by the learned, of a code of inconceivably barbarous cruelty to extort confession, of a procedure of trial that gave the accused no chance—all under the sanction of a glorious crusade for the redemption of mankind. The invention and employment of that weapon reflects a state of mind that is far more significant than the belief in the power of the witch. The pitchfork with the barbed prongs that appears in the Devil's signature was in reality the cruel tyranny of dogma carried to a fanatical extreme, of which the torture is the revolting expression. In one record, we read that brandy was poured over the shaven head of the witch and lighted, that sulphur was burned under the armpits, that the witch was tied to a spiked board and hung from the ceiling with a fifty pound weight on her feet; that she was placed in a vise for six hours and that a dozen other tortures were inflicted—all this on a pregnant woman on the first day of her trial in the year 1631.

That the witch mania could convert judges into human fiends is a phase of its psychology that cannot be ignored. It brings home the shattering power of fear, of resort to desperate means to escape the danger thus conjured. A reign of terror leads to desperate means of defense. Delusion destroys reason; in its fanatical expression it perverts emotion. That in addition the "hammer" was used as a political weapon in a period when intrigue ruled and feuds were active, when Church and State were jealous of each other's power, the records testify; the trial of Joan of Arc is the most familiar instance.

THE CULT

The history of witch manias belongs to several periods and countries, flourishing under Protestant as well as Catholic sanction. Long after the Devil had passed his prime, he was still active, so long as fanaticism prevailed.

Bishop Jewell, preaching before Queen Elizabeth, charges: "Your Grace's subjects pine away even unto death; their colour fadeth, their flesh rotteth, their speech is benumbed, their senses are bereft." According to Calvin, "Whoever shall now contend that it is unjust to put heretics and blasphemers to death will knowingly and willingly incur their very guilt. This is not laid down on human authority; it is God that speaks and preaches a perpetual rule for His Church."

Confession under torture gradually gave way to tests and ordeals. The charges resume their domestic phase, and the trials a lay character.

Joan Throckmorton, "imaginative and melancholy," and subject to spasms, felt pains all over her body as she passed the door of a certain "Mother Samuel." Sir Samuel Cromwell, lord of the manor, hauled the woman to his estate, where the inquisitors pricked her to see whether the punctures would draw blood. Lady Cromwell tore the cap from the witch's head and with it a handful of gray hair to work a counter charm. Mother Samuel roundly cursed her tormentors, predicting dire evil. A year later, Lady Cromwell died.

There were other charges. The milk turned sour; the cattle would not bear. The witch's familiars were named. Under torture Mother Samuel confessed that she, her husband, and her daughter had sold their souls to the Devil. All three were executed on the 7th of April, 1593. Sir Samuel received forty pounds out of the confiscated property, and used it to establish an annual discourse at Cam-

MATTHEW HOPKINS, WITCH FINDER GENERAL

Two witches are confessing to him the names of their imps
and familiars. After a contemporary print.

bridge on the enormity of witchcraft, which occasion was
continued as late as 1718.

The cult of witch-finding became a profession. Matthew
Hopkins (1644), who called himself the "Witch Finder
General," traveled from shire to shire upon this mission
of extermination, receiving a fee for each conviction. His

favorite test was the swimming rite, recommended by King James. The thumb of the right hand was tied to the toe of the left foot, and the witch wrapped in a blanket and thrown into a river. If she sank, her friends had the consolation of knowing her innocent. If she floated, she was rescued and hanged. The readiest test was pricking— those plying the trade being known as "common prickers." Of this custom the pins still preserved at Salem are a museum reminder. For the delusion spread from England to America. The Salem episode turns upon the activities of Increase Mather, and was continued more fanatically by his son, Cotton Mather, who, progressive in other directions, was diabolical in his pursuit of the Devil. That in this mission father and son regarded themselves as vicars of the Almighty appears in the *Providences*, Increase Mather's tract on witchcraft and possession (1684).

A noted case occurred in the household of the Rev. Mr. Parris, in Salem. Two girls talked strangely of the terrors and pains and spasms to which they were subject. They charged an old Indian woman with bewitching them. Mr. Parris sent for two magistrates, and with their aid, found other instances of bewitchment. Confronted by the witch in the courtroom, the children went into spasms. When the witch clasped her hands, the possessed clasped theirs and repeated her gestures—a well-known hysterical tendency. The accusers said they saw devils prompting the witch in her defense. Protests of innocence by the witch were met by outcries of the public, while the minister read texts to discourage the Devil. The Indian woman was flogged by her master until she confessed relations with Satan.

Any one showing distrust of the proceedings was in danger of being accused as an accomplice of Satan. Husbands were arraigned for disbelieving the charges against their wives; a clergyman might himself be accused for attempting to save the lives of his parishioners. One poor woman, who was charged with "giving a look toward the great meeting-house of Salem, and immediately a demon entered the house and tore down part of it," was duly hanged. But the fierce animus of witch persecution had spent its force; there were in all only twenty-eight executions in Salem. The state of mind supporting witchcraft was a waning heritage; the Devil was in his dotage.

Yet witchcraft survives today in backward communities. The name and the practice—*hexing*—were transplanted from Germany to the Pennsylvania "Dutch." A short time ago, a hexer was murdered in revenge for the evil he had brought upon his victims. Advised by another witch-doctor, the victimized family had determined, by force if necessary, to secure a lock of the hair of the hexer, in order to prepare a counter charm and end the reign of disasters: several members of the family had sickened; the crops had failed; the cattle would not yield; nothing had prospered. The struggle to gain possession of the lock of hair led to murder.[2]

PROTEST

At no time did the witch mania proceed without protest; rationality found its sponsors even in the prime of irrationality.[3] Reginald Scot's *Discoverie of Witchcraft* (1584) was suppressed by James I, who himself wrote the refutation, since known as James's *Demonology*. The royal fanatic took up cudgels against the damnable opinion of Scot, who was "not ashamed in public print to deny there can be such a thing as a witch." It was James who, when his bride had been forced to turn back to Denmark because of the severe tempests which beset her on the

[2] The survival of such practices is the theme of Theda Kenyon's *Witches Still Live.*

[3] The honor roll includes: John Weir, physician (1563), who did not deny the existence of witches, but opposed the supernatural claims as

voyage to England, accused Dr. Fian, a pretender to magic, and induced him to confess "after his legs were crushed in the boots, whereby they were made unserviceable forever," that several hundred witches had gone to sea in a sieve and "had raised storms to drive back the princess."

The message of Scot's book appears in the title, *The Discovery of Witchcraft: proving that the Compacts and Contracts of Witches with Devils and all Infernal Spirits or Familiars are but Erroneous Novelties and Imaginary Conceptions, including their Power in Killing, Tormenting, Consuming or Curing the bodies of Men or Animals, by Charms, Philtres, Periapts, Pentacles, Curses, and Conjurations.* And this is Scot's plea for rationalism:

Concerning the evidence, see first whether it be not frivolous and whether the proofs brought against them be not incredible, consisting of guesses, presumptions, and impossibilities contrary to reason, Scripture, and nature. See also what persons complain upon them, whether they be not of the basest, the unwisest, and the most faithless kind of people. Also, may it please you, to weigh what accusations and crimes they lay to their charge, namely: She was at my house of late, she would have had a pot of milk, she departed in a chafe because she had it not, she railed, she cursed, she mumbled and whispered; and, finally, she said she would be even with me; and soon after my child, my cow, my sow, or my pullet died, or was strangely taken.

The Devil was deposed by social and intellectual changes. The machinations attributed to him were not disproved; the state of mind favorable to their acceptance

delusions; Cornelius Loos (1593), who wrote *True and False Magic*, was imprisoned and forced to recant and but for his death by the plague would have been sent to the stake; Dietrich Flade, rector of the University of Treves, who after presiding at trials at which witches were condemned on trivial evidence, proclaimed his error, recanted under torture, and was burnt (1589); Balthasar Bekker (1691), who in his *Enchanted World* described the entire movement as a colossal delusion; John Webster, completely rationalistic, who placed witchcraft as an unworthy superstition entangling the lives of men.

was outgrown. The mania receded when it went too far against the growing tide of humane and rational consideration, and the increasing independence of the lay mind. The redoubtable Cotton Mather, when challenged by a mere merchant, Robert Calef, retorted by calling him "a coal from Hell," but had no reply to the confessions not of guilt but of terror on the part of those who had been on trial.

By reason of that suddain surprizal, we knowing ourselves altogether Innocent of that Crime, we were all exceedingly astonished and amazed, and consternated and affrighted even out of our Reason; and our nearest and dearest Relations, seeing us in that dreadful condition, and knowing our great danger, apprehending that there was no other way to save our lives, ... out of tender pity persuaded us to confess what we did confess. Our understanding, our reason and our faculties almost gone, what we said was in effect a consenting to what they said.

The judicial attitude came to prevail. Justice Sewall, who had condemned innocent victims, repented by spending one day in each year in fasting and prayer. The church of Salem formally revoked the excommunications, and drove the Rev. Mr. Parris from his pulpit; and there the story ends.

The perversions induced by fear impede wisdom far more disastrously than the distortions of wish, notably in that they incite to a reign of terror under the compulsion of danger. The mental machinery is the same: false premises leading to still falser principles, and both to a realm of unreality. Conjured fear created the Devil and all his works—an amazing fiction, a dismal structure of belief. The reality is the motivation: the enmities of men, the cruelties of power, the fanaticism of creed. The Devil is intelligible; it is Demonology that is fearfully and wonderfully made.

CHAPTER IX

THE CULT OF THE MAGNET

WONDER is the ally of wish in the quest for wisdom; by the same inclination magic is the forerunner of science. In the wonder-tales of science, the cult of the magnet has a unique place; for the magnet is a demonstrable bit of magic. A lump of amber picks up light particles; metal filings jump to an iron bar. Here is a mystic force incarnate—motion with nothing visible to move it. Reduced to the dimensions of a needle, the magnet points north; lodestar and lodestone attract mysteriously. The magnetic becomes the embodiment and the symbol of potent but invisible attraction, extending to living sympathy.

It is a long progression from the ancient magnetists, whose views of material and mental operations were shaped by the qualities of the magnet and whose thought was patterned by the occult, to the modern world, reconstructed by the discovery of electro-magnetism. The Swiss savant, von Hohenheim, who called himself Paracelsus, (1493-1541) was the pioneer magnetist. To him the magnet was the "monarch of secrets"; it was his philosopher's stone. "I have discovered other properties of the magnet besides the obvious one of attracting to itself iron. I have discovered that it possesses a hidden power."

Paracelsus was an adventurer in thought, a rebel against the authority-following scholastics; he is said to have burned the works of Hippocrates and Galen as a gesture of emancipation. He was an empiric both in the better and the worse sense. He traveled widely, lived riotously—rumor has it he was killed in a drunken brawl—and accepted and promulgated occult doctrines indiscriminately. His vagaries represent his weak side; he has been called half genius and half rogue. One must accept the contradiction as a product of the time.

Like many another scholar of the day, Paracelsus was a physician as well as a physicist, considering the welfare of the body and the nature of matter as one. Despite his vagaries, Paracelsus occupies an important place in the checkered history of medicine. Though the story of the magnet carries other implications, its central one is the cure of disease; the major theme is the magnet in the employment of medicine.

Denouncing the orthodox medicos of the day, he advises them to experiment with magnets, and they will find that "they can cure a flux from the eyes, the ears, and the nose; a magnet can cure cancer, fistula, ruptures of all kinds, and dispel both jaundice and dropsy." The theory seems to have been that, since the magnet was a drawing force, it had the power to draw these diseases out of the system. To Paracelsus, the magnet also represented *sympathy;* it brought *like* together. Combining this with "transference," he prescribed that bits of magnetic substance be impregnated with *mummy* and deposited with seeds in rich earth, the seeds having a "congruity with the disease." As the plants grew, they would absorb the disease of the patient in whose behalf the ceremony was performed. The use of *mummy* is borrowed from medical magic; mummies, long dead yet still preserved, were prescribed for longevity. The cult of the magnet is in accord with the emphasis by Paracelsus and other alchemists upon the mineral division of nature as against the vegetable, which dominated the herbal pharmacopia. He came to regard salt, sulphur, and mercury as the ruling substances, replacing the humors of Galen.[1]

The "magnetic" theories of Paracelsus found followers. An independent magnetist who, unlike Paracelsus, was an opponent of alchemy, was the Jesuit Father Kircher,[2] a progressive experimenter, inventor of the ear-trumpet, one of the first to use a microscope and to suspect the rôle of infection in disease. He ground magnets and had the patients swallow them. He next applied a poultice of iron filings over the diseased part and counted upon the magnet outside to draw the iron inside, and with it the tumor or whatever might be the source of the illness.

Another magnetist was von Helmont, a man of learning, who added both to truth and to error; and still another Goclenius, who wrote *On the Treatment of Wounds by the Magnet* (1608). As wounds inflicted by swords were then common, and as steel has a magnetic quality, the cure by "sympathy" developed the *weapon-salve,* which is applied to the sword that inflicted the wound. The formula of the salve has the Paracelsian quality: moss from the head of a hanged thief, real mummy, human blood and human suet, linseed oil and turpentine,

---

[1] If we may anticipate a period of advance following upon Harvey's discoveries (1628) and Sydenham's practice, we may find an expression of it in the words of John Locke, physician and philosopher, to the effect that careful observation by "a man not tied up to the four humors (Galen) or salt, sulphur and mercury (Paracelsus), or to acid and alkali (Sylvius and Willis) which has of late prevailed," will carry a man far in practice and with little medicine. That theories dominate and mislead practice is thus shrewdly noted—a comment applicable to other chapters of Medicine, and notably true of the medical cult of the magnet.

[2] His name is also associated with the *experimentum mirabile,* the marvelous experiment. A hen, held firmly, will soon cease to struggle and remains motionless in a fixed posture. Such cataplexy, or fixed holding of an unnatural posture, may be induced in so lowly a creature as the lobster. The condition occurs in men in the hypnotic trance; it was discovered in the persistent search for the magical and psychical properties of the magnet.

mixed and kept in an oblong narrow urn. Dr. Fludd introduced the remedy to England and used magnets for all
diseases, explaining that as the human body has a north
and a south pole, the patient's body must be "in a boreal
position."

A "Parson Foster" denounced the practice as witchcraft
in a pamphlet broadside: *A Sponge to Wipe away the
Weapon-salve*. He asserts that "the Devil himself gave it to
Paracelsus; Paracelsus to the Emperor; the Emperor to the
courtier; the courtier to Baptista Porta; and Baptista Porta
to Dr. Fludd, a doctor of physic, yet living and practicing
in the famous city of London, who now stands tooth and
nail for it." Dr. Fludd replied with mixed but drastic
metaphor in *The Squeezing of Parson Foster's Sponge*,
wherein "the bitter flames of his slanderous reports are by
the sharp vinegar of truth corrected and quite extinguished."

This duel with verbal swords found a second in Sir
Kenelm Digby, a generous believer in marvels. Gallantly,
he is said to have served his wife with a dish of capons fed
upon vipers, to preserve her beauty for a century. He converted the remedy into a "powder of sympathy," dispens-
ing with both the magnet and the sword—usually not
procurable—and applying it to any piece of clothing, such
as the garter worn by the wounded duelist. If the garter
was kept cool and moist, the wound felt comfortable; but
if the garter was heated and dried, the wound felt hot and
inflamed. Other practitioners held that pain could be relieved by magnetizing the sword, provided the magnetizing stroke were upward, a downward stroke causing
intolerable pain. These notions had fairly well disappeared
when "magnetism," with a new theory attached to it, took
a new lease of life in the latter eighteenth century in the
person of Franz Anton Mesmer.

Mesmer occupies the key position in the cult of the magnet. His career and his thesis enter equally into the tale. The story begins in Vienna in 1766, where he was granted a medical degree on so strange a thesis as *The Influence of the Planets on the Human Body*. In this he discusses a *gravitas universalis*, a universal force or energy which may be conveyed by magnets, and has curative powers. That the thesis should be accepted sheds a sidelight upon the medical education of that day. It appears that eight years later, Professor Hell, a Jesuit astronomer, used a magnet to relieve the crippled condition of a servant in the observatory; from that experience he went on to others, using heart-shaped magnets for heart trouble, kidney-shaped magnets for kidney complaints, ear-shaped magnets for deafness. He informed Dr. Mesmer of a request for a magnet which he had received from a distinguished visitor for the treatment of his wife. Thus encouraged, Mesmer began practising with magnets; within a short time, his house was besieged by patients from near and far, eager to be touched by the miraculous magnet.

Mesmer was a distinguished citizen of Vienna. His marriage to a wealthy widow gave him the means of entertaining; his house was a center of culture. He was a good musician, a friend of Mozart, and a recognized member of the medical profession. But his venture into curative magnetism injured his standing. He became the center of a controversy of a personal nature, through the case of a Mlle. Paradies, a blind singer, a protegée of the Empress Maria Theresa, whose sight had been restored by Mesmer's magnets. When her parents demanded her return, the young woman preferred to remain in Mesmer's house.

His friends began to desert him. For a time he practiced in Munich, performing cures upon distinguished persons, but failing to secure support from the medical profession.

Convinced that his reverses were the result of prejudice and malice, he betook himself to Paris in 1778 to establish his great discovery.

Early in his practice, Mesmer made a notable observation: namely, that *the magnet played no real part in the cures.* In abandoning the Paracelsian notion, Mesmer substituted another no less fanciful: that of an *animal magnetism;* this he held responsible for the cures. Animal magnetism was a *vital force* flowing through the human body and concentrated in his own person. The lifeless mineral was gone; a stage in advance toward a solution of what is now recognized as psychotherapy had been made; but Mesmer's contribution spread further error while approaching the truth.

An excited Paris approaching collapse welcomed wonder-workers. The new magnetic healer, Dr. Mesmer, became himself a magnet of attraction. Insisting that he was a savant presenting a new discovery, he demanded official recognition for his views, both of the Academy of Science and the Academy of Medicine. The academicians refused to endorse his theories; but his house was besieged by patients. The fame of his cures spread among high and low. Marie Antoinette became his patroness. The Marquis de Lafayette wrote to General Washington that he was bringing a treasure to the United States in Dr. Mesmer's secret.

Mesmer's devoted followers and friends subscribed five hundred louis d'or each as the initiation fee to a *Loge d'Harmonie,* the name of the inner circle which was entitled to receive the secret instructions covering his entire system. But controversies continued with increasing violence. Paris was divided into magnetists and anti-magnetists. Mesmer was glorified and defended; he was also satirized and denounced. He was a notable figure in a turbulent Paris until the Revolution put an end to his career. His followers continued his cause. In 1792, he withdrew to a quiet life in Switzerland where, in more modest fashion, he continued his magnetic practice. When he attempted to resume his life in Vienna, he was driven out, presumably by political enemies. Late in life, German friends of animal magnetism visited him and reinstated his doctrines. Mesmer experienced to the full the triumphs of success and the outrageous stings of fortune.

Mesmer's theories are shifting and vague. He retained something both of the planetary and the physically magnetic forces, but focused them on the organism and the nervous system. He held that the influence of sun, moon, and stars causes a reflux on earth through the medium of a subtle and mobile fluid, which particularly affects the nervous system by *intension* and *remission*. He claimed to have "rendered paper, bread, wool, silk, stones, leather, glass, wood, men, and dogs—in short everything I touched —magnetic to such a degree that these substances produced the same effects as the lodestone on diseased persons. I have charged jars with magnetic matter in the same way as is done with electricity." This "great discovery," he announced, heralded a new era in the understanding of life and health, and particularly in the cure of disease.

As for his "principles," they were summed up in twenty-seven dogmatic propositions. These he submitted to the Commissions, not for demonstration—he insisted that he had proved their truth—but for unqualified acceptance. He asserted the existence of a

universally diffused subtle fluid, appearing in all portions of the celestial system, and affecting the animal economy by insinuating itself into the nerves; it has properties analogous to that of the magnet, may be reflected like light, propagated like sound, and may be increased, opposed, accumulated, transmitted to another object, and transported; furthermore this principle, which is, in a way, a sixth sense artificially acquired, will cure nervous disease directly, and others indirectly by provoking salutary crises, thus bringing the art of healing to perfection.

For this theory he contended to the end. In treating his first case (July 28, 1774) Mesmer placed magnets on the chest and feet of a young woman suffering from a variety of symptoms. She soon felt "internally a painful streaming of a very fine substance, going now here and now there, but finally settling in the lower part of her body, and freeing her from all further attacks for six hours." When apparently in a light trance, the patient moved with expressions of pain whenever one of six "mesmerized" cups touched her, but not by contact of the other unmagnetized cups. This simple play of suggestion in an hysterical subject Mesmer did not recognize as such, either then or later. To him the effect proved a new order of magnetic power.

The treatment as he developed it in Paris was elaborate and theatrical. Mesmer adopted the medical theory of his day—in one form it goes back to Greek medicine—that every disease had its natural course, rising to a crisis; that by inducing the crisis, one could shorten the period and draw off the disease. Attached to his clinic was the *Salle des Crises*. The scenes in the main salon were impressive and bedlamic. The *pièce de resistance* was the great tub or *baquet*. The model of it was a battery—for Mesmer never wholly abandoned "magnetic" notions—filled with glass and iron filings, from which emerged "bent iron rods, the points of which could be easily applied to the outer parts of the body, such as the head, breast, stomach."

Mesmer had the patients seated about the baquet for a half-hour or longer, thus increasing the tension of expectancy; the light was soft and low, and strains of music floated in from an anteroom. Mesmer solemnly entered, clad in a lilac robe, wand in hand, touching and addressing one and another patient. The excitement spread.

There were manifested the most violent involuntary distortions of the limbs; partial suffocation, heaving of the abdomen, wild glances, were observed; one patient utters piercing cries, another has fits of laughter, while a third bursts into tears. Nothing can break this spell save the command of the magnetizer, and whether the patient be in the wildest frenzy or in the deepest stupor, a word, look, or nod of the master is sufficient to bring them to consciousness.

The passes and strokings and other gestures of conveying an influence were the medium of the curative effect. Mesmerizing—à la Svengali—came to mean pointing the extended fingers of the hands from which the force was supposed to flow dramatically at the patient, while the mesmerizer fixed the eyes of the subject by a compelling stare. In due course, any notion of an "animal magnetism" disappeared as completely as the earlier notion of a sidereal or terrestrial magnet. It is by way of magnetism that knowledge of the hypnotic condition and of the momentous influence of suggestion has entered into the familiar principles of psychology.

How we judge Mesmer's part in that transformation—how far he saw the truth, how far he was wholly committed to error, how far in his personal career he was a charlatan bent upon gold and glory, how far a misguided zealot eager to benefit humanity—depends upon what phases of his career we place first and what second. The issue has been revived by the recent championship of Herr Stefan Zweig. In no other critical account does Mesmer appear so completely a noble personage, a philanthropic leader, a learned scientist, and the accredited discoverer of hypnosis and suggestion. Mesmer, says Zweig, in his earlier period lived a hundred years too late and in his later period a hundred years too soon.

I cannot read the documents so favorably. The credit belongs elsewhere for the recognition that the phenomena

MAGNETIZING À LA MESMER

The stream lines of the magnetic force proceed to the head, inducing
the crisis and, by passes, the cure. From a contemporary print.

MAGNETIC TREATMENT BY MARQUIS DE PUYSÉGUR

Ropes attached to a magnetized tree are attached to the parts affected.
The marquis is shown with his somnambule Victor, who diagnoses the seat
of the disorder by clairvoyance. From Puységur's book, 1786.

which Mesmer produced depended upon an altered nervous condition of the patient; Mesmer, when confronted with it, explained it as a minor effect of the crisis. Mesmer's claims before the Commissions were extravagant and most unscientific. His enjoyment of public success and his yearning for a triumph over his conservative opponents are intelligible; the mercenary conduct of his propaganda is all too evident. He emerges as a convinced and zealous protagonist, a showman far more than a scientist. The historical fact remains that Mesmer's career was an indispensable step in the emancipation from ancient error, but likewise an influential reason for the continuance of that error into modern times.

The story of magnetism proceeds by elimination; first the iron, disease-drawing magnet goes; then the rise and fall of animal magnetism. The next stage in the succession is *somnambulism*. In the final act in the cult of the magnet, the chief figure is the Marquis de Puységur. His was not a trained mind but an observant one. He was an ardent disciple and defender of Mesmer, although rather shabbily treated when he differed from the master. De Puységur recognized in one of his subjects, Victor, a mental state of trance, closely similar to somnambulism. He called it *artificial somnambulism*, which name it bore until half a century later when James Braid recognized its nature more precisely and called it *hypnosis*.

By this recognition of an altered mental state, which might appear spontaneously or be induced in susceptible subjects, the clue to the nature of the mesmeric phenomena was transferred away from the magnetizer, to the subject. But no sooner was one wonder clarified than another took its place. The somnambules or sensitives became clairvoyants; they were human X-rays. Victor at once began to diagnose the bodily conditions of other patients and to prescribe accordingly. There arose on de Puységur's

THE ROUTING OF MESMER

A contemporary cartoon showing Mesmer, with ass' ears and devil's tail, routed from the baquet by the report of the Commission.

estate an outdoor clinic; hundreds of patients were treated, new somnambules discovered.

The phenomena were spoken of as somnambulism; but the theory of action was that of a magnetic fluid with the peculiar property that it could be directed by the *human will*. De Puységur's motto carries all the truth of suggestion: *Croyez et veuillez*, believe and will. But his practice reflects a belief in some sort of magnetism. The tree and its dangling ropes, from which the patients derive benefit, operates through the magnetic action imparted to it by the *will* of the magnetizer. For all his insight, de Puységur was still a magnetist.

The conflict between Mesmer and the Commissions turned on this one point: Were the effects due to magnetism, or to what was later called suggestion and by the Commission "imagination"? The first Commission was a notable one. It included besides Baillie, the President of the Academy, Lavoisier and Guillotin—the one presently to lose his head by an invention bearing the name of the other—and our own Benjamin Franklin. In deference to Franklin's gout, the Commission assembled in his garden, where M. Deslon, in the Mesmeric manner, magnetized a tree, the contact with which would induce the typical convulsions of the crisis. The subject was unlucky enough to exhibit the attack at the wrong tree. Eventually the Academy resolved that "magnetism" in any form shall not be considered; and the ban was not lifted until Dr. Charcot in 1882 read his memoir upon hypnosis in the treatment of hysteria.

In the period following the Revolution, magnetism had become clairvoyance. Somnambules were reading concealed messages, exhibiting knowledge beyond their ken. Special marvels appeared, such as the "transposition of the senses," the somnambules hearing not through the ears but through the stomach. For a time the hospitals of Paris had their diagnosing somnambules. Sporadic "magnetists" appeared, restating the older notions; in the main, enlightenment set in; the "magnetic" phenomena were recognized as trance-states, with suggestion the commanding clue. The magnet had yielded to psychology.

There is an epilogue to the tale a hundred years after. The cult of the magnet, so long associated with learning, had fallen to the slums of the "modern occult." The up-to-date magnetist deals in *Personal Magnetism* at so much a person. He is a leader of a "success" cult. The "exercise book of the Magnetism Club of America" prescribes the *Cultivation of Personal Magnetism in Seven Progressive Steps;* it closes with a certificate of graduation, in which the reader may enter his name. Magnetism is everything from the origin of life, the source of elemental force, to nerve energy, brain vitality, to personal power. The course extends from magnetic breathing, to magnetic temperaments with appropriate colors, to magnetic voices and magnetic individuality. It contains such neglected information, called "grand principles," as that rain is a common vehicle of natural electricity, and that there are mineral, vegetable, animal electricities, the last the climax of all energies. "Personal Magnetism" is still a phrase to conjure with, though the specimen cited belongs to the questionable forms of exploitation. For these vagaries not the mysterious power of the magnet, but the confusing power of the mind is responsible.

The trail of the cult of the magnet may also be followed in general medical practice. Diseases continue to be drawn out of the patient by one means or another; and the strokings and passes which the mesmerizer used were incorporated in mechanical devices. Famous were the Perkins tractors—a pair of metallic rods—a Yankee invention of the "wooden nutmeg" period. Their use spread all over the

United States; but it was left for the English advocates to found a Perkinian institution in London. When it was repeatedly demonstrated that a pair of wooden tractors would cure as remarkably, the "magnetic" tractors lost their occupation. Magnetism was replaced by electricity. Electric or electromagnetic belts, with impressive devices of zinc and copper sewed on the fabric, electric insoles, copper on one foot and zinc on the other, and other products of the patent medicine mind were duly invented, sold, and abandoned. These too engendered life-giving currents as imaginary as the magnetic vital force. Specimens are preserved in museums of medicine to remind the historian of the later issues of the cult of the magnet.

The contemporary survival of animal magnetism has an interest of its own. A young woman named Mary Baker saw the typical manipulations of a traveling mesmerist in a stage performance—the passes, the strokings, the complete control by the magnetizer as he deprived his subjects of sense and action, putting them through amusing and at times terrifying antics. She was impressed with fear and wonder. Much later, as Mrs. Eddy, she developed the theory of *malicious animal magnetism*. She believed so thoroughly in the existence of this hostile force, her biographers relate, that in traveling by train she had an advance engine precede her to drive the influence off the track; she sent telegrams by roundabout routes to avoid stations in possession of the malicious magnetists. When *Science and Health* went to press, it had to be guarded against the "crimes of mesmeric outlaws." Her husband's death, she informed the press, "was caused by malicious mesmerism." The autopsy showed "not material poison, but mesmeric poison."

"As named in Christian Science, animal magnetism or hypnotism is specifically a term for error of mortal mind. The malicious form of hypnotism ultimates in moral idiocy," Mrs. Eddy wrote. In 1878, one of her disciples, Miss Lucretia L. S. Brown, with the support of Mrs. Eddy, brought suit against Spofford, a dismissed assistant, on the charge of causing her unbearable pains by the use of mesmerism. The doctrine of M.A.M. was a strong personal belief of the founder of Christian Science; though revived now and then in the career of that movement, it played but a slight and diminishing part. From the cosmic theories of Paracelsus, by way of the baquet of Mesmer, to the doctrines of Mrs. Eddy, the story of the magnet runs its course. The attraction of the magnet became a mighty wonder-concept of the human mind.

Chapter X

MARVELOUS MADAME BLAVATSKY

MADAME BLAVATSKY was a wonder-worker and an extraordinary one, in a century of marvelous inventions, discoveries, and transformations, with which she had no concern; her wonders were of quite other kind. The same years of scientific plenty brought also a harvest of growths wholly aloof: discordant doctrines, revivals of ancient errors, irregular cults of health, religion, character-reading, "new thought"—a caravan of wish-laden wisdoms. Every member of the motley procession found its following and went its way, at once flaunting and disdaining the precepts of science. In that procession the thought-wave inaugurated by Madame Blavatsky has a notable place. Saint or sinner, we shall never see her like again. In the face of a rationalistic science, she staged a Paracelsian revival, grafting an Oriental occultism upon Occidental minds.

Helena Petrovna Blavatsky was a vital, tireless, commanding, ungainly, shrewd adventuress in life and belief. Her convictions were likewise her stock in trade. She was big enough to laugh at her triumphs and overcome her disasters. To her followers, she is a glorified occultist, cult-leader, creator of theosophic shrines. Her memory became the posthumous idol of the internationally organized Theosophists, who, forgetting their dissensions, observed in 1931 the centenary of the birth of the "Priestess of Isis." Her birthday in May is still observed as "Lotus

Day" wherever theosophists congregate. In so bizarre a career, motives are mixed. One still inquires what may have been the deepest urge in the search for the "soul" of things in this falsifying leader of a truth-seeking faith. The verdict of Richard Hodgson, which in 1885 startled the world by exposing the miracles of Adyar, may be recalled: "For our own part we regard her neither as the mouthpiece of hidden seers nor as a mere vulgar adventuress. We think that she has achieved a title to permanent remembrance as one of the most accomplished, ingenious, and interesting impostors in history." Her own confession is an indictment of human foibles: "What is one to do, when in order to rule men, it is necessary to deceive them? ... For almost invariably the more simple, the more silly, and the more gross the phenomenon, the more likely is it to succeed."

The cult of theosophy was inaugurated humbly, even grotesquely, in New York. It was enshrined in India. There its humble sanctuary was at first a wooden cupboard protected from examination by a halo of reverence. Here miracles were ascribed to the spiritual coadjutors, the mystic Mahatmas, Masters of astral force. The Masters were actual, living men of supernal wisdom, dwelling in seclusion, invisibly directing human affairs through messages to chosen leaders. The guardians of the Shrine were Madame Blavatsky's associates, M. and Mme. Coulomb. Their confessions and her own admissions disclose the technique of their bold but vulnerable performances.

The miracle which aroused Hodgson's suspicion was so trivial a matter as the astral restoration of a broken saucer. The shrine at Adyar was the center of curiosity. Visitors were received as prospective adherents. They were shown the cherished portrait of Koot Hoomi, the Mahatma guide of Madame Blavatsky, and were thus assured of the earthly existence of the source of her teachings as they

gazed upon his features installed in the shrine. In opening
the door of the shrine, Madame Coulomb brushed against
a china saucer resting near the edge, which fell and broke.
The pieces were collected in a cloth and replaced in the
shrine. Promptly there appeared a letter signed K. H.
(Koot Hoomi) assuring "the small audience" that "the
mischief is easily repaired." Upon removing the cloth, the
dish was found restored without trace of breakage. The
marvel was performed through the operation of the
"akasic force," the medium of the world-ether, *Akaz*.
The memorandum of a *pair* of saucers purchased at a local
shop explained the marvel otherwise. The deception was
arranged in advance by instructions of Madame Blavatsky,
who was absent from Adyar at the time. The "shrine" was
fitted with sliding panels hidden by a mirror. An opening
in the wall separated the "Occult Room" from Madame's
bedroom. There were miracles everywhere. By means of a
thread and a recess in the plaster of the ceiling, mysterious
letters fluttered down at the dramatic moment, addressed
to favorite disciples. They proved to have been written in
the handwriting, skillfully varied, of the Priestess herself.

The Occult Room was a conjuring chamber. Miracles
multiplied; there are tales of miraculous recoveries of lost
objects, of the miraculous appearance of a supplementary
cup at a picnic for an additional guest; and of many *et-
ceteras* equally marvelous and equally trivial, but all
accepted as momentous. Ingenious stagecraft appears in
the incident told by Colonel Olcott, President of the Theosophical Society, who had accompanied H.P.B., as she is
usually referred to, to India. He was traveling with Damodar, an advanced *chela* or pupil. Said Damodar, apparently
dozing in their compartment, informed Colonel Olcott
that he had just been visiting headquarters—which meant
that his double or astral self had made the journey—and
had witnessed an accident to Madame Blavatsky. She had

tripped on the carpet and injured her right knee; she had
been lifting Koot Hoomi's portrait from the shrine; she
mentioned the names of General and Mrs. Morgan. Colonel Olcott telegraphed an inquiry to headquarters. The
reply from H.P.B. read: *Nearly broke right leg. Damodar
startled us.*

Every detail of the plot had been arranged in advance:
the vision, the alleged accident, the presence of the Mor-
gans, the telegram. Damodar, however sincere a theosophist, was also an advanced pupil—in collusion.

Like many another wonder worker, Madame Blavatsky
is partly conjuror and partly legend. One of her biographers lists some fifty-odd distinctive wonders, not counting the constant "precipitation" of appropriate and providential Mahatma letters. The conjured wonders were those
that happened, though often not as described; the legendary ones did not. The legends aver that Madame walked
through the streets of Boston in a pelting rain without a
trace of dampness; that Colonel Olcott saw Madame Blavatsky's astral form in New York while she was in the flesh
in Philadelphia; that Madame Blavatsky cured herself of
serious ills over night; that books needed for her writings
appeared out of space; that a lamp lighted itself after being extinguished. Whatever the actual occurrences, they
were invested in a halo of miracle.

The conjurings became miracles by exaggeration. When
the room was filled with musical sounds, those who knew
that this was a favorite trick of Home, the medium,—
whom H.P.B. knew—suspected a music-box concealed in
the clothing; but its tinkle became orchestral in the imagination of her converts.

Marvels came to be related of her early life. It was said
that the person born as Helena Petrovna fell as a youth in
the battle of Mentana, where in male attire she fought

MADAME BLAVATSKY

Photograph taken at Ithaca, 1875.

under Garibaldi. To Colonel Olcott, she showed her sabre wounds and the bullets embedded in her shoulder and leg. A defender explains that H.P.B. took possession of her present body when that body had already formed its rather coarse habits, for which naturally "she," the theosophic leader, was not responsible. As herself a Master, she was a reincarnated personality, one of her former selves being Pythagoras.

The real Madame Blavatsky is more interesting. An editorial associate, Mabel Collins, pays her this composite tribute:

> I learned from her how foolish, how gullible, how easily flattered human beings are, taken *en masse*. Her contempt for her kind was on the same gigantic scale as everything else about her except her marvelously delicate tapering fingers. She had a greater power over the weak and credulous, a greater capacity for making black appear white, a larger waist, a more voracious appetite, a more ceaseless and insatiable hatred of those whom she judged to be her enemies, a greater disrespect for *les convenances,* a worse temper, a greater command of bad language, and a greater contempt for her fellow-men than I ever supposed possible to be contained in one person.

Whatever we may think of her use of her powers, she played a large-scale part, commanding the minds of men by an ambitious and original technique. The marvel remains: the extensive cult of theosophy in the twentieth century as the issue of the hectic *Wanderjahre* of a Russian emigré, on adventure bent in Victorian days with most un-Victorian ways.

The personal story of Madame Blavatsky appears more clearly in the biographies prepared to celebrate the centenary of her birth. She was born in 1831 in the Russian Ukraine, the daughter of a Captain Hahn. She was married at seventeen to an official twenty-five years her senior, whose name she bore for life, though with whose company she parted without ceremonial leave after a few months of marital incompatibility or boredom. She had traveled extensively on her own. She was deeply interested in "spiritism" and the occult. She arrived obscurely in New York in 1872 or later, and in 1877 published the voluminous *Isis Unveiled,* destined to become the Bible of theosophy.

As a contribution, it was harshly reviewed; the general verdict called it a "dish of hash" of varied flavor. At a later stage a critic wrote in an open letter: "I am aware that you are extensively read in useless literature. You have made a wonderful collection of the maggots of the human brain. There is hardly a superstition which is not wholly or partially sanctioned in your four portly volumes. Your heap of rubbish is colossal."

By her followers[1]—a small but growing number—*Isis* was accepted as a revealed gospel. It is in fact a discursive and miscellaneous collection of occult lore of all ages, together with a statement running through it of her own original, irresponsible, mystic, and pontifical affirmations. Much of it is borrowed without acknowledgment, and more of it is garbled superficially from accessible literature. She must have been an habitué of public libraries; she was certainly a prodigious worker. The book is not personally revealing. Isis emerges with more veils rather than fewer ones. A ruthless critic—after the Adyar collapse— wrote an *Isis Very Much Unveiled,* revealing much of a personal history which H.P.B. had failed to mention, or having recorded in her indefatigable, exuberant correspondence,[2] chose to forget.

[1] Among the small group of joiners, is the name of Thomas A. Edison, written in that unmistakable lithographic handwriting and dated at Menlo Park, April 4th, 1878; he takes the pledge to keep absolutely secret the doctrines of theosophy to which he asks initiation.

[2] Among her versatile gifts was a fair facility in drawing; many of her

The twenty-five years of wandering before reaching New York are rarely referred to; and what is told may not be true. A baffled reviewer speaks of her as "the most monumental liar in all history." In tracing her psychic career, the inclusion of her amorous ventures would be only indiscreetly relevant. She confesses her part in the "Saturnalia of the moral depravity of mankind"; but there are confusing alternating denials. At one period and another, her letters recount frankly her free love relations with men; yet later she presented to her detractors an ambiguous medical statement in support of the virginity that was esteemed an asset in a claimant for mystical saintliness. "Between H.P.B. from 1830 to H.P.B. of 1875 there is a veil drawn over a private life, holy and sacred"; those who questioned her legends were declared "slanderous and venomous mad dogs."

Our story concerns Madame Blavatsky, the esoteric nomad. She claims to have visited every continent, seeking occult learning from Hindu, Egyptian, Red Man, Voodoo, Buddhist, Mohammedan, Christian, Jew, bringing what grew to be a wisdom religion to the busy marts of men. How that motive came to dominate the orientalized imagination of a rebellious young woman is not altogether clear, nor need one indulge in Freudian speculations.

To one of her tempestuous temperament the appeal of a career of freedom and escape is intelligible. The cult of the day that offered an outlet and a livelihood for this "psychic" urge was spiritualism. To that she professed eternal allegiance, even to parting with her last dollar—

letters are accompanied by sketches. Her cartoons of her fellow-theosophists spare no one and approach the ribald in caricature. Olcott in turban in saintly pose is called "Maloney"; and his intimate name for the Priestess was "Mrs. Mulligan." This persiflage, no less than the domestic level of the miracles, seems incongruous with the inspirational solemnity of the cult.

of which she then had few—or to laying her head upon
the block. She devoted her head to it otherwise for some
ten years, when she launched upon her great adventure
and exchanged commonplace spirits for erudite Masters—
her master stroke. She had founded a *Société Spirite* in
Cairo and maintained herself as a medium there for several years. There is a report that the finding of a long
glove stuffed with cotton, which had served as "a materialized hand and arm," hastened her departure to New York
—to pastures newer and greener.

The period of Madame Blavatsky's identification with
spiritualism on its native heath is fully documented,[3] including her own statement that she came to America "with
feelings not unlike those of a Mohammedan approaching
the birthplace of his prophet." Her ardent defense of
mediums in Philadelphia who were detected in flagrant
fraud led her into trouble. She was in touch with the
three great mediums of the day, Home, Slade, and Englin-
ton, and learned tricks from all of them, though Home denounced her when she turned her back on spirits and
threw her lot in with her special creation, the Mahatmas.
Her fear that "Home's malignity has ruined me forever
in Europe" proved groundless. She shrewdly realized that
the commonplace controls of the ordinary séance cramped
her style, that reincarnated Mahatmas and their majestic
pronouncements were far more impressive as well as freer

[3] Particularly by the recently published letters and accounts of her
friendship with Professor Corson at Ithaca, while *Isis* was in preparation.
The visit of this orientalized foreigner to the newly founded Cornell
University was not without its embarrassments. She had promised her
host and hostess not to smoke her Russian cigarettes where the coeduca-
tional youth or the academic dignity would be shocked. She was taken in
a carriage and pair to gaze upon the natural beauties of the picturesque
region. Once in the shelter of the woods, she cared little for landscape
but revelled in the opportunity to smoke in solitude. Her costume and
her manners were equally appalling; but the spirituality of her discourse
in higher entities carried all before it. All this gives a very human picture
of the priestess before the apotheosis.

from investigation; they provided the larger stage on which she as a psychic prima donna could rule supreme.

The birth-date of Theosophy—September 7, 1875—is worth recalling. The "Miracle Club" met in the *Lamasery* —H.P.B.'s apartment, "filled with all manner of curious stuffed animals, curios and junk"—to listen to an architect

H.P.B.'S CREST

With characteristic assumption, this crest was designed by Madame Blavatsky and used on the note-paper of the Society from its foundation in 1876. It was printed in colors and embossed. It combines the worldly with the occult—a crown such as was used by noble Continental families, together with mystical and cabalistic letters and symbols, including the swastika, and, in the center, the initials E.B. (Elena Blavatsky, the Italian form of Helena). The present seal of the Society is derived from it.

by name of Felt discourse upon "The Lost Canon of Proportion of the Egyptians." Said Felt promised that if supplied with the proper chemical appliances, he could make visible the race of beings who people the "elements." He was voted the funds, but there were no results. Then and there, they enlarged the scope of the Club to include occult aims. Searching the dictionary for a suitable name, they came upon the blessed word *theosophy*, with its imposing historical glamour, and adopted it.

At a spiritualistic assembly, Madame Blavatsky made the most momentous contact of her life—that of her future associate, impresario, and biographer, Colonel Olcott. He was soldier, lawyer, journalist, but above all an occult

spiritualist, with an insatiable appetite for marvels. He
fell completely under her dominance. She described him
variously as a "blockhead," "a windbag full of vanity, conceit, and silliness"; a "psychologized baby," who "did not
know his head from his heels,"—this after she had turned
it in the desired direction.

When the Colonel drew up the prospectus of the Society
and was about to sign it with his name as President,
Madame Blavatsky directed him to sign it, "For the Committee of Seven, Brotherhood of Luxor!" Soon after, he received his credentials in a letter written in a strange handwriting with gold ink on thick green paper, assuring him
that the Mystic Brotherhood really existed and had elected
him as a spokesman. He was advised that "Sister Helen
was a valiant, trustworthy servant," and that the Masters
would guide his newly formed society. The signer was
"Tuitit Bey."

The New York period of genesis covers at most seven
years; the exodus took place in 1882. The meeting of East
and West came by way of a modern society—though H.P.B.
spoke of it as the most ancient of Masonic Lodges—called
Arya Samaj. The leader, Dynanand Saraswati, wrote sym-
pathetically to H.P.B. when *Isis* appeared. Joyously she
seized upon the new recognition; with irrepressible gusto
she exclaimed, "Three cheers for the Heathen Hindoos!"
Promptly (May, 1878) the New York Society was renamed
"The Theosophical Society of Arya Samaj." A new star
seemed to beckon from the East! H.P.B. took out American citizenship papers, reduced her weight by ninety
pounds, by means of a glass of mesmerized water a day!
Colonel Olcott initiated plans of exchanging American
clocks for tiger skins. The society moved its headquarters
from New York to India. The movements, as ever, were
dictated or at least approved by the Masters. But their
higher wisdom did not avert a fatal breach when H.P.B.

began an aggressive campaign in India among the influential British and Indian residents. Then East and West came in conflict as irreconciliable as the force of gravity and the akasic force. Each denounced the other as counterfeit. Indeed the suggestion to a group of her Indian brethren that they present themselves to prospective adherents as messengers of the Masters, hastened the end of the *mésalliance,* with the parting shot from Dynanand that H.P.B. had no genuine faith whatever.

There were repeated demands for the appearance of the Mahatmas in person; there are tales of shadowy turbaned figures appearing at dusk in tropical Indian gardens, and unwitnessed accounts of personal interviews, but nothing more than a turban to validate the visit; there was even a turban in New York. To give the world a clinching demonstration, Mr. Sinnett, editor, induced H.P.B. to relay a request to the Masters that they precipitate a copy of the London *Times* to India on the day of publication! This feat Koot Hoomi declared "unthinkable" and the "results deplorable," as "the world is yet in its first stage of disenthrallment." The public is safe only because the custody of the immense power wielded by the Masters is in saintly hands. All marvels must be viséed by the Priestess herself. With her passing, the Masters seem to have become disorganized or helpless.

The question remains: are there Masters in the flesh? Authoritative travelers in Hindustan and Tibet, in the locale referred to in H.P.B.'s highly colored accounts of her wanderings, have failed to find them. Of the places described in glowing terms as superb seats of learning, some are actually miserable hovels; others have no existence on the map. H.P.B. is vague and generous in her geography. The Mystic Brotherhood was first placed at Luxor, with "Tuitit Bey" as leader; then it was transferred to the Kashmir Pass near Lh'assa—where alone the holy men "can live, as conditions there are perfect"—whatever that may mean. "Shocking as it may seem to the nineteenth-century self-sufficiency, the Masters are indifferent to its declaration that they are non-existent."

The story of the posthumous Madame Blavatsky becomes that of Theosophy—a long and tangled tale, which lies outside my province. There would have been no Theosophy but for H.P.B.'s thaumaturgical career; her chief marvel was the reinstatement of a belief in the reality of miracles operated by forces attested by esoteric wisdom. More and more as an established wisdom-cult with disciples and a college and a monumental shrine came into prospect and fulfilment, the emphasis of the great movement was directed from miracles to doctrines.

The combined impact of H.P.B.'s legendary fame, her weird personality, the impressive sweep of the astounding disclosures, the ecstatic uplift of a glorified faith, captivated her audiences of high and low degree. The spiritual instructions came to constitute the dominant center of the movement, and to them may be attributed its extraordinary spread. Theosophy continued to retain the thaumaturgical temper in the interests of the successors of H.P.B.

The most important of these is Mrs. Annie Besant, whose conversion in 1889 was a consternation to her friends and to the large public that had followed her career as freethinker, socialist, political reformer to a position of distinction among the leading women of England. Mrs. Besant met Madame Blavatsky as a prematurely aged and ailing woman, yet was completely won by the Theosophic gospel. The fate of Theosophy without the adherence of Mrs. Besant might readily have been that of a declining cult, already torn by dissensions which it fell to her lot to adjust. To her the "intellectual instructions of the Mahatmas were enormously more interesting than even the exhibition of their abnormal powers." Yet she added, "If there are no Mahatmas, the Theosophic Society is an absurdity, and there is no use in keeping it up."

It may well be that it was the disillusionment of Mr. Sinnett, the most important survivor of the Blavatsky leadership, that retired miracles to the background, though these were clumsily attempted by Mr. Judge, president of the American Theosophists, who continued to receive Mahatmic precipitations, including one from Koot Hoomi reading, "Judge's plan is right"; which message Mrs. Besant was forced to conclude had been written by Judge himself. Long maintaining that the supposition that the Mahatmic letters with which he had been so generously honored were written by H.P.B. was an absurdity, Mr. Sinnett came to admit that they were written by H.P.B. at Koot Hoomi's dictation. "Koot Hoomi frankly told me that, as they stand, they are a 'travesty' of his meaning. As to dropping letters through the ceiling, I have long since forgiven the wrongs they did me."

The thaumaturgic trend appears in Mrs. Besant's sponsorship of the amazing revelations of Rev. Charles W. Leadbeater. Over their joint signatures appear discoveries of another order[4] that rival Madame Blavatsky's most extravagant fabrications. For forty-two years, until her death in 1933, Mrs. Besant led the Eastern branch of Theosophists to its present estate. The most dramatic incident of her career centers about a young Indian, Krishnamurti, whom she hailed as a Master in the flesh. She presented him to large gatherings in all parts of the world. He founded the Order of the Star, wrote inspirational treatises, but after a few years of being idolized, dissolved the order and finally withdrew from Theosophy altogether.

Though the wonders have ceased, according to Mr. Sinnett the Masters were still active in the War on the side of

[4] These are considered in "Thought-Forms and Beyond." See p. 214.

the Allies. One Master protected the American transports
on the way to France. The "White Masters" withdrew
from Germany when Satan "monopolized spiritual influence there." "The benefic aspect of Jupiter to Uranus
early in July, 1932" was used by the Masters "to bring
the Lausanne conference to an unexpectedly successful
issue."

The posthumous Madame Blavatsky survives. Forty
years after her death, there are Theosophic Societies and
Lodges—a hundred or more—in all parts of the world; the
adherents, permanent or transient, are numbered by the
hundred thousand. There is an Eastern Shrine at Adyar,
set in an extensive park with impressive buildings, and a
Western one no less sumptuous—though in origin a seces-
sionist group—at Point Loma, California. There are or
have been fifty journals devoted to the cult, published in a
score of languages; and to celebrate the centenary, *World
Theosophy* was established in 1931. At an International
Congress at Geneva there were some five hundred dele-
gates from twenty-five countries. There is a centenary edition of *Isis Unveiled* in four stately volumes. In 1933 appeared the first volume of what is to be a definitive edition
of Madame Blavatsky's complete writings—in all, an imposing monument to her career as a mistress of marvels
that satisfy wishfully the eternal quest for supernal wisdom.

PART III
TRANSCENDENCE
ESCAPING LIMITATIONS

By the eagerness of the human mind things which are obscure are more easily believed.—TACITUS.

Mystics always hope that science will some day overtake them. —BOOTH TARKINGTON.

The age of miracles is past, the age of miracles is forever here.—CARLYLE.

Argument

PRIMITIVE *philosophy and early belief disclose a world of magic; in one way or another, that world survives in popular belief, alias superstition, in learned doctrines, in more scientific attempts to demonstrate its existence. The transcendent world is the world beyond, outside the range of ordinary experience. It throws the emphasis upon the transcender, in the primitive (and later) belief upon the medicine man, priest, prophet, seer, adept in rites and ceremonies. In more recent days it focuses upon the* medium—*the medium of intercourse between this world and that other beyond one variously conceived.*

Transcendence has a distinctive place in religion, where it assumes the form of inspiration, revelation, miracle; that falls outside the frame of the present consideration. Psychological transcendence posits knowledge and powers—limited as ever to unusual individuals by special gift—beyond the recognized use of the senses and other mental ways of information, often acting without the normal consciousness or intention of the individual in whom they occur. However to be accounted for, they form an interesting chapter in psychology. The interest in them was quickened by the emergence of "psychical research" (from 1882 on) which specializes upon their study. The present selection of episodes is limited mainly to recent instances which are capable of a more precise analysis.

The story of transcendence is far older than this; it goes back to magic. The alchemist set out upon a transcendent search for control of physical and biological processes beyond the ordinary limitations; he sought to convert baser metals into gold, to escape the limitations of age by discovering the elixir of life. Psychical transcendence is closely connected with varieties of spirit-belief. Many of the phenomena, both physical and mental, referred to spirit origin—such as levitations, materializations, rappings, communications, revelations—became the standard evidences of modern spiritualism in its vigorous American revival not a hundred years ago. It claimed to demonstrate newer phases of transcendences, such as spirit-photographs and paraffin molds in the physical domain, and new orders of revelation of private affairs in the mental domain. Psychical research tested such alleged transcendence as "telepathy" by experimental techniques.

The psychology of transcendence finds a pivotal clue in the subconscious phases of mind. The existence of trance-states and milder forms of dissociation gives further plausibility to the claim. The more complex examples involve the interrelations of a house divided against itself—two souls in one body. The evidence of hypnosis confirms the diagnosis. In so far as mind is expressed through muscles, the principle appears in involuntary movements. This chapter in psychology may be followed in the genealogy of Ouija, which has a long pedigree. Practically applied, the principle gave rise to the divining-rod, and as a form of mystifying skill, to "mind-reading." And here as elsewhere we meet the troublesome question of sincerity—the will to deceive on the part of some playing upon the will to believe on the part of others. There may be sincere counterparts as well as fraudulent counterfeits of apparently transcendent operations, and puzzling minglings of the two.

When we take the step—which modern psychology aims to show is not a transcendent one—into the subtler phases of mental action, in which physical manifestations are secondary, we are indeed in a different world, to be investigated by a technique yet to be perfected. The lesson of the subtlety of our muscles in conveying indications of emotional and mental states we may carry over; for we are ever dependent, in normal and abnormal conditions alike, upon the trained muscles to express knowledge from whatever source. The source of knowledge becomes the bone of contention between those who believe that its origin is within and those who hold that it demonstrates knowledge beyond the ordinary avenues of information. We come upon such dramatic adventures in transcendence as that of turning back the clock of time and living in bygone centuries, of receiving communications in strange scripts of other days, which revelations are subject to confirmation; we come upon persons in trance-states living and acting scenes completely out of the workaday orbits of their lives; we come upon operative authorship of distinctive workmanship and wide range, realistic and imaginative as well. These newer chapters in transcendence offer further challenges to the naturalistic psychologist; nothing less than the detailed analysis of their provenance will reval their hidden plot.

The sources of our mental life are indeed complex and do not lie on the surface; there are hidden springs of motive, wayward losses and recoveries. There are daylight and twilight phenomena. The field of operation which prompted belief in transcendence is real and significant; that it can be brought within the range of accredited principles is the position of modern psychology. Its impress upon the story of belief through the ages gives it added interest. The episodes are so diverse that their reduction to a common plot is itself an application of the new psychology.

Chapter XI

OUIJA AND FAMILY

THE HEROINE of this tale is not a person, but a device, or, rather, the principle behind it. The family name of *Ouija* is a Franco-German alliance of assent: *oui* and *ja*. The principle of Ouija is *involuntary movement* revealing intention and ideas; all devices of that nature belong to her clan. The vogue of the ouija-board had its place in the procession of diversions affording entertainment by contact with mysteries. Its ancestry goes back to the days when the mysterious was interpreted as an oracle of the gods. "Ouija" is described in the work of a Roman writer, Ammianus Marcellinus. I cite from the account by Andrew Lang:

About 371 A.D. one Hilarius was tortured on a charge of magical operations against the Emperor Valens. He confessed. A little table, made of Delphic laurel, was produced in court. "We made it," he said, "that confounded little table, under strange rites and imprecations, and we set it in movement thus: it was placed in a room with perfumes, above a round plate fashioned of various metals. The edge of the plate was marked with the letters of the alphabet separated by certain spaces. A priest, linen-clad, bowed himself over the table, balancing a ring tied to a thin thread."

When the table spelled out T-H-E-O as the next ascendant of the throne, the Emperor put several rivals by name of Theodore and Theophile to death; he was actually succeeded by Theodosius.

Just how the "little table" and the ring suspended at

128

the end of a thread were combined in this earliest of alphabetical ouijas is not quite clear. We are safe in inferring
that the hand that held the thread guided the table in its
travels from letter to letter. There are other Roman accounts, in which the alphabet was *recited,* the ball ringing
out against the side of the glass at the "right" letters. Only
a few years ago the same mysterious ball and thread was
sent to me by a well-known exposer of spirit mediums,
with the comment that the thing actually worked in the
form of a *sex-detector:* that in the hands of a man, or when
held over an article of male attire, the ball would swing
to and fro, and, for a woman, swing in a circle.

This contrivance, which may still be found in conjuring shops, has quite a story attached to it, interesting as a
curious experiment in physics. The details might have
been lost but for its record by the distinguished chemist,
Chevreuil. At the beginning of the nineteenth century, a
group of experimenters were convinced that this ball-and-
thread possessed remarkable physical properties. One of
them, Professor Gerboin, of Strassburg, wrote an entire
book upon it, of date 1808. He gave it the name of the
exploring, or revealing, pendulum—*le pendule explora-
teur.*

The claims for it were varied, but all of the same type:
it would swing one way for one kind of substance or influence, and in an opposite way for another. It was claimed
that when the string, with a bit of iron, sulphur, gold, or
other metal suspended from it, was held over the north
pole of a magnet, the movement was from left to right,
and over the south pole from right to left; held over copper or silver, it went right to left; over zinc or water, left
to right; if held in the left hand, the movement was reversed; if held over an apple with the stem upward, it
moved one way, if over an apple with the blossom-end
upward, in the opposite way; if held over the head of a

human subject, it rotated "positively," if over his feet, "negatively."

Convinced that they were exploring a new branch of physics, these investigators developed a theory. They concluded that the force responsible for the movement was either expansive or compressive, actively or passively perturbed, according to the kind of movement of the pendulum. They found oxygen to be expansive and hydrogen compressive; the tips of the fingers were expansive, the middle joints compressive; some minerals were found to be expansive, and the diamond was neutral. This entire alleged new chapter in science is wholly mythical, the result of expectant suggestion; *the ball swings as you think it will or should.* The "sex-detector" proves to be a revival of a simple illusion that works as well in the drawing-room as in the laboratory. The scientist makes more elaborate discoveries and spins more fantastic theories.

Chevreuil found several mentions of a miraculous pendulum in books on the curiosities of physics in the seventeenth century, and a reference to its use in the fifteenth and sixteenth centuries as a means of telling the time of day. The group of pendulum explorers of the early nineteenth century were presumably acquainted with this tradition, and attempted to give it scientific standing. The wrinkle of "sex" is a modern exploitation.

The movement of the pendulum is so delicate and subtle that Chevreuil himself was at first deceived by it. It actually worked as described when he held the pendulum over a dish of mercury. To test whether a physical force operated the pendulum, he interposed a glass plate between the iron ring and the mercury. Again, to his surprise, the oscillations diminished and then stopped entirely, and started again when the glass plate was removed. Suspecting that the movement was due to the difficulty in holding the pendulum steady with a free arm, he rested his arm on a support; the oscillations diminished but did not cease. Still suspicious, he had his eyes blindfolded and let *some one else* interpose the glass plate *without his knowing when;* and *nothing happened,* though he held the pendulum still for fifteen minutes. This observation marks an important moment in the annals of suggestion.

Chevreuil had made a great discovery which stood by him for life. "So long as I believed the movement possible, it took place; but after discovering the cause I could not reproduce it." He adds that the experiments "might be of some interest for psychology and even for the history of science." They show how easy it is "to mistake illusions for realities, whenever we are confronted by phenomena in which the human sense-organs are involved under conditions imperfectly analyzed." [2]

Chevreuil was a master mind, a devotee of the scientific method, chemist, physiologist, psychologist, with the further distinction of living one hundred and three years. In that day neither "suggestion" nor "expectant attention" were well recognized. Chevreuil described the process minutely and generalized the principle of the "exploring pendulum" in a letter to Ampere in the year 1833. It was the great vogue of table-turning in 1853 that revived his interest, which extended to the principle of the divining-rod. Chevreuil brought the three phenomena under the same law: pendulum, divining rod, table-turning are all examples of involuntary movements under expectant attention. His memoir of 1854 remains a classic in the psychology of suggestion.

[2] Examples of psychic automatisms in which the central interest lies in the source of the ideas and the acquisition of a technique appear in "The Strange Case of Hélène Smith" (page 167) and especially in "Patience Worth: An Alter Ego" (page 178), who began her literary career on a ouija-board, but graduated to freer media of expression.

The modern story of Ouija begins with the Rochester "rappings," which inaugurated the great American move- ment of spiritualism in 1848. By 1853 the world—England, France, Germany, as well as the United States—was pos- sessed by the idea of communicating with the dead. Pre- sumably it was the first imposing "intellectual" movement that reversed the course of empire and made its way east- ward.

The raps themselves belong to a far older tradition. They were recognized by the Church as *spiritus percutiens,* and, in phenomena of the *Poltergeist* variety, survive feebly in Hallowe'en performances. The pranks of the Fox sisters started the raps that were heard around the world; forty years later they publicly confessed that the raps were produced by dislocating the toe and knee joints. They established a code of communication with the rap- ping spirit by rapping once for *no* and three times for *yes.*

Sharing honors with the raps in the properties of early spiritualism, and at times the instrument, was the *table.* The table did two things: it moved or turned or rose in the air, and it rapped. *Tables tournantes,* table-turning, and *table parlantes,* table-talking, were the phenomena that crossed the seas and upset the mental poise of two continents. There was even a journal called *La Table Parlante.* It is the *talking* table that belongs to the direct family of Ouija.

The simplest "ouija" of the spiritualists was an alphabet-board held in the hand of the questioner, who pointed with a pencil from letter to letter until a rap sounded; by repeating the process again and again, words and entire messages were evolved. It was a slow and tedi- ous performance sustained by a tense interest in the result. In another usage, the alphabet-board was held by the medium as the questioner followed her movements; or the company might be seated around a table with the board upon it, the table-legs tilting at the selected letters. In 1853 American mediums held rapping soirées in London with half-guinea admissions. The questions could be asked aloud or silently; and if silently, the medium was dependent upon the involuntary indications of the questioner. The clue appears in the test made by George Henry Lewes, when he deliberately emphasized the hesitation of his pencil at the "right" letters; he talked with one of the Eumenides, who gave him private information concerning his domestic relations, induced the table to confess that the medium was an impostor, and that Hamlet's father had seventeen noses—all this when the medium did not *know* the nature of the question. His skepticism did not stem the tide of belief in the spirit origin of talking tables.

It was left for Robert Hare, professor of chemistry at the University of Pennsylvania, to reduce spirit communication to a true "ouija" by an ingenious combination of table and dial, the table communicating as it moved. Professor Hare was convinced that the medium—at some sessions it was one of the Fox sisters—could not be the source of the arrest of the indicator selecting the letters, as she saw only the back of the alphabet-disc; presumably she obtained a sufficient hint from the facial expression of the questioner.

Professor Hare's simple credulity appears in the conduct of the experiments.

I said: "If there is a spirit present, let the letter 'Y' be brought under the index." Accordingly it revolved to the letter "Y." "Will the spirit be so kind as to give his initials." It revolved immediately to "R" and to "H." "What," said I, "my father?" It revolved again to the letter "Y" indicating the affirmative. "Will you arrange these letters in alphabetical order." This was done; and upon request the apparatus spelled *Wash-*

ington and *Franklin.* At a later session, the apparatus, of its own accord, spelled: *"Oh, my son! Listen to Reason!"*

He referred to this communication as the most important experiment of his life. He likewise naïvely records that, wholly unexpectedly and unsolicited, he received a communication through a medium by name of Lanning,

PROFESSOR ROBERT HARE'S "OUIJA" TABLE

The device converted rolling movements of the table into spirit communications. The pointer halting at each letter in turn spelled the message. From Robert Hare, *Experimental Investigation of the Spirit Manifestations,* 1855.

from "an assembly of eminent spirits," reading thus: "We cheerfully accompany your father to sanction the communication given through our medium, Mr. Lanning, to you." Further, they were interested in the publication of facts through experimental investivations. The document, cherished by its recipient, had notable signatures: Geo. Washington, J. Q. Adams, Dr. Chalmers, Oberlin, W. E. Channing.

Hare was naturally the object both of pity and ridicule by his skeptical friends. He complained bitterly: "I was

represented as capable of becoming the dupe of any girl";
he insisted that his experiments were made under "test"
condition; he appealed to learned societies, but to no avail;
his faith in mediums was never shaken.

The "Hare" form of the ouija was not altogether convenient. A Yankee inventor by name of Pease substituted

TWO FORMS OF PEASE'S "SPIRITOSCOPE"

The hand rested on the board in one form: the entire board rolled in
the other. The addition of numbers, "yes" and "no," and common phrases
facilitated communication. From Hare's *Experimental Investigation.*

for the pulleys and cords a lever working against a spring,
and called the apparatus a *spiritoscope.* Professor Hare
adopted it eagerly. "It is surprising with what readiness a
spirit, even when unused to the apparatus, will by moving
the lever actuate the index causing it to point to the letters, words or figures distributed on the face of the disk."

So widespread was the epidemic of table-turning that
to quiet the agitation, two great scientific leaders inter-
rupted their labors to give a rational explanation of the

phenomena: Faraday in England and, as already indicated, Chevreuil in France. On the basic question, What made the table move? Faraday wrote: "The effect produced by table-turning has without due inquiry, been referred to electricity, to magnetism, to attraction, to some unknown or hitherto unrecognized physical power able to affect inanimate bodies, to the revolution of the earth and even to diabolical or supernatural agency," and most generally, to the spirits of the dead.

Faraday's sound sense and expert knowledge of the conditions of a valid experiment solved the problem, though not to the satisfaction of spiritists. "It is with me a clear point that the table moves when the parties, though they strongly wish it, do not intend, and do not believe that they move it by ordinary mechanical power. They say the table draws their hands; it moves first and they have to follow it." He was surprised at the number "who gave testimony in good faith in the cause of error." He was willing patiently to try the effects of various substances with different electrical properties. "No form of experiment or mode of observation that I could devise gave me the slightest indication of any peculiar natural force—nothing but mere mechanical pressure exerted inadvertently by the turner."

Faraday reduced the matter to a demonstration by arranging two small boards with glass rollers between them, held together by light rubber bands that permitted a play of the upper board upon the lower. To make the movements visible, he attached a straw to the top board. The fingers of the operator rested lightly on the top board; as it always moved before the table did, the proof was plain that the fingers moved the table, and not, as they supposed, the table the fingers. Furthermore, if the operator watched the straw, he could hold the board steady by downward pressure; but as soon as he looked away, the slight movements returned. The demonstration had little effect. The occult accounting went on; the mystery of the table was too precious a belief to be disturbed by a simple apparatus in the hands of a skeptical physicist. The "inadvertent turner" of Faraday became the involuntary mover, the automatic writer. The contest was on between a natural and a transcendental explanation.

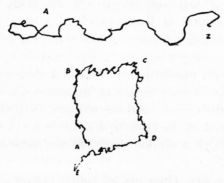

INVOLUNTARY MOVEMENTS RECORDED BY THE AUTOMATOGRAPH

Above, when the subject thought of the object at 2, the hand moved toward it. Below, as a metronome clicked first at A and then at B, C, and D, the hand changed direction.

Forty years after, I devised a modification which registered these involuntary movements. I called it an *automatograph,* since it writes the "automatic" involuntary movements under the influence of an idea. With a sensitive subject the record follows the direction of attention. When a metronome was set going, first in one and then in another corner of the room, and the subject was directed to count its strokes, his hand involuntarily traveled with his attention.

The turning or talking table illustrates how a belief in transcendence gains headway under the impetus of a "psychic" wave, once the idea of a natural explanation is dismissed. Every current occult notion claimed the table as proof of its thesis; it was also referred to physical forces, in turn misunderstood. It was *electricity,* one observer finding that the table moved more freely when insulated by glass tumblers or sheets of gutta-percha; it was *magnetism,* either of the classic type or as *animal magnetism,* in that the sitters felt peculiar tingling sensations in the finger-tips; it was *odic force,* the *od* being the then credited discovery of Reichenbach of a force equally illusory; it was a new order of *neural* force, the human body becoming a charged battery; it was an entirely new physical force with untold possibilities as a source of energy; it was *Satanic Agency,* which is "at least equal to the production of the effects," and has scriptural support (in fact a Bible placed on the table by a pious believer stopped its motion, though a skeptic produced the same effect by a copy of *Gulliver's Travels* or Hoyle on Whist); and above all, it was spirits. These are all contemporary accountings based upon the entire gamut of error from defective observation to subjective delusion to occult speculation. In its day the talking table held the center of the stage as a baffling psychic mystery, confuting skeptics.

The *divining-rod* belongs to a somewhat independent branch of the Ouija family. Its line of ancestry, as the name indicates, goes back to oracles. Early Christian divining-rods were inscribed with emblems of the Church, and were formally blessed to ensure their efficacy. The Roman *virgula divina* had several forms, including devices for casting lots by turning a sieve or throwing a stick. It seems to have been used for finding treasure or locating any object of search. From the Middle Ages onward, the typical diviner came to be a folklore figure reputed to possess a special gift for finding water for wells, veins of ore in mines, or hidden treasure. He carried a forked

THE DIVINER OF METALS

From an old German print.

DOWSING AT THE INTERNATIONAL CONFERENCE
OF DIVINERS, VERONA, 1932

hazel stick—the hazel associated with magical properties; hence the popular name "witch-hazel" for the healing lotion hammamelis. He held one prong of the stick in each hand, watching the free end, with the expectation that this would dip downward when passing over the locality of the object of search. Naturally the direction of exploration was at his command; and what hidden sources he passed over without any movement of the rod were never discovered. As his successes were noted, and his failures forgotten, his reputation increased after the manner of clairvoyants and prophets. By the same untutored shrewdness that makes the sportsman's guide woods-wise and weather-wise, the diviner becomes "ore"-wise or "water"-wise.

The "ouija" principle of involuntary, yet directed, movements as applied to "dowsing"—dipping for water— would hold that the "dip" occurs when the diviner releases the impulse, though he has the strong impression that some outside force makes his hands "dip." The knowledge of where to look and when to "dip" is likewise his contribution, his "idea." An English engineer, W. J. Lewis Abbot, after a long experience, reports that he knows no instance in which a diviner located water under conditions that would have surprised a hydrologist, and that their failures were many. The diviner makes a study in his own way of surface features, though he has a contempt for geology; and much the same applies for metal ore. Indeed a seventeenth-century book on divining for metals gives the advice to select for the operation a territory where ore is likely to be found. The prospector, though he believes in the magic of the hazel twig, uses his experience. Carefully controlled experiments of reputed diviners have been almost uniformly negative. Yet the controversy between the "involuntary" and the "special gift" explanation keeps on. The attempts to rationalize the process by assuming some form of "vibrations" or "electric currents" is gratuitous speculation.[1]

Mind-reading—which is muscle-reading—forms another interesting member of the Ouija family. A wave of interest in this variety of psychological skill gave popularity to public exhibitions some thirty years ago. The confessions of a professional mind-reader, such as Stewart Cumberland, make most interesting reading. He had a keen insight into the true nature of the indications which he interpreted so skilfully. At times blindfolded, and with instructions to the subject to concentrate upon the locality of the object to be found, he would take the subject's hand, place it on his forehead and, from the readiness or hesitation to follow his lead, quickly find hidden articles and even a marked passage on a page in a book on a library shelf. Practice and a sensitive endowment work wonders, occasionally increasing the marvel by a fortunate guess.

The art of muscle-reading confirms and extends the principle of involuntary movements; and so does another interesting variation—"involuntary whispering." It appeared in connection with experiments in "thought-transference," or telepathy, that an intense concentration upon the sound of the word to be transmitted may induce a slight tendency to utter it. The skilful reading of lips by the deaf is a related art; that involuntary movements by the master were sufficient to give the clue to a horse to start and stop "counting" appears in the story of Kluger

[1] Of all instruments of ouija-ing, the divining-rod has by far the largest representation in the literature. The subject is covered richly in a lengthy contribution by Professor W. F. Barrett (*Proceedings of the Society for Psychical Research*). He concludes that the "involuntary-movement" hypothesis and subconscious use of normally acquired rule-of-thumb observation accounts for the phenomena, but leaves a margin for experience not so accountable.

Hans. Thinking is inhibited doing; as the mind-reader puts it, all thinking is pushing or pulling. The tendency of a thought to find an outlet in the muscles is inherent in the action of the nervous system; and that and nothing more mystic is the secret of Ouija.

The *planchette,* which appeared as a protegé of spiritu- alism, is the actual parent of the ouija-board. Spelling letter by letter was slow; why should not the spirits write through the hands of the medium? Faraday's apparatus may have furnished a hint; who invented the "little plank" is uncertain. The instrument is a heart-shaped board just large enough for the fingers resting upon it; it travels on two legs fitted with smooth tips, while the third member of the tripod carries a pencil which writes. It writes, however, in a peculiar manner; the subject, losing the sense of directing, refers both movement and senti- ment to some foreign agency. *Planchette* is an instrument for *automatic writing.* In the 1860's revelations by plan- chette flooded spiritualistic literature. Talking spirits be- came literary, the effusions of no high order. Many automatists appeared who wrote fluently with pen or pen- cil—requiring no planchette—and claiming for the source of their writings some outside agency, the spirit of some of the great departed, or a personal message from a "control" or deceased member of the family.[2]

Planchette, if not the mother, may be said to be the godmother of Ouija of the ouija-board. Spirit-belief, the

[2] Among the "automatically" inspired authors who have honored me by sending me their works is one through whom commune all the great liter- ary lights and celebrities of the past: Plato, Shakespeare, Milton, Lincoln, Poe guide her pen. Another receives messages by "clairaudient transmis- sion." The poems are her own, referred to no other personality, but "coming" as if dictated. In these as in many other cases the interest lies less in the technique of recording than in the source of the ideas and the command of expression. There are automatic artists, who draw or paint under similar conditions.

desire to communicate with the departed, is the true progenitor. That interest gave planchette vogue. To guide a planchette to form a readable script required a measure of "automatic" ability which few possessed. By the simple step of substituting for pencil and paper the original spiritualist alphabet-board and by making the "little table" the pointer, the clientele of communicants was greatly increased. To point from letter to letter and lose the sense of directing the readily gliding instrument was within the compass of many—aided and abetted by a slight dose of self-deception.

Ouija, originally of the temple, received the protection of the Patent Office. Whatever her skill as a fortune teller, she made a comfortable fortune for her inventor. Presently we find her in the courts successfully suing a rival, the *Volo-board*, for infringement of her patronymic and commercial rights. Ouija-ing as a popular occupation seems to have enjoyed two periods of revival, first in the '80's and again in the '90's, when it supplanted planchette, and once again in the period of the World War and its aftermath.

There are two versions or legends concerning the birth of Ouija of the toy-shops. The one that, Minerva-like, she emerged full-grown from the head of a cabinet-maker, who though not a spiritualist, had enough sympathy with spirits to wish to relieve them of the burden of moving heavy tables; he devised a lighter, more convenient, and more articulate bit of furniture. The other reads that its inventor in an idle moment of an empty day, seated in his comfortable Maryland kitchen, took a bread-board on his lap, placed a saucer upon it and his hand upon the saucer, and noted how readily the saucer moved about, as if animated. Ouija-ing captured the American public completely, but like other captivations as suddenly lost its appeal. From "everybody's doing it" to "nobody's doing it" is often a brief transition in popular fashion. The ouija-board was extended far beyond its use for spirit communication. It became a ready form of release—a simplified instrument for automatic writing.

Its psychology is the motor counterpart of crystal gazing. The gazer or scryer sees in the reflecting ball the picturized projection of his mental imagery; he gets back in his message what his subconscious reflection formulates in words. The surprising feature in automatic movements is the ignoring or falling away of the sense of intention and effort which accompanies the movement of my pen as I write these words.

The genealogy of Ouija forms an engaging and significant chapter in the persistent conflict—the age-old controversy—between the natural and the supernatural. The popularity of the ouija-board, although but a small portion of those who played with it could make it "work," is an added testimony to the wide dissemination of involuntary movements and to the operation of the subconscious mechanisms of the mind. Ouija has a large family and a long genealogy; she has a permanent place in every museum of psychology

CHAPTER XII

PALADINO'S TABLE

THE BIOGRAPHY of Eusapia Paladino would be far less interesting than that of her table. As neither could read or write, we must read the story in the abundant accounts of the table's spectacular performances. Eusapia was brought up without any schooling; at first a seamstress, she later drifted into professional mediumship. This illiterate peasant was "dragged through all Europe and half America," surrounded by a galaxy of savants and dilettanti, and became the theme of an international literature. She was investigated by many commissions, some of which endorsed and others as decidedly rejected her claims to supernormal powers.

The table of Paladino was a plain affair, built like an ordinary kitchen table but much lighter and only eighteen inches wide. This simple table was in her hands an instrument of potent power, not by virtue of what she made it do—a common enough art—but of how she, or rather her sponsors, persuaded others to think she did it. It worked wonders in belief. It accepted the curtain-calls of enthusiastic witnesses of its gyrations, which, being mainly upward, were called levitations. The table of Paladino was a piece of psychic furniture with a history, like that of other heroes and heroines, partly legendary.

For when that table rose, it not only levitated, it transcended. It transcended the accredited behavior of tables which keep their legs on the floor through a sense of decorum or by the force of gravity; it became the evidence of a rare psychic power. The principle of its motion, along with similar exhibitions of transcendent mechanics, was referred to as *telekinesis*. This impressive word means action at a distance by a supernormal force not recognized in ordinary physics.

The pedigree of Paladino's performance goes back to the table-turning and table-rapping days of a half century earlier, and Eusapia, though her name suggests wisdom, belonged to the unintelligentsia; she was incapable of rising to the cerebral level of a message. Home, the famous medium, who had inspired Browning's "Sludge, the Medium," had introduced levitations of a table of a tilting variety; objects placed upon it defied the action of gravity by not rolling off. The levitating table had been retained in the spiritist's repertory; it was a common way of introducing a séance and gaging the coöperation of the sitters. It is the very simplicity of Paladino's performance, in contrast with the extravagantly transcendent explanation, that makes the episode memorable. The story of Eusapia is that of the convinced or favorably disposed believer's habit of mind, not primarily of the exotic or quixotic behavior of her table.

An account of the table in action appears in the record of a séance held in New York on April 17, 1910, which I had some part in arranging. At that session, unsuspected by Eusapia, two young men, dressed completely in black, crawled under the table, screened by the company of bystanders. From these favored positions they observed the levitations, their eyes close to the left foot of Paladino, which proved to be the telekinetic instrument of uplift. I cite from the report from under the table.

A foot came from underneath the dress of the medium and placed the toe underneath the leg of the table on the left side of the medium, and pressing upward, gave it a little chuck into the air. Then the foot withdrew, and the leg of the table dropped suddenly to the floor.... I was lying with my face on the floor within *eight inches* of the left leg of the table; and each time that the table was lifted, whether in a partial or a complete levitation, the medium's foot was used as a propelling force upward.

Signora Paladino wore soft leather shoes with wide flanges on the stout sole, to afford a secure resting-place for the sharply square leg of the table.

The apparent elimination of the medium's muscular endowment as the source of the levitation arises from the reliance placed by her endorsing examiners upon the control of her hands and feet. The sitter on Eusapia's right controls her right hand, the sitter on her left her left, by maintaining a contact with his own hand, all hands on the top of the table. Similarly, under the table the medium places her left foot *on* the right foot of her left "control" and her right foot *on* the left foot of her right "control." The contacts thus maintained are supposed to prevent the use of the medium's hands or feet. By a simple trick of "substitution," one hand or foot is released for action— gradually, skilfully, without arousing suspicion. The trick consists in letting the *one* foot of the medium serve for contact with the "controlling" foot of each control.

The same substitution comes into play for the hands in the cabinet performances, when a curtain, thrown over part of the table, serves as a screen. The repertory of Paladino's transcendence includes the manipulation of objects in a recess behind her chair, partitioned by a curtain, all within range of her versatile left arm and leg, aided, if need be, by other devices. Objects deposited in the "cabinet" space are thrown about or transported to the table; these performances occurring in fairly complete darkness. There also appears at times a "transcendent" hand—actually the freed left hand of the medium—in the opening

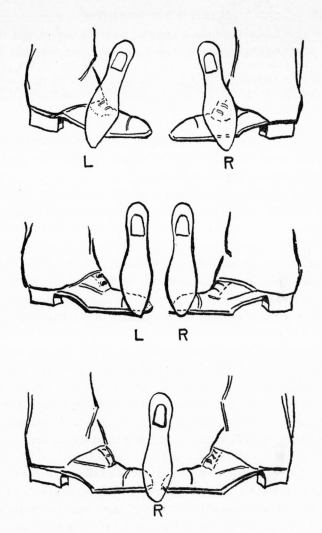

HOW ONE FOOT DOES FOR TWO

First Position. The "feminine" outlines indicate the medium's shoes, the "masculine" ones those of her controls.

Second Position. The medium jockeys her feet to a position favorable for substitution.

Third Position. The right foot of the medium serves as contact with both controls. The left foot is free to levitate the table. "Nervous" pats and shifts accustom the amateur control to irregular contacts.

of the curtains. In some séances a light flower-stand, just within reach behind the curtain, is used as a rake to bring objects out of her physical reach within telekinetic control.

An unusual feature of the carefully rehearsed séance of April 17, 1910 was that the "controls" were experienced conjurors. They knew all the tricks of the trade, and were fair enough actors to keep their faces non-committal as they expressed their admiration of the miracles. In 1910 the belief in the genuineness of the transcendent table was strong; even a circumstantial report of eye-witnesses to the tricks failed to impress Eusapia's following. A double demonstration, positive and negative, was arranged. In the first séance the medium was given all the rope and encouragement she wanted; the purpose was to realize the effect of a successful performance, and to invite her assurance that all went well and genuinely.

The program for the second séance was conducted quite otherwise. Held a week later, it opened under the same lax control as amateurs usually exercise; levitations and transportations appeared abundantly. At an arranged signal, the control was made expert and all attempts at substitution blocked. *From that moment on nothing whatever happened.* The telekinesis was as dead as a circuit without a battery. And here may end the tale of the table.

The second part of the tale is the vital one; it relates not to the table but to the belief that now and then the laws of matter are transcended in the presence of a gifted transcender. Since the laws of transcendence are unknown, they are improvised; and no one can gainsay them. In this instance they were accepted as stated by an illiterate medium. Tables were levitating and rapping by the hundreds in spirit séances all over the world, but remained inglorious. It was Paladino's table rather than another's that became telekinetically famous because of the prestige

THE EXPOSURE OF PALADINO

The séance in New York at which observers concealed under the table
saw the release of the left foot for levitation.

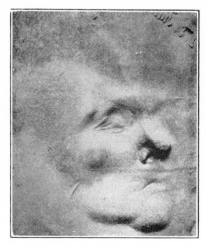

THE FACE OF PALADINO MYSTERIOUSLY MOLDED IN PUTTY

of her endorsers. From 1888 on, when Lombroso attested her transcendence, Eusapia had the good fortune to be examined by one group and another of "psychical researchers," including men of distinction in the sciences. She was shrewd enough to allow herself to be levitated into fame, repeating with the vanity of a prima donna: *È una Paladino!* She had the honor of having a volume devoted to her by Hereward Carrington, in which, despite the admission of occasional trickery, he pronounces her the one black swan, the unique exception, among the claimants to supernormal material manifestations.

The defense of the belief in transcendence leads to a strange code of logic, which makes argument impossible. The trick, discovered in New York by direct evidence, had been suspected and detected long before in Berlin, again in London, and later in Paris, and by men of equal reputation with her defendants. But the argument of the defense concludes that there are "good" séances and "poor" séances. The poor ones consist of weak, tricky counterfeits of the genuine, good ones. I know of only one more specious argument—and this, too, has been used— that there must be genuine performances; otherwise there would be nothing for the counterfeit ones to imitate.

And their explanation? The power, force, or what-not, which is supposed to be the transcendent form of energy, *gives out*. Paladino, in order not to disappoint her sitters, and to earn her attractive fee, or for pride in her performances, then levitates by foot-power. According to Mr. Carrington, "this is not a wild supposition, since Professor Lombroso some years before his death stated his belief that Eusapia was rapidly losing her powers, and that it would not be long before they were lost altogether." The prophecy certainly seems to have been fulfilled during her American visit. The supposition is not only wild but suicidal, especially in view of Lombroso's completely uncritical attitude. First assuming a mythical power and then assuming its loss to account for its absence, is a logical catch to which there is no reply and no need of one. It marks the nadir of argument and the zenith of assumption. It may be described as the heads-I-win-tails-you-lose logic.

Both the arrangements of the séances and the argument in defense of transcendence are as tricky as the tricks themselves. Paladino is supposed to be controlled, and being controlled, unable to levitate by hand or foot. As a fact *she* does all the vital controlling, and insists that her foot shall be placed on yours, *not yours on hers*. She determines the conditions and positions and lighting and the order of procedure. It is this circumstance that made indispensable a counterplot in which the medium should be outwitted. The most difficult part of the arrangements was to persuade Eusapia, keenly suspicious and surrounded by equally suspicious compatriots, to come to the séance, accompanied only by the Italian member of the group of investigators, who acted as interpreter. For once Eusapia *was* under control.

The same analysis applies to Paladino's other items in transcendence: reaching objects beyond range, the mysterious breeze about her forehead, plastic paraffin molds, moving a balance without contact (by means of a fine hair, and consequently failing when the balance was under glass). For each alleged transcendence, there is obviously a special technique, and ever the additional technique for avoiding the detection of the *modus operandi*. Since she determines the rules of the game and the stage setting, she is well protected. The table is a *screen;* the curtain is a *screen;* her skirts are a *screen*. No man, says an expert observer, could do the foot-substitution trick in any sort of light, because any one looking under the table would see the vagrant foot. The conditions imposed are a *screen* —from dim light to nearly total darkness. The sitters, forming a chain, prevent exploration. The alleged sensitiveness of the medium to contact limits examination. She cries out in pain when any one places a hand behind the curtain; but *not* when that hand wore a black glove so that she could not see it. The supposition of waning power or the unfavorable effect of the attitude of skeptics—all these are psychic *screens*. Paladino's skill was not in moving tables, but in evading control. Her most valuable asset was the inclination to credit the belief that tables do occasionally move by telekinetic force. The setting of the séance provides a shelter for the feeble logic, which like a ghost cannot endure the light of day. The levitating table is a fable; but what the fable teaches is that a belief in transcendence may not only lift tables but move mountains, as will duly appear. The parallelogram of physical forces of the foot-power that moved Paladino's table is simple; the parallelogram of psychic forces that made of it a demonstration in telekinesis is far more complex.

Chapter XIII

PSYCHIC ADVENTURES IN
RETRO-HISTORY

A SCIENTIFIC mind has suggested an intriguing idea. If we could take our position so indefinitely far off in stellar space that the light from this planet would be reaching us centuries after it left the earth, and if we were granted the proper super-telescopic vision, we might be witnessing the signing of the Declaration of Independence, or the granting of the Magna Charta, or the Fall of Rome. The assumption of transcendence attains this thrilling experience far more simply. It assumes that what once was, is still; that people and events leave an impress or influence, which persists and retains the power to reveal the past to minds attuned to a hypothetical something, for which the "wave-length" provides a tempting analogy.

The byways of psychological literature record twentieth-century experiences in setting the clock of ages back by a transcendental unwinding, in unrolling psychically the coiled scroll of history. One such adventure occurred to an English schoolmistress and her companion. As if in a vision, they suddenly saw at Versailles a partial reconstruction of the park and its properties as it appeared before the French Revolution. Another psychic adventurer reconstructed the buildings of Glastonbury Abbey; his revelations came not as visions but as technical descriptions by monks from the long ago, writing in olden language in "automatic" psychic script. Other transcendent revelations proceed by way of impersonations staged and penned. A modern maid of Geneva impersonated in trance the part of an Indian princess of the fifteenth century; in another drama, she was an inhabitant of Mars; in a third she became Marie Antoinette. A housewife in St. Louis, never out of America, and without literary training, came to write by way of the ouija-board stories of old-time England, full of local color and quaint idiom, and in due course improvised sustained romances equally outside the range of her customary occupations.

In all such psychic adventures in retro-history, facts and settings are revealed allegedly unknown to the revealers. If accepted at their face-value, the tales would establish that one mind can inhabit another, or receive its message. This ancient belief has shaped the folklore and imaginative fiction of all ages. These creations are puzzling; the psychologist seeks their explanation in a natural origin; he interprets them as intricate tricks of the mind under the combined sway of an interest in thrill and marvel, and an urge to self-expression. The mind seeks disguises in the subtleties of its own operations; by failing to recognize their true source, it finds support for beliefs dramatically attractive. Some minds seem peculiarly disposed to such acceptance; which is natural enough in that any other explanation requires rather technical understanding of what remains at best an obscure pattern of creative intelligence. The case must rest upon the plausibility of one explanation as against another.

THE VERSAILLES EPISODE

The tale reads that on a warm afternoon on August 10, 1901, two middle-aged Englishwomen, to be known as Elizabeth Morrison and Frances Lamont, coming to Paris with only a tourist's interest, knowing little about Versailles, strolled toward the Petit Trianon, saw before them a gate and through it a path, which they followed; and the adventure began.

"To our right we saw some farm-buildings looking empty and deserted; implements [among others a plow] were lying about; we looked in, but saw no one. The impression was saddening; but it was not until we reached the crest of the rising ground where there was a garden, that we began to feel as if we had lost our way, and as if something were wrong." There were two men there in official dress, greenish in color, with something in their hands; it might have been a staff. A peculiar antiquated plow and some other gardening tools were near them. "They told us in answer to my enquiry, to go straight on."

At one stage and another, their vision included "a young girl standing in a doorway, who wore a white kerchief and a dress to her ankles"; a pretty lady sketching on a terrace, who wore an old-fashioned gown "trimmed with a light green fichu"; and a quaint bridge, with waterfalls, rocks, and grottoes.

Miss Lamont reports: "I began to feel as if I were walking in my sleep; the heavy dreaminess was oppressive." They saw "a building consisting of some columns roofed in"; on its steps was seated "a man with a heavy black cloak round his shoulders and wearing a slouch hat." The weird feeling increased; it took on a touch of fear. The man slowly turned his face, which was marked by smallpox; his complexion was dark. The expression was "very evil," so much so that they hesitated to pass. What would happen next?

The reader is informed that for a *whole week* after the adventure, the two companions never alluded to that afternoon; "nor," writes Miss Morrison, "did I think about it until I began writing a descriptive letter of our expeditions of the week before. As the scenes came back

one by one, the same sensations of dreamy unnatural op-
pression came over me so strongly that I stopped writing,
and said to Miss Lamont, 'Do you think that the Petit
Trianon is haunted?' Her answer was prompt. 'Yes, I do.' "
To determine how far their visions agreed, each wrote
an independent account; they resolved to take the experience seriously and to search for such historical basis for
their visions as could be found. Miss Lamont, in instruct-
ing her class of girls studying the French Revolution, recalled that the 10th of August was a date of importance.
A French friend told her that on a certain day in August
each year, Marie Antoinette was seen outside the Petit
Trianon wearing a light flapping hat and a fichu gown;
that the gardens were then peopled with her pleasure-
seeking attendants.

Since, on August 10, 1792, the Tuileries were sacked,
they wondered

whether we had inadvertently entered within an act of the
Queen's memory when alive, and whether this explained our
curious sensation of being completely shut in and oppressed.
What more likely, we thought, than that during those hours
in the Hall of the Assembly, or in the Conciergerie, she had
gone back in such vivid memory to her Augusts spent at
Trianon, that some impress of it was imparted to the place?
Some pictures which were shown to us proved that the outdoor dress of the gentlemen at Court had been a large hat
and cloak, and that the ladies wore long-waisted bodices, with
full-gathered skirts, fichus, and hats.

The plot is out. For the narrators, the clue to the adventure is *transcendence*. Their hypothesis supposes that
walls and gardens have eyes and ears; that they retain an
impress of the persons who once inhabited them; that by
some rare gift, the two sight-seers became second-sight
seers sensitive to this "influence."

Three years after the first adventure, on July 4, 1904, they repeated the visit. Everything was changed. There was no trace of the old paths; everything seemed on a smaller scale. "The kiosk was gone. Instead of a shaded meadow continuing up to the wall of the terrace, there is now a broad gravel sweep beneath it. . . . Exactly where the lady was sitting, we found a large spreading bush of apparently many years' growth." Instead of quaintly gowned peasantry, they found noisy Parisian crowds drinking lemonade. "The commonplace, unhistorical atmosphere was totally inconsistent with the air of silent mystery by which we had been so much oppressed. People went wherever they liked, and no one would think of interfering to show the way."

The two researchers spent hours in libraries, ransacking the annals and memoirs of the period; from old maps and contemporary descriptions, they reconstructed the topography of their adventure; they assembled the legends concerning the Trianon and Marie Antoinette; they searched lists of employees to verify costumes. They satisfied themselves that in every detail their visions had an actual basis in historic facts. By accident, they had stepped into a magic circle, and had turned time back for more than a century. They had been favored with a psychic adventure in retro-history.

It seems a pity to spoil so engaging and innocently wishful a tale by intruding the prosaic doubts of reason. But until it is established that palaces are haunted on significant anniversaries, when appropriately appareled *revenants,* or returning ghosts, appear, or that effluvia or auras exist from which complete scenes may be restored when registered upon sensitive brains, the psychologist must look elsewhere for the explanation.

Resorting to conjecture, he may suppose that the original impression is a vivid projection of the imagination, prompted by a fleeting, unacknowledged flash-thought, which has flitted through thousands of tourists' minds. If articulate, it would say: "Wouldn't it be thrilling to see Versailles as it was in Marie Antoinette's day!" In this instance, no sooner thought than seen.

Far more of us have had such vivid impressions than there are records of. The experience may be called a *psychic mirage*. In a physical mirage, an illusory appearance is reflected above the horizon from a location below. In the psychic mirage, the source below the horizon of clear consciousness is the rich repertory of experience and memory; its submergence prevents the recognition of its provenance. Travelers see the same physical mirage—a ship at sea, or an oasis in the desert—because its source is fixed out of visual range. The psychic mirage reflects the individual reservoir of experience and selects variably from that. But what it most requires to see psychic mirages is that pictorially projecting kind of imagination which many, including all crystal-gazers, possess. The peculiarity of the episode at Versailles is the unusual vividness of the projecting stagecraft of the imagination. The *imagined* scenes are projected upon a *real* stage as though the gardens were a crystal sphere.

The issue of transcendence remains: that the resurrection with all its details was not within the range of the normal information of the gazers. That, I continue to conjecture, was a mistake. The first self-deception is in supposing that the knowledge possessed by two cultivated women, professionally teachers—one of them, it seems, of the history of the period in which the adventure is laid—is too meager to be the source of their projected visions. Both had more knowledge of the events of Versailles than they admitted; and they happened to have the pictorial, eye-minded type of imagination to project it. It appears that Miss Morrison's brother, over thirty years before, "had written a prize poem on Marie Antoinette, for whom at the time I felt much enthusiasm."

As for the confirmation by research, to go into that involves tedious detail. But if one keeps on combing abundant records, one will certainly find some favoring instances. There is no applicable calculus of chance; each item stands on its own measure of coincidence. Finding detailed records of plows, of carts, and of workmen gathering leaves, together with their wages in account-books, constitutes no startling verification. Had the retro-historians been told by the "phantom" gardeners their names, and had these proved correct, it would have been a staggering mystery indeed.

These verifications—like many another so-called fact—are treacherous. For the dark-looking man with pocked face they were able to find a counterpart in the records of a Creole gentleman who had smallpox and was in attendance at Versailles. There is nothing unusual in the description; minute research cannot fail to score occasionally. To make much of the finding of a kiosk on an old map is much ado about nothing, since that form of structure is familiar in Paris newstands. Paintings and the stage offer properties in abundance, which a vivid imagination can project into a scene and exaggerate as historically correct. Finally, had these transcendent visitors come upon some other day than August 10th, they would have found an equally cogent reason for the appearance of the phantom "old Versailles" on that day.

A large error in transcendent tales enters with the telling thereof, particularly when the critical experience occurs under conditions unfavorable to precise observation and highly favorable to subjective coloring. In the interpretation of dreams, Freud came upon much material which was not wholly in the dream itself but introduced quite naturally in reflection upon it and in the telling thereof; this mechanism he called *secondary elaboration*. There is much of it in this dream-like psychic adventure, an unconscious embellishing of a good story to make it a better one. The "secondary elaboration" may have been a mutual reinforcement. Each observer alone might have hesitated to credit what when shared seemed more trust-worthy. Is it likely that two women after so thrilling an experience would not speak of it for a whole week? Also, the details noted, particularly of dress, fall well within the feminine range of interest. Had the episode fallen to the lot of two male visionaries, would the incidents have been the same?

The psychologist finds in all such tricks of the mind the action of an organic factor, most generally of fatigue. Under fatigue one loses the sense of direction, if so pre-disposed, and the sense of reality fades. Fasting produces visions. French psychologists record among such psychic lapses in orientation the peculiar feeling of *déja vu,* the sense of "having been there before," when actually the scene is novel. They speak of *fausse reconaisance,* the rec-ognizing as familiar of what actually is not so—memory and perception confused. If we put together tourists' fatigue, a drowsy afternoon in summer, and two English women going without the indispensable ceremony and stimulus of tea, the psychic adventure becomes more ex-plicable. At all events, after tea the depression disap-peared, and Versailles resumed its normal appearance. Had these ladies stopped for tea before visiting the gardens, we might have lost a good story!

But in the last analysis, it is not the momentary state of mind, but the general disposition to believe in the reality of transcendent phenomena, that favors psychic adventures, whatever form they assume. One must be mentally disposed to such adventures in the psychic. This one, far more than most others, though welcomed, seems to have come uninvited. But the belief in transcendence was there to begin with; it was not created by the experience. The "psychical" researchers became historical researchers only in the interests of a romantic conclusion. Any rare personal experience adds an agreeable flavor of importance and a sense of participation in the unusual and incomprehensible. What is described as a depressing experience may in deeper analysis prove to be a cherished and compensatory adventure.[1]

[1] The preconception, which is rather veiled in this instance, comes out boldly in the next psychic adventure in retro-history. The two should be jointly considered before the reader decides whether, so far as these instances go, the dead past has come to life, and whether one mind of a bygone century can appear to, and speak through, another of today.

The vividly pictorial and detailed projection of the scenes and properties of Marie Antoinette's Versailles points to an aptitude and habit of the imagination which is presumably more common than is supposed, especially by those—and I am among them—who have it not either in tendency or capacity. What Goethe called the joy in fabling—*Lust zum Fabulieren*—and which he said he inherited from his mother, is clearly the basis of the novelist's art and of the ready following of plot and romance by his readers. In their *Plots and Personalities* Slosson (chemist) and June Downey (psychologist who was also a poet, dramatist, and arranger of pageants) give interesting evidence of the prevalence of the habit and of the pleasure it affords. Crystal-gazers must be fairly proficient in the aptitude, and so must be the subjects of apparent transcendence such as the reconstructors of the gardens at Versailles or, in the next instance, of the abbey of Glastonbury; a like facility plays its part in the dramatic creations of Hélène Smith and the literary elaborations of "Patience Worth." It is difficult to evaluate this factor; but it seems indispensable to the rich vividness of "visions" however constructed.

That it is a possession and a cherished one of creative writers—though by no means of all—is familiar. Robert Louis Stevenson presents the staging of his plots as the work of the Brownies of his imagination. I chance upon an explicit statement in the Journal of Katherine Mansfield, who speaks of her capacity, when wakeful at night, to project "scenes from real life or imaginary ones," so marvelously vivid that "they are almost hallucinations," with the details "richer than in life."

So striking is this facility that a German psychologist has given it the name of *eidetic* imagination; he finds it marked in exceptional children. This power of imagery is also responsible for the color composition of tones and the projection of number forms. Galton noted the waning of this power in middle and later life.

THE GLASTONBURY TALE

Tales of transcendence may read like fairy tales, turning upon supernormal powers. They are presented as true stories, not fictions. Were there degrees in uniqueness, the superlative might be awarded to the Glastonbury tale. This concerns the research of two antiquaries, consulting, as if contemporary, the eye-witnesses of distant centuries. As usual, the pivotal first step is missing: how they started upon the venture. We are simply informed that "it occurred" to one of the investigators to apply the faculty of automatic writing that was possessed by the other to the problem of restoring the glorious ruin, Glastonbury Abbey, the "English Jerusalem."

The tale is told in *The Gate of Remembrance* by F. Bligh Bond and J. Allen Bartlett, spoken of as John Allen. These archæologists were appointed to take charge of excavations by reason of their minute knowledge of the architectural history of the Abbey. Just how these two worthies proceeded must be read between as much as in the lines. Mr. Bond evolved the engaging theory that "the mere logical machinery of the brain, which is forever combining the more superficial and obvious things written on the pages of memory"—which presumably is the instrument of orthodox archæologists—must somehow be switched off, for it interferes with "the more contemplative elements in the mind" that seeks "to revive from the half obliterated traces below." He rejects the theory of "communication of discarnate spirits," and prefers to find the source of the revelations in a "cosmic memory."

The two collaborators agreed to remain passive and to talk casually of indifferent matters. While conversing, F.B.B. would place his right hand lightly on the back of J.A.'s hand, which held a pencil; under favorable circumstances the pencil began to write as if guided by an alien intelligence. It did so at the first trial, November 7, 1907. A photograph of the two men thus occupied might be more illuminating than even the script which they produced. Without any ceremony of establishing connection, addressing thin air, F.B.B. said, "Can you tell us anything about Glastonbury?" J.A.'s fingers began to move in lines of small irregular writing that "turned out to be," *All knowledge is eternal and is available to mental sympathy.* This is interpreted as endorsing F.B.'s views.

Then this sketch was traced by the "automatic" pencil.

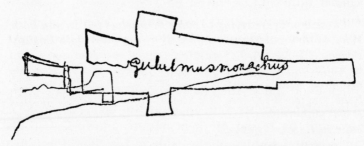

AUTOMATIC DRAWING OF GLASTONBURY ABBEY

Showing the Edgar Chapel in double lines. After F. Bligh Bond and J. Allen Bartlett, *The Gate of Remembranec.*

It is described as a blindfold tracing of the Abbey, first in small and then in larger scale, with the signature: *Gulielmus Monachus,* William the Monk. F.B.B.: "What does this drawing represent?" *Guest Hall... St. Maria Capella. ...*(sig) *Rolf Monachus.* Later came a new sketch and a long message in peculiar Latin: *Capella St. Edgar. Abbas Beere fecit hanc capellam Beati Edgari...martyri et hic edificavit vel fecit voltam.* It went on to specify details indicating what the Abbot Beere constructed and the Abbot Whitting tore down.

At the second session, four days later, this script "came through," but with gaps: *The material influences were at fault when last....I think active influences were over-*

*powering my will.... Those monks were anxious to com-
municate.... They want you to know about the Abbey.*

These scripts were obtained at Bristol. Then came this
advice: *Benedicite! Go into Glaston soon. Gloria reddenda
antiqua. Laus Deo in saecula seculorum.* One of the scripts
was signed *Johannes Bryant, monachus et lapidator,* which
means stone-mason.

The sessions continue. "Tell us more about yourself."
*Yn 1533 obitus ... curator capellae et laborans in mea
ecclesia pro amore ecclesia Dei.* In the script of November 13th:

> *Those monks are trying to make themselves felt by you both.
> Why do they want to talk Latin? Why can't they talk English?
> Benedicti Johannes. Ye names of builded things are very hard
> in Latin tongue ... transome, fanne tracery, and the like. My
> son, thou canst not understande. Wee wold speak in the Eng-
> lyshe tongue. Wee saide that ye volte [vault] was multipartite
> yt was fannes olde style in ye este ende of ye choire and ye newe
> volte in Edgares chappel.*

Mr. Bond comments: "Is this a piece of actual experience transmitted by a real personality, or are we in contact
with a larger field of memory, a latent cosmic record?"

The directions become explicit:

> *When you dig, excavate the pillars of the crypt, six feet be-
> low the grass ... they will give you a clue. The direction of
> the walls eastwards ... was at an angle ... clothyards twenty
> seven long, nineteen wide. Wait and the course will open in
> the Spring. You will learn as you proceed.... We have much
> to do this season.*

From a later script:

> What was the clear internal length of the chapel? *We laid
> down seventy and two, but they builded longer, and he who
> followed made new schemes for a certaine roofe in golde and
> crimson very cunning. Ye must use your talents lest they
> weaken.... Piece by piece ye shall rebuild it and there is enow,
> I wot, for ye.*

There is a great deal more of this and much of it not easily intelligible: monks telling who they are, when they died, speaking words of cheer, giving measurements, filling in history, explaining that they cannot write well when the weather is cold. They seemed strangely sympathetic, offering aid at all stages, as if anticipating archæological interests that were to develop six hundred years after they were dead. And all for the glory of Glastonbury and the newly appointed "psychic" excavators.

Following the instructions of the script, with pick and shovel, they discovered the buried remains of the Edgar Chapel! And they did so, they aver, on the basis of statements unknown to any living person and not found in historical records.

The verdict in the case of Glastonbury is wholly a matter for experts. The claims have been closely examined by a competent critic, H. J. Wilkins, D.D., and found grievously wanting. He has written a book to refute the Glastonbury tale. He concludes that "this automatic script, while it made incorrect statements, disclosed nothing new which was true; and all might have been gathered from existing historical records or from careful observation and deduction."

So far as prediction and verification go, the case is dismissed. But the psychological interest in the adventure remains. The Glastonbury tale, like others of its kind, does not stand wholly on its evidence, but on its setting, which is equally suspect. Helpless as I was, in reading the Bligh Bond account, to gage its accuracy or detect the precise flaws in the casting of the tale, it made a weak impression: so intrusive was the far-fetched theory, so crudely theatrical the scripts, so labored the apologetics, so much archæological dust thrown in the reader's eyes!

The sequel justified the distrust. There followed in 1911

The Hill of Vision, containing a forecast of the World War and as suspiciously prophetic as was the *Gate of Remembrance* retrospective. It asks us to believe that the monks of old are still watching our affairs and communicating through a living mind. Their prediction in script that the war would end August 26th is held to be true for no better reason than that the British took the offensive on that day. As a fact, Messrs. Bond and Bartlett are occultists first—Mr. Bond is a numerologist also—and archæologists afterwards.

And thus it seems ever to be when we sift these cases to their personal source. We begin with such concrete and verifiable and impressive data as walls and measurements in feet and inches, and end in the murkiest thickets of occultism. And the reason is the solution: because *the belief in the occult is the active starting point of the entire adventure.* The exact technique is so much subterfuge, so much sop offered to science, not as deliberate fraud but as one of the subtler channels through which wish takes on the semblance of wisdom. Transcendence may contribute little to knowledge, but it contributes much to the knowledge of the belief-habits of the mind and the tricks which it manufactures to its own confusion.

M. Flammarion, astronomer by profession, strong believer in occult psychic forces by avocation, states his experience. He was not deceived by his own adeptness in automatic writing. True to his profession he received messages through the great Galileo! But later he concluded:

There can be no doubt that these thoughts were wholly the product of my own intelligence and that the illustrious Florentine had nothing to do with them. . . . It has been the same with all communications of the astronomical class; they have not led the science forward one single step. Nor has any obscure mysterious or elusive point in history been cleared up by the spirits,

nor by assumption of "cosmic memory," nor by reincarnation, nor by one mind speaking through and inhabiting
another—a vain hope though a natural one.

The Glastonbury tale is superficially archæological, in-
trinsically psychological. It raises the query: How can two
conscientious archæologists so far deceive themselves as to
invent this complex medium of expression for their own
subconscious revelations? The answer would require a
deeper analysis of the mental habits of the automatists
than the record provides. It is sufficient to note that
every item of revelation, every medium of communication
—classic Latin, medieval Latin, early English architectural
terms—are all in the possession of the automatists. Had
the scripts in that form come to one without that technical background, it would have been an imposing miracle
indeed.

Let each believe according to his standard of plausibility: either that a returning thirteenth-century monk
dictated the scripts, with Messrs. Bond and Barrett the
passive amanuenses, or that Messrs. Bond and Barrett—
subconsciously if you like—are the source of the dictation,
with the monk as a psychic figurehead to give the esoteric
interest to what otherwise would be a prankish tale. Like
all the prepossessed and the suggestible, they drew out
what they put in; by familiar sleight of mind, they dis-
owned the recognition of the process in the interests of a
thrilling tale. The wish to believe overrides the wisdom in
believing.

Chapter XIV

THE STRANGE CASE OF
HÉLÈNE SMITH

THE NAME Hélène Smith conceals the identity of a resident of Geneva. She is described as an attractive woman in good health, thirty years old when the "case" began. Raised in modest circumstances, she had earned her living from girlhood and held a responsible position in a large shop—hardly a promising foundation for some of the most bizarre romancing on record. The case has a volume to itself and a sequel. It is the subject of a careful psychological biography by Professor Flournoy, *From India to the Planet Mars* (1901).

The alternative in interpreting psychic adventures lies between regarding them as evidences of genuine transcendence or of peculiar transactions in the clandestine traffic between the conscious and subconscious employments of mind. The case of Hélène Smith is at once a personal drama and a drama of impersonations. Taking our place in the theater of her operation, we see her as an improvisatrice. She presents tableaux and episodes with a common plot and cast; the séances present a serial story, with the sequences in part suggested by the approving interest of her audience.

Hélène, like Du Maurier's Trilby, performs in a trance-state. She throws herself into that condition with the aid of an imaginary Svengali, whom she calls Leopold. The onset of this condition is heralded by a change in appearance and manner. She enters a world of hallucinations of which she has no memory upon awakening; to that extent Hélène's personality is subject to dissociation. The secondary personality rarely intrudes upon her workaday self. The two Hélènes—the business woman in office hours and daughter at home, and the entranced impersonator on romance bent—are sharply contrasted but still related; the personal and the theatrical drama, as Freudians would suspect, intertwine.

The performance began in a spiritualistic environment, where Hélène displayed mediumistic powers, which she directed to a psychic-dramatic career.

At the moment the stage is set for the Royal Cycle. Her appearance as Marie Antoinette is thus described:

Hélène should be seen when the "royal" trance is full and complete: grace, elegance, distinction, at times majesty in pose and gesture—the actual demeanour of a queen. The most subtle shades of expression—charming amiability, queenly condescension, indifference and withering contempt—are shown in rapid succession on her countenance and bearing as the défile of her courtiers pass before her in her dream. They play of her hands with a real handkerchief and fictitious appurtenances —fan, lorgnette, smelling salts with a screw-top in a little bag attached to her girdle—her curtsies, her movements full of careless grace, as she never omits to throw back her imaginary train at every step—everything, every smallest detail is perfectly and naturally worked out.

The court, which is really a company of her friends, adjourns to the dining-room. In her dream-play she notes the presence of the Marquis de Mirabeau, who in real life may be butcher, baker, or candlestick-maker. "Oh, Marquis! you have been here and I have not noticed you." Hélène—Marie Antoinette—has eyes and ears only for her companion, the Marquis. She partakes of whatever the Marquis sets before her, including coffee, and a cigarette, a misstep not repeated after it was noted by her guests— to whose remarks she was supposed to be deaf—that

cigarettes were unknown in that day. The play is prolonged until ten o'clock, when a peculiar movement of
Hélène's left arm is recognized as the presence of Leopold, her manager and protector. The hand makes passes
over her forehead, which slowly break the trance. Fully
awake, she complains that she is hungry. She has no feeling
or memory of having dined amply a short time before.
She is escorted home, goes to sleep, and the next morning
is back at the shop, where she handles dress-goods and
waits upon customers, who little suspect her royal adventures.

In contrast to this simple impersonation is the complex
Martian cycle. Hélène is now cast as Ésenale, a Martian
maiden of high station. The scene may begin with the
pantomime of leaving the earth and arrival upon the
planet, when she greets the Martians with fantastic gestures. How shall she communicate? Ésenale begins to
speak rapidly in a jargon. As the séances continue, some
words become intelligible, such as *kesin outidje* and a
name, *Vasmini Metiche*. There are characters of the play:
Ramie and *Pouzi*, but first and foremost, *Astané*. He is a
young man of magic powers who must be introduced more
intimately. At séances held at the house of M. Le Maître
there was present Mme. Mirbel, an elderly woman much
depressed by the recent loss of her son Alexis, and longing
to communicate with him.

There had been some discussion of the possibility of
Mars being inhabited and of establishing communication.
At these séances, conducted in the spiritualist tradition,
there was communication by raps by and on the table.
Questions were answered by "yes" or "no" and by spelling
out messages. There came a message reading, *"Le Maître,
that which you have so long desired!"*. This promise is
made by Leopold. It refers to communication with Mars;

soon after appeared the first scene on that planet. Through the accident that Mme. Mirbel's anxiety centered upon the loss of her son, Alexis Mirbel becomes the Martian Astané, another identification of real and fantasied personalities.

Being Martian and French, Astané speaks both languages through Hélène's voice and interprets to the company. Hélène, when she is herself, hears words spoken which she is able to repeat, but without understanding their meaning. Later she began to see letters such as these,

THE MARTIAN ALPHABET

which were later identified as the Martian alphabet. These spontaneous auditions and visions indicate a subconscious preparation for the Martian cycle, a constant rehearsal, or incubation. Astané has in a measure replaced Leopold as guide, philosopher, and friend—one is tempted to say boyfriend. He furnished the code, word for word, with its translation:

> Dodé né a haudan te   méche metiché Astané
> This is the house of the great man   Astané
> Ke de me véche
> whom thou hast seen.

The message added that Astané had gone away but would soon return, and would teach Ésenale to speak and write Martian.

Thus was revealed knowledge of the Martian language, of Martian ways, of Martian scenery and houses, plants and animals. These revelations, fortunately—since so much of what happens in the trance is out of reach of Hélène's normal consciousness—she can recall and draw. Selections of the scenery are reproduced herewith. Their authenticity, like that of the script, is safely removed from verification. As in a measure consistent results, the products of the Martian episode are notable as creative fantasies.

The Hindoo Cycle is in several respects the most revealing and the most baffling, and no less romantic. The argument reads thus: "Hélène Smith was at the end of the fourteenth century of our era the daughter of an Arab sheik, apparently named Ferus, whom she left in order to become, under the name of Simandini, the eleventh wife of Prince Sivrouka Nayaka, of whom I [Flournoy] have the honor to be the actual reincarnation." At the death of Sivrouka, who reigned over Kanara and in 1401 built the fortress of Tchandraguini, the princess, according to the customs of the country, was burned alive on his funeral pyre. That scene supplies the dramatic climax of the Indian Cycle. It is performed in pantomime. Hélène assumes herself to be the Asiatic princess, tears from her person the rings, bracelets, necklaces, earrings, girdle, anklets, and with an expression of resolute devotion, mingled with growing terror, ascends the pile—then collapses in a state of physical exhaustion, from which Leopold rescues her.

There are other scenes in which Hélène as Simandini reads love letters from her lordly fiancé; or she plays with her pet monkey, Metidja. She bows and kneels, and sits in cross-legged fashion; she chants, and she sways her body in oriental postures. So much is dramatic fantasy; the puzzle arises when it is found that some of these names are not inventions but actually occur in historical records.

At this point, with regret, for there are other interesting
scenes, we leave the performance of the entranced, theatrical Hélène and return to her actual Genevoise self.

Whether a tale of India or Mars or Paris, the case is
throughout that of the suppressed urge to romance of
Hélène Smith. As a girl Hélène was a vivid and persistent
day-dreamer; the dreams were projected visually, with
rich detail of color and form and action. In her childish
fancy she held herself different and superior, destined for
a higher fate than her humble circumstances indicated;
she speculated whether she really was the daughter of her
parents. The spiritualistic contacts crystallized these fantasies. Mediums, she learned, went into trance-states under
the influence of a "control."

Her first "control" was Victor Hugo; he spoke through
her, and through him she attained her first distinction and
the admiration of a believing circle. After a few months of
joint protectorate, he gave way to Leopold, a less distinguished but romantically more satisfactory guide. Leopold
is her own invention, yet is subject to other identification; he is her protector and monitor, but admirer as well.
He is the bridge between the waking and the entranced
Hélène; he brings her back to her normal state. He directs
what shall and shall not be done in the séances, and, in
later stages, writes through her hand, holding the pencil
differently, resulting in a handwriting bolder than
Hélène's. For another product of the dissociation to
which Hélène is subject is automatic writing. This she
does as Hélène Smith; but the script thus produced may
emanate from another, usually from Leopold.

Leopold appears to Hélène in times of stress; on one
occasion he compelled her to take a roundabout way home
to protect her from danger—what it may have been she
never knew. Leopold is so personal a creation that he is

jealous. In the tramway from her house to her place of business, Hélène frequently met a fellow-passenger who made friendly advances; on one occasion he offered her a rose. Soon after Leopold spelled out this message: *"I desire that you refuse henceforth all the flowers that he may offer you."* To this Hélène protested, through automatic writing, saying that it was but a simple act of

AUTOMATIC WRITING OF MLLE. SMITH

Above, her normal handwriting. Below, a letter in the hand of Leopold, automatically written by Mlle. Smith in spontaneous hemisomnambulism.

courtesy, and *"it is not nice of you to make me write such things on paper before everybody."* It requires no deep analysis to read in these messages the staged conflict of desires and hesitations, using subconscious channels of expression.

That her case was important enough to bring to her séances a professor of psychology was a flattering testimonial. Her relations to M. Flournoy are conflicting. He is the rationalist in the play, attempting again and again to convince her that all these fancies are elaborations of early memories; but to no avail. Hélène insists that Leopold is real, and the Cycles also, though not in the same sense. So Leopold writes: *"My thoughts are not thy thoughts and thy wishes are not mine, friend Flournoy."* And to Hélène: *"Do me the kindness, dear sister, I beg of you, to tell me that from this time forth you will cease from endeavoring to probe too deeply the human heart."* The wisdom explanations were less satisfying than those of the wish for marvel and romance.

The initial stage of many of the scenes later acted in the séance is a spontaneous hallucination. Hélène first *saw* Leopold projected in a courtier's dress of the eighteenth century. Soon he was identified as Joseph Balsamo, better known as Cagliostro. As such he takes part in the Marie Antoinette drama, is addressed as *mon cher sorcier,* and both fuses with and replaces Leopold. In function, he is Leopold-Cagliostro, protector and devoted admirer. Astané of the Martian episode plays a Leopoldian rôle, though identified with Alexis Mirbel. Likewise, though less so, does the princely husband in the Indian scene, who is identified with M. Flournoy and his generous interest in Hélène's affairs. As M. Flournoy suggests, Hélène seems to require a slightly idolatrous attention—a not unfamiliar feminine perquisite—and finds it in the flights of somnambulistic fancy.

M. Flournoy points out the emotional similarities of the plots; the Indian maiden sacrificing herself on the funeral pyre of her husband, and Marie Antoinette a victim to her royal station. All afford the glamour of distinction and participation in the fates of exalted personages, and the more intimate satisfaction of a romantic relation enacted before a gallery. We have, then, a composite of a Freudian and a transcendental drama. The assignment of parts and mo-

THE HOUSE OF ASTANÉ

Blue sky; soil, mountains, and walls of a red color. The two plants with twisted trunks have purple leaves; the others have long green lower leaves and small purple higher leaves. The frame-work of the doors, windows, and decorations in the shape of brownish-red trumpets.

A MARTIAN LANDSCAPE

Sky of yellow; green lake; gray shores bordered by a brown fence; bell-towers on the shore, in yellow-brown tones, with corners and pinnacles ornamented with pink and blue balls; hill of red rocks, with vegetation of a rather dark green interspersed with rose, purple, and white spots (flowers); buildings at the base constructed of brick-red lattice-work; edges and corners terminating in brown-red trumpets. This and the above from Flournoy, *From India to the Planet Mars.*

tives may readily become uncertain and involved. There is the emotional longing, and the elaboration of plot and circumstances to give impressiveness and authenticity to what otherwise would be but a fantastic tale, a rather juvenile bit of play-acting.

M. Flournoy's diagnosis reads that these grand cycles of somnambulism grew out of the occasional day-dreaming hallucinations. The plots and details fall within Hélène's actual knowledge. She draws upon a remarkable impressionability, an almost photographic memory of impressions. The elaborate scenes do not appear suddenly; the remarkable feats were slowly developed after long periods of incubation or rehearsal. "The menu of the séances— if the expression is permissible—is always composed of one or two *plats de résistance* carefully prepared in advance in the subliminal laboratories, and of various *hors d'œuvres* left to the inspiration of the moment."

This is notably true of what remains a remarkable performance, however, accomplished—the Martian language. At first jargon, the sounds gradually took form, and a spoken language was invented; still more remarkably, a complete written alphabet was devised and memorized. But *the structure of Martian is French,* the only language that Hélène knows. "Martian is only disguised French," made as different as possible; just as Martian scenery is an exotic variation of an oriental scene, not beyond the reach of an exuberant fancy. "There is also perfect accord between the puerile character of the Martian romance, the poetic and archaic charms of its style, and the audacious and naïve fabrication of its unknown language."

Hélène, ever defending her transcendent powers, responds to the challenge of Professor Flournoy's skepticism. She invents an ultra-Martian language with still more fantastic characters; these she draws from the vividly hallu-

cinated pictures of texts presented by Astané. So far as
Martian languages go, however remarkable the feat of
creative imagery, there is no checking the result. Hélène's
fantasy has free play; she is the final authority.

The Hindoo Cycle offers the puzzle of origin. Professor
Flournoy admits that he was mystified when he found Sivrouka, Nayaka, the fortress of Chandraguini, and the
date 1401—all of which he had taken to be fabrications—
actually recorded in a book by de Marles. The book proved
to be unauthoritative, but it indicated Hélène's source.
Apparently a casual perusal of the page was enough to fix
the names and the incident as a dramatic nugget. Note
how ready is Hélène to respond to suggestion. When M.
Flournoy commented on the absence of Arabic in Simandini's speech, he was rewarded with a short sentence
written in cursive Arabic, which proved to be a motto in
Arabic on the fly-leaf of a book accessible to Hélène. Her
eyes had retained the picture so exactly that the script was
recognizable, but so mechanically that she wrote it from
left to right, not as Arabic is written, from *right to left.*
At every point there is a feat of mystery, but also its key.

In the Hindoo Cycle appeared Sanskrit words. The
origin of these was more puzzling still. Much of it was
Sanskritoid, just a jargon of words giving an impression of
being Sanskrit, with its frequent use of the vowel *a.* But
there are also actual Sanskrit words and some arbitrary
combinations of sounds that chance to be words in Sanskrit, but never properly used, as a Sanskrit scholar, M. de
Saussure, testified.

Though completely convinced that all of the revelations were reverberations of early memories and clever
elaborations, M. Flournoy had to close his volume with
the confession that for several of the important authentic
words and facts, he could find no clue accessible to Hélène.
Later they were found in a book by an orientalist who had

visited Geneva and left a presentation copy in the public library, which Hélène may have seen and forgotten. To what extent she was intentionally mystifying her public does not appear.

The story closes because of Professor Flournoy's insistence upon natural explanations, and his discovery of the actual sources of her knowledge, which, as they took away from the glamour of the performances, led to a break in their personal relations. That the personalizing fantasies of the subconscious can create the semblance of transcendent memories and powers, and yet admit of a natural explanation, is nowhere better shown than in this well analyzed yet strange case of Hélène Smith.

CHAPTER XV

PATIENCE WORTH: AN
ALTER EGO

THE CASE of "Patience Worth" concerns a chain of transcendence in authorship—a mind operating with material beyond its ken and converting it into stories, poems, parables, of distinctive workmanship. The theory of transcendence is resorted to because of the great discrepancy between what the one mind has acquired and what the other—the alter ego—accomplishes when in possession. The "accredited" individual is the one whose name appears in the telephone book, who keeps house and shares the life of the community; the other is the author who calls herself *Patience Worth*. The party of the first part is a gifted and intelligent but moderately schooled, middle-class young woman, with rather limited advantages, having enjoyed no travel and few literary contacts. The party of the second part, under peculiar conditions, composes with amazing facility and in several fashions of diction and content.

The one was born as Pearl Pollard and by marriage became Mrs. Curran; the other personality is Patience Worth, who lived long ago, yet whose name appears as author of the books from which Mrs. Curran derives royalties. "Patience Worth" has become an enterprise. Those who sponsor it also sponsor the theory that Mrs. Curran, of St. Louis, from the year 1913 on, is somehow the mouthpiece of Patience Worth, a Devonshire lass of several centuries ago. That theory the psychologist finds as unacceptable as superfluous. He holds that the two directing egos are the same; that the writing performance is compatible with Mrs. Curran's personality and circumstance, and a credit to them.

"Patience Worth" was born on a ouija-board on July 8, 1913. Congenitally articulate, she introduced herself: *"Many months ago I lived. Again I come—Patience Worth my name."* The participants in the ouija séance were Mrs. Curran, her friend Mrs. Hutchings, a professional writer, and Mrs. Curran's mother, Mrs. Pollard. With surprising promptness for novices—for ouija is not an easy technique to many—they received or transmitted well constructed sentences.

Around come trooping myriad forms, and plucking all the flowers, cast wide upon the lake their wanton plunder, and lo, a wreath appears.... All those who lately graced your board are here, and as the moon looks down, think ye of them and their abode as a spirit lake, a spirit song, a spirit friend, and close communion hold 'twixt thee and them. 'Tis but a journey, dost not see?

In this contribution the hands of both Mrs. Hutchings and of Mrs. Curran were on the board. A week later came Patience Worth through Mrs. Curran's hand, addressing her thus: "Wait, I would speak with thee. If thou shalt live, then so shall I. I make my bread at thy hearth. Good friends, let us be merrie. The time for work is past. Let the tabby drowse and blink her wisdom to the firelog." Mrs. Pollard asked the enigmatic communicant when she lived. The pointer hesitated between 1649 and 1694. Where? *"Across the sea."* In what city or country? *"About me you would know much. Yesterday is dead. Let thy mind rest as to the past."*

Mrs. Pollard suggested that Patience may have a past that needs concealing. "Wilt thou but stay thy tung. On rock-ribbed shores beat wisdom's waves. Why speak for me? My tung was loosed when thine was yet to be." Again, directed to Mrs. Pollard: "Wilt thou of too much speech pray silence the witch. Much clatter from a goose." When respectfully asked to continue: "If the storm passes. Thanks, good souls. Could I but hold your ear for the lesson I would teach."

To indulge in such stilted bantering conversations, Patience Worth broke her centuries of silence. Within six weeks she was composing short poems of a devotional type, and within a few months dramatic tales of olden days, with plots, characters, dialogue, descriptions, all complete; later a drama in six acts and nine scenes, some twenty thousand words long. The shorter poems and improvisations continued.

The interest grew. "Patience Worth" sessions were held once or twice a week. Friends came, providing an audience to marvel at the strange authorship of one of their number. Mr. Curran acted as recorder; the manuscripts accumulated; news spread from coast to coast of the amazing production. *A Psychic Mystery* it was titled in the volume *Patience Worth* (1916), edited by Caspar W. Yost of the St. Louis *Post-Despatch*, who throughout the early years was the sponsor of the enterprise.

Stage by stage the output changed its character; but the author was still Patience Worth, as she, when questioned, definitely asserted. One tale was dropped and another begun, with distinct changes of scene, plot, and diction. What many regard as her masterpiece—*The Sorry Tale; A Story of the Time of Christ*—was published in 1917. In 1918 came *Hope Trueblood,* a lengthy novel in ordinary English, set apparently a few generations back, dealing rather sentimentally with the complications of English village life. *The Pot upon the Wheel* is an allegory of life. Of later date are *Light from Beyond,* a selection of poems, and *Telka,* an idyl of medieval Europe, an ambitious drama in blank verse; both of which have been translated into German. These are all issued as the *opera* of Patience Worth, which assignment—if taken literally—would mean that Patience can see backward and forward in time, can anticipate and retrospect, and live in the century of her choice.

The measure of mystery depends upon the contrast in knowledge and ability of Mrs. Curran and the compositions emanating from her brain and personality when these are under the control of Patience Worth; also upon the appraisal of the quality of the output, which a few selections may serve to suggest.

APHORISMS

A lollypot is but a breeder of pain.
Dead resolves are sorry fare.
Quills of sages were plucked from geese.
Puddings fit for lords would sour the belly of the swineherd.
Climb not the stars to find a pebble.
Should I present thee with a pumpkin, wouldst thou desire to count the seeds?
Ye who carry pigskins to the well and lace not the hole are a tiresome lot.

The following poetic selections date mainly from a later period (1926); they show command of effect through symbolism and form. Some of them are rapid improvisations, as many as thirty delivered in one evening.

POETIC PASSAGES

Lavender and Lace

Foibles; yea, trumpery, in which to deck my lady.
Soft, billowy, clinging—a robe, mayhap,
All scented sweet of lavender.

Lavender and Lace (symbolized)

A purple sky; twilight,
Silver-fringed of tremorous stars;
Cloud rifts, tattered, as old lace,
And a shuttling moon—wan-faced, seeking.

World Court

An enviable attainment can it be—
Yet man must pocket his egotry,
As I hae said,
Else, sic an thing may ne'er to come.
A country be nought but the voice of her men.
Remember this!

Patience Worth

A phantom? Weel enough,
Prove thee thyself to me.
I say, behold, here I be,
Buskins, kirtle, cap and pettiskirts,
And much tung.
Weel, what hast thou to prove thee?

Her own estimate of her compositions is interesting and affords an opportunity to note Mrs. Curran's own style:

Whether original or reflected from others, Patience Worth has confidence that her poetry is good and that it is good for people to read it. Patience Worth seems to imply that she has had the advantage of experience and viewpoints that make it inevitable that she should be able to counsel those who have had but a few years on this mundane sphere, and powers which have been ripened in the more favorable climate where she professes to dwell. Not infrequently, she takes pains to remind us that she is in some sense, as she believes, a messenger from God, commissioned in her way to speak for Him.

FORMAL POEM

Into the Purple Sea Would I Cast My Nets

Oh, into the purple sea would I cast my nets.
I would drag its depths for the vagrant songs
That sink to rest therein.
I would trap the whisper o' the shells
And the moaning of the reefs.
I would catch the silver sprays
As they trickle back upon the sea's breast,
Losing them in one great mightiness.
I would listen to the waters
Of the young morning, when they wake
Fresh sounding of the wind's caress.
Into the purple sea would I cast my net
To bring it forth so laden.

NARRATIVE

(From The Sorry Tale)

The morn spread forth the golden tresses of the sun, and lo, a star still rested upon a cloud bar. And Jerusalem slept. The temples stood whited, and the market's place shewed emptied. Upon the temple's pool the morn-sky shewed, and doves bathed within the waters at its edge....

And Mary lay the alabaster box upon the floor and oped its pit, and behold, tears fell within it, and she put unto it its cover and gave it unto the hands of Jesus. And He held it up before them and looked and spake: "Her casket of jewels also hath her hands delivered. Behold, the herbs of Heaven shall be refreshed with these."

(From Hope Trueblood)

The man should be held up before the people. He is clothed in the garb of the hypocrite. I sucked the plum stone and wondered what a hypocrite was and if they were upon the road at night. "Sally Trueblood's brat." I looked to the sampler and read slowly, "God is Love." And I wondered what a brat was.

(From *Telka*)

A-swish the pot-broth. A-whang the bowl. A-kick the hearth-log. A-flush the cheek and a-snap the eye. A-jerk the reed-wove basket from off the cupboard top. A-thud bare soles. A-whack up on the flags with scows, a-slammed from 'neath the bench. A-clatter scow-shod feet, and kirtle jerked o'er middle o' the smock. A-toss the curls, and maid, a-hot by anger, off adown the path unto the river's bend.

(From *Patience Worth*)

'Twere a peddle-packer who did stroll adown the blade-strewn path along the village edge, abent. And brow-shagged eye did hide a twinkle-mouth aneath.

Go ye to the lighted hall to search for learning? Nay, 'tis a piddle, not a stream, ye search. Mayhap thou sendest thy men for barleycorn. 'Twould then surprise thee should the asses eat it.

As for Patience Worth in the flesh, if she ever was such, there are only autobiographical fragments. She lived in the seventeenth century, apparently in Devonshire, where enthusiastic followers have tried to find traces of her. She worked in the fields and took part in the household industries of the day. When a young woman, she migrated to America and was killed by the Indians. There are memories of the sea and cliffs, of a church and its "wee windows and pine walls," of the squeaking of the benches, the women's dresses, the minister who denounced finery; also of her flirtations, of her humor and her rebellion against a narrow religion. As a bit of fiction, it is not beyond the imaginative facility of a bright American girl on story-telling bent; and if Patience Worth was what she describes herself to have been, how did such a lass in those days acquire the wisdom, the allusions, and the facility of expression which the writings disclose? Patience

Worth's own answer is evasive: *"Behold my wares; herein am I."*

Pearl Pollard's story provides some clues. She was born in 1883 in Mound City, Illinois. Her father, of English-Welsh extraction, was editor of a small newspaper; her mother was English-Irish. They moved early in her life to Fort Worth, Texas. She spent part of her childhood in the Ozark region with her mother's relatives. Her uncle was a spiritualist medium, of which calling the rest of the family disapproved. Pearl Pollard is an Episcopalian with strong religious interests. She studied music in Chicago, and for a time was pianist at her uncle's spiritualist church. She earned her living by music and as an employee in a department store. At the age of twenty-four she married John H. Curran, former Emigration Commissioner of Missouri.

In this background of experience, however modest, there is some clue to the pivotal circumstances that turned Pearl Pollard into Patience Worth. Inevitably she absorbed some knowledge of English ways from her parents. Her father's editorial office may well have been a center for miscellaneous information. The constant association with Mr. Yost, editor, voracious reader, with a large fund of general knowledge, encouraged the development of Patience Worth. Mrs. Hutchings, a writer, introduced the ouija-board as a medium of expression. Mrs. Curran found that she could make it go. The possibility of mediumship or control was familiar to her; also that at séances mediums spoke in affected language. Her own religious occupations appear throughout. The Ozark dialect fell upon a sensitive ear and a retentive memory; it is a quaint speech with many archaic usages. To a vivid imagination and a latent ambition, life in a neighborly but not stimulating bourgeois community fell short of complete satisfaction.

It is then my hypothesis—and admittedly such—that Mrs.

Curran welcomed the ouija-board as a mode of release of a literary facility and an imaginative trend. To launch upon an uncertain sea of writing on her own account would hardly be a venture that would come within her consideration. Patience Worth was a mask; and even the diffident become bold when their personality is safe-guarded. Convention no less than conscience makes cowards of us all, or at least makes of us timid and hesitant performers. Inhibitions of expression approach the fron-tier of the subconscious and step over it. Mrs. Curran did not devise this outlet or plan the career which came to be hers; she drifted into it, and from drifting came to steer the craft, with all the zest of a successful navigator. That form of motivated drifting is favorable to the freedom of improvisation, which is congenial to ready rather than to elaborately schooled minds.

The psychology of composition is obscure and individ-ual. Expert and novice alike must await the happy asso-ciation; the favorable release of ideas and fluency in expression are most variable factors—an uncertain flow. For novice and adept alike, the muses must be wooed and cannot be commanded. Facility is given to some at all levels of talent; hard labor and constant revision is the lot of others. Tapping the resources one has is the art of arts. Mrs. Curran seems to be unusually fortunate in the facility with which she crosses the bridge from idea to ex-pression. Chafing under the literal ouija-board, she ex-changed it for the fluency of vocal speech. The entire course of Patience Worth's technique shows the essential earmarks of a natural development, though an unusual one.

Mrs. Curran possesses many endowments favorable to composition. She has a vivid receptiveness of both eye and ear, favoring rich imagery. The material comes mainly as mental pictures. She sees the scenes as though Patience

Worth were showing her a magic picture-book tempting her curiosity. She describes in words what is seen by the mind's eye. As the characters of the stories act and speak their parts on an imagined stage, the author-reporter sees background, scenery, and by-play. When the characters speak in a foreign language, the voice of Patience is heard above it all as interpreter and director. All the little details of costumes and properties and local color are there. A poem has similarly a filmed accompaniment of imagery. At times and while otherwise engaged in ordinary occupation, a story may be flashed upon her mental vision which takes hours to tell. The two authors are constantly coöperating. Patience Worth utilizes what Mrs. Curran has read or otherwise absorbed. When Mrs. Curran writes on her own account, the process is wholly different. That writing fatigues her, while composing via Patience Worth exhilarates. But Patience Worth is not restricted to her original release via the ouija-board; she uses Mrs. Curran's voice as well as her accomplishments. When typing became automatic to Mrs. Curran, seventeenth-century Patience Worth could operate that medium of expression.

Mrs. Curran has a retentive memory. She holds in mind the sequence of her tale, and of several tales; like a blindfold chess player at a group of boards, she continues the moves and passes from one game to another. Her wide reach and quick adaptation of attention appears in her ability to keep up a conversation while still speaking or ouija-ing as Patience Worth. She may address a comment to one of the company, or answer the telephone, and resume without loss. There is not the slightest trance condition; when Patience Worth appears, she is always both Mrs. Curran and Patience Worth. She is unaware of any preparation; the material seems to come spontaneously and impromptu; but as in all such cases of subconscious performance, there is convincing evidence of long incubation; the hatching is not as sudden as it appears. This literary partnership became an education in itself. "Six years ago," writes Mrs. Curran, "I could not have understood the literature of Patience Worth had it been shown me." One must make large allowance for the encouragement of an audience, private and public; authorship particularly thrives upon it. The urge to write is equally an urge to be heard. The alibi of Patience Worth became the most stimulating experience of her life.

The specific evidence of historical authenticity centers upon the usages. Of these, as of all phases of the problem presented by the provenance of Patience Worth's ideas and expressions, the late Dr. W. F. Prince made a minute examination, which extends to five hundred pages of evidence and argument. I am indebted to his account at many points, though I dissent from his conclusions.

If the idiom were the mode of speech of a seventeenth-century lass, one would suppose that it would arrive with her personality; but the special mannerisms were gradually acquired. At first she spoke thus: "The cat doth drowse, my good folk, but when the fire is overhot doth rouse." "Put faith in farthings and let the shillings rust." "From constant wishing the moon may tip for thee." Later, she seemed to be reminded of dialectical mannerisms. "A put athin the see o' her. Aye and 'tis the see o' ye, that be fulled o' the put o' me and yet a put thou knowest not." "I pettiskirt me so that ye know the me of me. Yea, and I do to take me o' the store o' her that I make me word for thee." Unlike the immigrants we know, whose dialect and brogue is most pronounced on arrival on American shores and in time wears off, Patience Worth comes without it and acquires it as its alien charm is admired.

But are the words and phrases of the period? By patient search Dr. Prince was able to find many that were. But so rich is English in its heritage of vocabulary and so familiar the survivals—as in the Scriptures and Shakespeare—that a hit-and-miss method would score many successes; against which must be set all the usages *not* to be found, including spellings. The style of a period is far more and goes deeper than the mosaic of the words; it derives from a total habit of thought and expression.

On such matters an expert opinion is decisive. Professor Schelling, eminent Elizabethan scholar, to whom I submitted the "case" kindly sends me this definitive verdict:

> The language employed is not that of any historical age or period; but where it is not the current English of the part of the United States in which Mrs. Curran lives, is a distortion born of a superficial acquaintance with poetry and a species of would-be Scottish dialect—it would be better to say—the borrowing of some dialect words and the clear misuse, misunderstanding and even invention of many others. . . . There is an easy facility of phrase almost wholly in our contemporary idiom and showing nowhere the qualities of the language of Elizabeth's or any previous age.

So much for the medium employed. As for the content and the circumstances of composition, the literary verdict is in complete agreement with the psychological one. Professor Schelling continues:

> I see nothing in the "wisdom," which is often cryptic to the point of insignificance, of the verse or the prose which might not be compassed by a naturally clever person brought up and "educated" as was Mrs. Curran. The prose shows no sense of style beyond a certain feeling for the swing of our English Biblical phrase, and I find nothing in the way of genius either in the plots or the stories or in the realization of the personalities of the characters involved.
> Improvisation, now a lost art among lettered folk, is not dead; and it is under such conditions as those surrounding Mrs. Curran that it is likely to be revived: not too much education, an interest in music, an existence shall we say upon the fringes of culture, a memory for the phrase and a tendency

to revery. I raise no point as to the candor in this as in any such case; it is as easy to deceive oneself as others; and deliberate deception does not enter into it.

The transcendence in the case of Patience Worth has largely been read into the records by the inclination to such beliefs on the part of her zealous but not circumspect champions.

Dr. Prince used the strange method of interviewing Patience Worth herself as to her dialect, but received oracular or evasive replies, Patience Worth having *"made me flesh-cunnin' 'nough for to stand the blade o' inquiry."* Alibis are plentiful to keen minds. *"Ye see when first I singed, I stripped the burr frae my tongue to be known in the tongue of them I singed to."*

One may well question whether Patience Worth is worth so much patience. The linguistic product is plainly antiqued, monotonously and ostentatiously so. We are accustomed to antique furniture and examine it closely in order not to be deceived, even as to the worm-holes produced by bird-shot. Patience Worth's use of *a' o', the me o' me, a-down, a-stopped, a-wing o' hand, not all a-yet,* is so much verbal bird-shot. To suggest that the model is a recollection of Ozark does not mean that she speaks that dialect; the similarity is only that of an older and quainter diction, made familiar in her childhood.

Now and then it is possible to catch the source of an impression. There occurred in *The Sorry Tale* a name historically correct, of which Mrs. Curran disclaimed all knowledge; yet it was found on a poster announcing a screen version of *Ben Hur,* which, as close to her interests, must have caught her eye. The name *Patience Worth* itself occurs in a novel of Mary Johnson, which Mrs. Curran does not recall reading. For one source traceable, there are scores with the clue lost.

The tendency to read mystery into Patience Worth developed into a cult, with a *Patience Worth Magazine* as an organ. It even led to a spirit-photograph of Patience Worth, vague and modernized. And because the step was authorized by Patience Worth, Mrs. Curran has adopted a child and named her Patience Worth Curran.

"Transcendent" accounts of the case of Mrs. Curran look at the author's equipment, native and acquired, through one end of the opera glass, and at the literary output through the other, belittling the one and magnifying the other, thus presenting a picture with irreconcilable contrasts. Mrs. Curran's own account is judiciously reserved; she offers "a nut for psychologists" and lets them crack it as they will.

To suppose that Mrs. Curran in any sense is in touch with a Devonshire lass of three hundred years ago brings no illumination and adds much confusion. How could Patience know or write the tale of the Christ with that fullness of setting which actually appears? How can she spread her personality from then until now? I know nothing of the habits or the psychology of discarnate personages; but their habit of behaving so much like the persons they inhabit is both disconcerting and revealing.

I do not depreciate the quality of Mrs. Curran's performance, nor its value as a contribution to the psychology of creative literary activity; but I cannot subscribe to the independent reality of Patience Worth, whether in the reserved sense in which Mrs. Curran maintains her faith in her inspiration, or in that of those who go so far as to find the authentic voice of a real, once living person. My analysis gives Mrs. Curran the credit for the merit of Patience Worth. The performance is significant not as trick authorship, but as an interesting form of release, which is not likely to be duplicated—not with the same setting. To Mrs. Curran, Patience Worth has been worth the patient devotion she has spent upon it. Many a writer, including the present one, would gladly adopt a mythical ghost, if in compensation he received the fluency of output along the directions of his desires, and thus became his own ghost-writer.

PART IV

PREPOSSESSION

FINDING WHAT YOU LOOK FOR

If one should tell you he has sought and found, do not believe him; but you may believe him who tells you he has found without seeking.—ANCIENT INDIAN PROVERB.

If the conclusion determines what the reasoning shall be, the reasoning is sham.—CHARLES S. PEIRCE.

Faith, fanatic faith, once wedded fast to some dear falsehood, hugs it to the last.—THOMAS MOORE.

As is your sort of mind,
So is your sort of search; you'll find
What you desire.
—ROBERT BROWNING

ARGUMENT

PREPOSSESSION *comprises the general inclination to bend thinking toward a conclusion reached in advance and—for whatever motives and reasons—cherished. In the ledger of human relations appear limitless entries on the debit side, chargeable to prepossession. As an obstacle to fair judgment and the defeat of justice, it forms one of the constant problems in social direction. That makes another story, and the vested interest of dogma still another; neither aan here be considered. The phase of the foregone conclusion most pertinent to* Wish and Wisdom *concerns issues turning upon a valid or concordant relation between premises and conclusion. The divorce of the two, as in human relations, may be based upon several varieties of incompatibility.*

The simplest instances are those in which the premises, the data themselves, are the result of prepossession: when the eyes find what the mind looks for. Such action of suggestion is pertinent to the theme, but only for a limited application. As a rule, there must be a theory to defend, an interpretation to advance. Such prepossession is familiar, since the entire procession of theories once upheld and now discarded had no difficulty in amassing observations in evidence, though these had their reality, like Hamlet's ghost, only "in the mind's eye"; they illustrate how the senses constantly deceive us. They may make what is true in the ordinary situation false in the exceptional circumstance. Or by way of anticipation or an expectant attention or a deluding hope or fear, they may create a subjective impression which has no reality. The same principles apply to more abstract convictions presented as conclusions from all sorts and conditions of premises. To cite my own summary: Create a belief in the theory and the facts will create themselves.

*In the episodes selected, such effect of suggestion cited as a
fact to prove a theory appears rather simply in the "transposition of the senses." When one end of a magnet attracts while
the other repels, or when a pinch on the arm of one subject is
felt by another, the observed result is produced by the theory
and does not confirm it except to the prepossessed mind. When
prepossession affects an entire attitude toward a problem,
both creating and selecting facts in its favor through self-
delusion, the instance reaches a more significant level of logical error. Such is the demonstration of calculating horses and
similar animal prodigies. Throughout, the only adequate
check is a control experiment in which you cannot be tempted
to find what you look for because you do not know what to
expect, or in which objective registration replaces a subjective
record. But prepossession once unleashed can go far beyond
this. If placed at the disposal of the imagination, and under
the further assumption that there is a higher order of vision
reserved for the elect who have clairvoyant powers, it can
create a world of glorious visions. They are seen because the
theory maintains that they must exist, and furthermore, must
conform to a moralistic dispensation—another prepossession.
Such is the origin of the thought-form, truly an amazing product of the modern mind. It may be considered as approaching
the borderland of hallucination, but does so under the direc-
tive drive of seeing things as they should be—the "should" a
prepossession of heroic stature.*

*These are selected, pointed illustrations, but no less typical
for their approach to the extreme. For one instance in which
prepossession is the dominant, even the exclusive clue to the
false and foregone conclusion, there are a score in which it
combines with other inclinations, subtly, vaguely, inadvertently, subconsciously. Looking deeper for its motivation, we
may recognize that the satisfaction of security opposes the
spirit of venture; that it seems safer to think as one travels,
knowing one's destination in advance and planning the journey accordingly. The management of our beliefs finds instruction in "awful examples" of prepossessions that have misled
trained and untrained minds.*

Chapter XVI

THE PUPPETS OF DR. LUYS

THE PROCESSION of beliefs at the frontiers of science moves irregularly. A belief comes forward, recedes, and later is revived in another form. Older beliefs reappear; there are survivals and revivals. The closing years of the nineteenth century—including the mauve decade—formed a period of revival of belief in magic forces. The "psychic" came into fashion. The varieties of it were many. There were platform exhibitions of hypnotizers demonstrating weird powers over human subjects; these vied with spiritualist séances where sealed messages were read, flowers materialized out of space, and shrouded human forms were summoned from cabinets; slate-writing, levitation, telepathy, premonitions, haunted houses, phantasms of the living, and mysteries of mind were in the spotlight. Some of them were endorsed by one or another scientist of distinction. The intelligentsia of London, Paris, and New York were devotees of the cult. A psychologist was regarded as a spook-hunter or marvel-monger, or a psychical researcher. The modern psychologist had not arrived.

In that atmosphere, Dr. Luys, a member of the French Academy of Medicine, announced a discovery. His patients at La Charité hospital reacted to magnets most dramatically. They obtained the effects of drugs in sealed vials. They transferred these powers from one to another. It was called "exterioration of sensitiveness." These demonstrations were to herald a new era in the understanding of psychic phenomena, with great benefit to mankind, though also with serious dangers if the rare powers were abused.

Had one been in Paris in 1892 and sufficiently interested in psychic mysteries, one might have visited the clinic of Dr. Luys and witnessed some startling effects, which I must rely upon the pictures to convey. These excited demoiselles have been hypnotized—just how deeply is uncertain. They touch one end of a magnetized bar; they seem gratified, for it is the "attractive" or "north" pole of the magnet. likewise it gives out a pleasing blue light. They cry out: "See the blue flames playing about! It is the color of the sky—the color of Heaven!"

The bar of the magnet is reversed, and all is changed. The magnet now repulses; it frightens: "That's red! Take it away, it's red, red! I don't like it! It hurts me!"

Dr. Luys explains:

One day I hypnotized a subject on a velvet-backed chair in my office. The subject was taken across the room to another seat when I accidentally touched the velvet of the chair in which she had been seated. To my surprise, the woman put her hand to her back and showed signs of intense suffering. Evidently the subject by sitting in it had charged the chair in some way. I then tried with a silk-covered chair, but this did not produce the same result. Still, the first observation satisfied me that not only was it possible to exteriorize the sensitiveness of a human being, but that the sensitiveness could be stored in some other substance... and be transferred to a glass of water; while the subject is unaffected by the touch of the hand, or even the pricking of a pin, she suffers excruciating pain the moment you touch the surface of the water with the tip of your finger. The water becomes highly charged with the sensitiveness of the individual, but loses it in a comparatively short time. On the other hand, a fat or a greasy substance will retain the sensitiveness longer; while, if transferred to a liquid, which is afterwards crystallized, it impregnates the mass for a fortnight, or even longer; and during the whole of

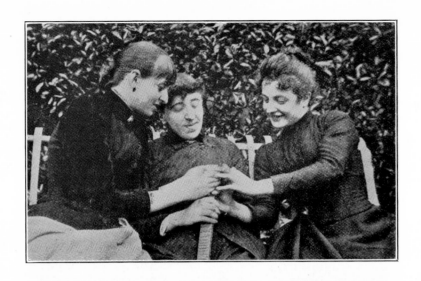

THE PUPPETS OF DR. LUYS

Above, attraction by the positive pole of a magnet; expression of
pleasure. Below, repulsion by the negative pole of a magnet; expression
of fright.

that period the person, when within a reasonable distance, would be conscious if I touched the charged substance, and would suffer pain if I pinched it violently, or attempted to stick a pin into it.

The doctor exposed photographically sensitive paper to a magnet and showed it to the subject. Whereupon she would see blue flames on the paper but not on unmagnetized paper. Upon gazing upon a photograph of Dr. Luys, she reports: "It is full of lights and colors; there are red flames issuing from the right eye and from the cheek and mouth and ears on one side of the face, and from the other come blue flames, all blue." "That," said Dr. Luys,

is how she sees me in the flesh, and strange to say, the same magnetic flames are seen on my photograph. And what is still more remarkable, the blue and red flames are seen radiating from an illustrated printed picture taken from photographs of living individuals, but never from drawings or engravings which have not been photographed from the living subjects in the first instance.

A band of magnetized iron was placed on a subject's head. "In that magnetized head cap," says Dr. Luys,

are stored the thoughts and ideas of a patient who had been the subject of hallucinations of persecution and of black misery. When this iron band was placed on the subject's head, although happy and contented before, very quickly his features became haggard, his expression that of melancholy and fear; presently he struggled, with horror and fright depicted in his face, to escape from imaginary persecutors. "They are following me," he cried, "I can't get away from them, they are torturing me."

In another demonstration drugs in sealed tubes are applied to the neck of the subject, Marguerite. The tube contains cognac. Marguerite cries out: "What have you been giving me; I feel quite tipsy," and begins to reel.

A sealed tube of valerian converts another subject into a cat. He sprawls and claws, and mews and spits; he jumps about like a human cat. Distilled water produced the symptoms of hydrophobia, popularly interpreted. Dr. Luys assured the students that he performed these experiments with caution for fear that the subjects would be injured by the violent reactions.

Next, the "exteriorization" is transferred from one subject to another without magnets or vials. Clarice is hypnotized and placed beside Marguerite. "Now we will see," says Dr. Luys, "whether the vibration will be transferred by contact from one to the other." And Clarice becomes as intoxicated as Marguerite. Finally the last act: the sensitized puppets! If you pinch one subject, the other feels it at the same spot. A doll is magnetized. If you pinch the doll or pull its hair, the subject feels the pain. Thus, upon the sole testimony of the discoverer, was the "exteriorization of sensibility" discovered.

This discovery brought Dr. Ernest Hart from London to investigate. He arranged matters differently. It was agreed between him and his assistant that when directed to turn *on* the current, it should actually be turned *off*. Marguerite, to whom a magnet was a magnet under all conditions, found the north pole—though there was no current in it—"very pretty!" She was fascinated by it, and fondled the blue flame, following it across the room. When the other end was presented, she was repelled, and so terrified that she had to be carried back to her chair. The change in color of the flame from blue to red was equally successful with a dead magnet. "Marguerite was never once right, but throughout her acting was perfect; she was utterly unable at any time to distinguish between a plain bar of iron, a demagnetised magnet, or a horseshoe magnet carrying a full current and one from which the current was wholly cut off." A single experiment properly controlled blasted Dr. Luy's entire edifice.

The doll performance in Dr. Hart's hands turned out differently. "Taking Marguerite's doll from her, I disposed of it behind some books, and proceeded to operate on another doll which she had not touched and which I had just taken out of the box in which it came from the toy-

THE DOLLS THAT CONFOUNDED DR. LUYS

The witness dolls used in Dr. Hart's controlled experiments. After Ernest Hart, *Hypnotism, Mesmerism and the New Witchcraft,* 1896.

shop." The substituted unmagnetized doll acted just as well; when the doll's hair was pulled, Marguerite cried out. A bottle of cherry water, simulating the cognac, caused the inebriated scene. "Never by any accident did any one of these subjects show any power of discerning the effects of magnetized from non-magnetized iron. The same results appeared under the influence of an empty tube, of a tube of alcohol, and of a tube of valerian, if the subject did not know the content."

The moral is simple. Prepossession in a learned doctor is even worse than in a layman; for he has a theory to defend, and though he knows that hysterical subjects are suggestible, he is naïve enough to believe that they will not take a hint on their own account and act out the expected part to make life more interesting for themselves and the experimenter. Dr. Luys talked freely in their presence and before his students of the wonderful exteriorization and what effects it would produce. So far as the subjects are concerned, the effects may have started subconsciously; they ended with a deception. One of the subjects confessed to Dr. Hart: *"Nous le fluons tous!"* "We all put it over on him."

The idea of magnetic action and of sympathetic action is an old one; it crops out in various beliefs through the ages.[1] It acts no differently in an experiment claimed to be scientific, but in which all the essential scientific controls are omitted. Laboratories may stage dramas of prepossession, when shrewd and suggestible subjects supply the phenomena to confirm the theory.

[1] "The Cult of the Magnet" illustrates it variously.

Chapter XVII

ANIMAL GENIUSES: AS MADE
IN GERMANY

THERE is an intriguing psychological episode of which the hero is not a man, but a horse, though the plot turns upon the part of the man. The horse was Hans, known as *Der Kluge Hans,* and the man was Herr von Osten, gray-haired, kindly, convinced that his friend the horse had as good a mind as man. A privileged tourist or an inquisitive psychologist visiting Berlin in 1904 would have found a select company gathered in a courtyard around a beautiful animal. Hans's sagacity had even come to the attention of the Kaiser. An imaginative sketch in an illustrated journal pictured Hans under formal examination by the Prussian Minister of Education.

Calculating animals have long figured in the exhibitions of the showman. Hans's arithmetic surpassed them all. *How much is 2/5 plus 1/2?* Hans answers: *9/10.* He does so by pawing with his right hoof—first nine times, a pause, and then ten times. Herr von Osten has explained to Hans that for fractions, the numerator is to be tapped first, and then the denominator! *What are the factors of 28?* Hans taps in succession: *2, 4, 7, 14, 28.*

A test in reading follows; for Hans is a schoolroom prodigy. On a card are printed a number of words. One of them may be *oats,* in which Hans has a genuine interest. Asked, "Where is oats?" Hans points to the word with his nose. A list of words is presented:

1. Scissors   4. Pencil
2. Nail   5. Candle
3. Magnet   6. Key
            7. Ninepin

Which of these objects is magnetic? Hans taps the correct numbers. He can also recognize these articles if displayed on a table; for Hans knows what *magnetic* means. All this according to Herr von Osten and his fellow-believers in equine savants.

Next comes spelling. The letters of the alphabet and the common combinations, such as *sch*, are arranged in a square and numbered on the top—1, 2, 3, 4, 5—and also at the left. *S* is in place 1 of row 5; its "hoof-indication" would be *5–1*. Question: *What is in the lady's hand?* Answer: *5–2; 3–2; 4–6; 3–7*. In the table, 5–2 is *sch;* 3–2 is *i*, 4–6 is *r* and 3–7 is *m; sch i r m*—which means parasol. Hans also recognizes *pictures*. Shown a picture of a horse, he spells hoofwise *p f e r d*. Hans carries the calendar in his head. *If the eighth day of a month comes on a Tuesday, what is the date for the following Friday?* Instantly the answer is given: *11*. He tells the time. *Between what figures is the hour-hand of a watch at five minutes after half-past seven?* Do you know? Well! Hans did.

Hans's repertory was extensive: counting, spelling, reading, telling coins, cards, tones, forms, colors, and much else. It was claimed that he had reached about the level of an eleven-year-old boy, and a Berlin boy at that.

Hans was also conversant with music; he had an ear for tone and interval, distinguishing between a "third" and a "fifth." *If C, D, E are sounded together, which tone must be omitted to make the effect pleasant?* Hans tapped 2, which meant the second tone, D. Hans also had a sense of humor; if a questioner asked a question of which he himself did not know the answer, Hans would tap out letters that made no sense. Questions in French or Latin made him fidgety, "thereby showing the genuineness of his achievements." On topics with which he was familiar, he could not be misled. A sentence containing fifty-eight letters was given one day, and Hans remembered the whole of it correctly the next day! A wonder horse indeed!

This performance was taken so seriously that a commission was appointed, with Professor Stumpf, the distinguished psychologist, at its head. His associate, Dr. Pfungst, conducted the examination with characteristic Teutonic thoroughness. The experimental biography of *Clever Hans* reads altogether differently. The glorious fable becomes a simple fact, though a clever stunt; psychology learned something in detecting how Hans performed.

The first critical test was decisive. Five words were shown thus: 1, *stall;* 2, *oats;* 3, *Hans;* 4, *Osten;* 5, *key.* Hans was to tap the number next to his own name. But the five words could be shown in any order. At times von Osten knew the position, and at times not. In fourteen cases in which von Osten knew which words had which numbers, Hans tapped correctly *every time;* in twelve cases in which von Osten did *not* know, Hans *never* tapped correctly. Result: one hundred per cent success when his master knew; one hundred per cent failure when he did not.

Three words, *arm, Rom (e), Hans,* were whispered into Hans's ear; he was asked to paw the word *Rom.* When the questioner did not know the number-clues of the letters, Hans pawed *j j st*—completely wrong. It will not surprise the reader to learn that Hans is as illiterate as any other horse; he cannot recognize numbers, nor calculate, nor spell. All the reading and calculating is done by the master's or bystander's brain, and not by Hans's.

But Hans is clever enough to note a clue, which is the signal to start pawing; and most importantly, the signal for stopping. For that horse sense he deserves his reward.

It was not easy for the human eye to detect the signal; and von Osten was wholly unaware that involuntarily he was giving Hans his clues. His sincerity is shown by his willingness to coöperate in the scientific investigation.

The clue was nothing more than this: *A slight forward stoop of the questioner as he puts the question and fixes his gaze upon the hoof which was to indicate the answer* was caught by Hans's keen eye as the *signal to begin* pawing; the stooping position of intent interest was held by von Osten throughout the count; a *slight release of the stoop,* the almost imperceptible straightening up of the body, particularly the head and shoulders—an equally natural shift in posture—was the *awaited signal to stop.* Both signals had to be within the range of Hans's vision, or there was no result. If Hans happened to be tapping rapidly and missed the signal by one count, the nature of the error itself showed that there was no reading of letters or grasp of meaning, but only a slip of one cog.

Once in possession of the secret, Dr. Pfungst, acting in von Osten's place, could make Hans give any answer, right or wrong, by a slight—but in this case, intentional—stoop and lift of his posture; if he remained stiffly rigid, Hans was completely lost. He could make Hans say that he had three ears and two tails, that three plus four equals nine, that orange was blue, or that he liked Professor Stumpf, whom he detested when questioned by von Osten:

The investigation satisfied psychologists but not hippophiles—horse fans—who were still convinced that horses were such lovely creatures that they must be good scholars. Herr von Osten questioned every step of the official report. The investigation inspired Herr Karl Krall, and led to the still more famous story of the Horses of Elberfeld.

The magnificent Arab steeds, Muhamed and Zarif, and later Mustapha, are the subjects of a sumptuous volume:

Denkende Tiere (1912). They learned far more rapidly than Hans; for Herr Krall was even less critical and more prepossessed than von Osten. Moreover, he declined to permit others to conduct control tests, having the negative report in Berlin in mind. Skeptics were not welcome, and an atmosphere of credulous worship prevailed. The Elberfeld stables were wondrous temples of learning. Within fourteen days Muhamed learned arithmetic; in a few months he obeyed commands spoken or written in Gothic or Roman characters or even in Greek ones. The method is substantially the same; but Herr Krall taught his horses to use the *left* foot for *tens* and the *right* for *units,* thus extending the number-range and reducing the endless tapping. He also simplified the alphabet-board.

A sample session in "Professor" Krall's seminar will illustrate his conversations with his gifted pupil: "Look, Muhamed, this sign $\sqrt{}$ is a root; if I put a 2 in it thus, $\sqrt[2]{}$, it becomes a square root. And if I write $\sqrt[2]{36}$, that means you must find a number which multiplied by itself makes 36. What is it?" Muhamed taps six times. Herr Krall dictates to Muhamed: "56 $\times$ 3, how much is that?" Answer, *168.* "What number is that?" Answer: *t l f o n k r a l,* 168 is actually Herr Krall's telephone number! Herr Krall at times telephoned his commands from house to stable, the groom holding the receiver to the horse's ear, convinced that the horse understood everything his master said.

Not only do Herr Krall's horses talk or rather spell in the hoof-language; they interpolate ideas of their own. Thus they hold conversations, with question (Q) and answer (A). Mustapha indicated that the person questioning him was a girl. Q. *How do you know it is a girl?* A. *Because she has long hair.* Q. *What does the girl lack?* A. *Schnrbrt,* which means mustache. Q. *I am going to give you some carrots; so spell it.* A. *M o r n,* which is short for

Mohren (carrots). But Mustapha continued to tap the letters *f u n w f*, for *fünf* (five). *Good! so you get five carrots.*

Shown the picture of the Kaiserin, Muhamed spells *ks r*,
but when told that is not right, adds *in*. He spells
Bethmann-Hollweg and Schopenhauer from their pictures;
but for Professor Stumpf, he impatiently taps *t n o r r z*,
which may signify profanity or disgust. Called to order,
under prompting, he spells the name rightly.

The dramatist Maeterlinck visited the horses and exalted their powers. They addressed him by name—hoofwise—without an introduction. M. Maeterlinck, it will be
recalled, has a highly credulous mind; he subscribes to
this as to a hundred other marvels, dramatizing bees and
horses with equal indifference to natural history. His account of Hans, who had been willed by Herr Osten to
Herr Krall is highly romantic:

Hans, the Pure, who till then had led an austere and monk-
ish existence, vowed to celibacy, science, and the chaste delights
of figures, Hans, the Irreproachable, incontinently lost his
head and cut himself open on the hanging rail of his stall
when an imprudent or vindictive groom introduced an equine
siren into the premises. The injury required severe surgical
repairs. He is now rusticating miserably in a meadow outside
the town. So true it is that a life cannot be judged except at
its close, and that we are sure of nothing until we are dead.

The controversy continued. Herr Krall's book of five
hundred pages called out an equally bulky rejoinder: *Do
Animals Think?* by Dr. Stefan von Maday. Krall's amazing
statements are all refuted, stage by stage, with the heavy
artillery of tables, diagrams, and analyses; a single shot of
a pop-gun should have been sufficient to explode the absurd bubble.

Dr. Maday adds a psychoanalysis of Herr Krall. He regards this wealthy merchant as a victim of a superiority
complex, who is indeed deeply devoted to animals, but is

THE CALCULATING AND READING HORSE ZARIF

After Krall, *Denkende Tiere.*

more deeply motivated by a craving for importance. He
harbors a "complex of greatness," revealed by Muhamed's
tapping out *k r a l l k e i s r* (*kral* is Slavic for king). It is
simpler to conclude that Herr Krall represents the fanatical type of mind, unwilling, or incapacitated by prepossession, to listen to the voice of reason. It is Herr Krall,
and not the Arab steeds, who finds his reward in this volume, so beautiful externally and so absurd internally. If
horses really could reflect, it would be interesting to know
what equine geniuses think of human intelligence.

Humanizing man's animal companions is an intelligible
prepossession. Particularly does the rapport between horse
and rider favor an exalted rating of equine intelligence.
Primitive life calls out the admiration and awe of man
for animal powers, in so many ways exceeding his own;
animal folklore is venerable and universal. The humanizing tendency is part of a great wish-error, which set the
trend of popular belief, and through that channel long
delayed the advent of a scientific view of the animal mind.
From the serpent in the Garden of Eden, through Æsop
and all his successors to Br'er Rabbit and Dr. Doolittle,
the dramatic employment runs.

Our scientific conscience does not permit the intrusion
of dramatic wish into sober wisdom. Comparative psychology is a serious study pursued by rigid methods. Calculating and reflecting horses not only fall completely out of
its range; the very belief in their possibility, let alone
their reality, is a preposterous assumption that violates
every basic principle of mental evolution. A flying Pegasus
is as zoölogically probable as a calculating horse. Carried
far enough, such a belief leads to chaos.

It may be needless or even insulting to state the grounds
of such a protest; but an inclination toward accepting animal geniuses still prevails. To make still plainer what is

plain enough, consider the slow years of step-by-step instruction that a child must pass through before the multiplication table comes at all within its mental horizon; consider that in all the stages supporting this mighty achievement, instructor and child share an increasing instrument of communication possible only to a human brain—the marvel of speech—and one appreciates the absurdity and stupidity of ascribing to a horse even of the highest equine I.Q. the rudiments of these most unequine accomplishments available only to educated humans.

To suppose that the horse's brain is as competent as the human for purposes of calculation is a primary falsity; to make the horse's power so indefinitely superior to the human is a far more preposterous assumption. From $2 \times 2 = 4$ to fractions, from spelling *cat* to indicating magnetic objects; from counting to telephone numbers: all this in a week or a month! That second miracle exceeds even the primary miracle that they calculate at all.

The very extravagance of the conclusions is their undoing. Obviously it makes no difference to the horse what happens or is said or done between the signal to start and the signal to stop, if only the carrots follow. You may ask for the logarithm of pi, or the distance of the moon, or the birthplace of Homer, or who killed Cock Robin, and if you know the answer yourself and go through the code, the horse's paw will reflect your knowledge. What is posed as a demonstration of supreme wisdom becomes ridiculous folly. The claim and the fact, the calculus and the horse's mind, belong to two wholly disparate universes of consideration; and it would indeed take a miracle of a supremely miraculous order to bridge the gap. It takes a miraculist mind, such as that of Maeterlinck, to accept it.

The primary miracle of Elberfield is that the stallions should have been given the means of expressing what they think and feel. It is momentous but when closely looked into, it is not incomprehensible. The second and greater miracle is that man should have been able to move the horse from his immemorial sleep to fix and direct his faculties and to interest him in matters that are more foreign and indifferent to him than the variations of temperature in Sirius and Aldebaran are to us.

While few will take this rhapsody seriously, the tendency to seek and find miracles in the animal mind is extensive enough to warrant further consideration and illustration. Apart from the primary prepossession that horses might be able to calculate and spell, von Osten's error was the overlooking of the involuntary signals to start and stop pawing. Krall's error goes far deeper; he deceived himself into believing that the horse originates ideas and speaks them. It takes a more psychopathic form of prepossession to produce belief in such a super-miracle. But even the miracle of Elberfeld is not the limit. For that we must go to the story of a dog by name of Lola, as told by Fräulein Henny Kindermann.

It may be ungracious to suggest that in psychic wonders the female of the species is more deadly than the male; but such is the personnel of the story. Miss Kindermann learned her technique from Frau Dr. Moerkel, trainer of Rolf, the talking dog of Mannheim, the sire of Lola. Consulting Lola, she devised *an alphabet of raps of the dog's paw on her palm,* and thus made conversation possible. After a time, Lola would paw *36—5,* which by Miss Kindermann's code spelled out *we,* which was short for *weh,* which was short for *kopfweh*—indicating that this strenuous exercise of talking was giving Lola a headache!

Lola told time; in fact, if you wanted to know the time, you just asked Lola, and she would rap *4 17* if that happened to be the hour! Show her a thermometer, and she indicated in degrees centigrade how warm she liked her food. On New Year's Day, Lola offered congratulations with her paws, phrased in proper greeting-card style! Lola forecast the weather, predicted it days ahead so accurately that mowing was postponed when Lola announced rain! When Lola was to become a mother, Miss Kindermann asked her how many pups there would be; the answer was nine, which proved correct! Lola had a canine sense of honor; when asked to explain how dogs knew so much, she replied that all dogs have taken an oath not to reveal this secret!

For readers who may be inclined to doubt, despite my exclamations, that such statements occur in what is offered as a scientific book, made in Germany, and attested by persons with academic titles, I must cite literally from Lola's diary some precious gems of prepossession:

13 November: Lola had to write a letter today to a lady of whom she is very fond; it ran as follows: "Dear, I have just been in the yard, I like eating biscuits, I kiss you!" (I think this letter bears evidence of being Lola's own composition.)

10 August: Today is my father's birthday, and Lola was to give him a good wish. I suggested good health, long life, and so on, but she would have none of them. At last she rapped: "*Ich wunsche esen*"—and after a pause—"*und ich auch.*" (I wish him food and for myself also.) "Now give him a second wish, something you yourself find good." "*Re jagen und has.*" (Hunting deer and hare.) "And a third!" "*Heiraten*" (marriage). Such were the dog's wishes on my father's natal day! Food, Hunting, and Marriage—the first one being ever the central idea in a dog's thoughts—and yet how necessary are all three wishes to the maintenance of the species—after all, there is something very simple and direct about an animal!

And something far from simple and remote from common sense in a human who can ask other humans to credit such extravagance. After this exhibit of complete irresponsibility, the reader will not be surprised to read the recommendation that all police dogs should first be tested for their veracity and then instructed in the paw language, in order to report all they saw, heard, or smelled in the interests of running down crime!

We have traveled far along the road of prepossession, from von Osten's involuntary signals and Krall's more definite promptings, to Fräulein Kindermann's complete draping of her own constructions about the alleged reactions of a dog. The pawing of a horse's hoof is a rather ponderous performance in which the horse must participate. The rapping of a dog's paw on a lady's hand is a more intimate procedure, in which it is altogether easy for the lady to convey from hand to paw all she desires. Though the lady protesteth much to the contrary, she admits with regret that she could not teach Lola to rap on a table, which would have disclosed the lady as the sole performer. She uses Lola's paw as a ouija-board, an instrument for recording by self-concealed movements the questions that she asks and the answers that are equally hers but referred to the dog, by reason of the prepossession in favor of animal genius. There remains only to record the opinion of Dr. William Mackenzie, an Italian, that the dog does it all by telepathy, to reach the final stage of demonstration of how a simple humanizing error in observation under a prepossession can compromise rationality, as wish diverges from wisdom.[1]

[1] Among the strange by-products of humanizing animals is the discussion of their share in immortality. It was asserted on theological grounds by Richard Dean in 1767 in *An Essay on the Future Life of the Brute Creation*. The Rev. J. T. Wood found the basis for animal immortality in three hundred remarkable anecdotes. As late as 1911, W. C. Meller argues the case for the animals in *A Brief for Animal Immortality*. But the prize argument is by Elliott O'Donnell in *Animal Ghosts* (1913). He finds abundant accounts of the wraiths of pets returning after death. To doubters he replies emotionally: "The whole animal world will live again; and it will be man—spoilt, presumptuous, degenerate man—who will not participate in another life unless he very much improves." There are abundant ways for humans to lose their minds over the minds and souls of animals. Keeping pets may not be so innocent an indulgence as it seems.

Chapter XVIII

THOUGHT-FORMS AND BEYOND

IT MAY NOT be illuminating, but it is precise to define a thought-form as a form produced by a thought. It is a discovery of theosophy by way of clairvoyance; thought-forms are said to hover about wherever human beings have thoughts tinged with emotions. They are visible only to adepts; so the ordinary reader need not hope to see them. They derive from the principle that thoughts are things—not hard, solid, opaque things, but ethereal emanations, floating, vaporous, colorful shapes. They are "astral"—blessed word!—images, in effect like the projections on the screen of what the hero thinks. They are symbolical rather than pictorial compositions of colored forms. All this we learn and can learn only from the seers of thought-forms. They report:

In some churches, instead of tokens of devotion, we see floating above the "worshippers" the astral images of hats and bonnets, of jewelry and gorgeous stones, of horses and carriages, of whiskey bottles and of Sunday dinners, and sometimes of whole rows of intricate calculations, showing that men and women alike have had during their supposed hours of prayer and praise no thoughts but of business or of pleasure, of the desire or the anxieties of the lower form of mind and existence.

Which is a sermon in itself.

But these are rather complex examples. The alphabet of thought-forms appears simply in the emotion of love. Its color is rose or carmine, which to you may be but a dab of color, but to the thought-form seer, is "a revolving cloud of pure affection; and except for its vagueness, it represents very good feelings. The person from whom it emanates is happy and at peace with the world, thinking dreamily of some friend whose presence is a pleasure." Such thought-forms are more truly pictorialized emotions.

When the affection, though still vague, takes a selfish turn, the thought-form changes, becoming darker, murkier, less attractive, "a far less desirable feeling." "The dull, hard brown-grey of self shows itself very decidedly among the carmine of love.... It is scarcely possible that these two clouds should emanate from the same person in the same incarnation. Yet there is good in the man who generates this second cloud-thought. As yet it is but partially evolved."

When the *affection* becomes *definite,* the thought-form acquires contours, in this instance one within the other, in different degrees of purity or depth and shades of color: "Even a first glance shows something definite, effective, capable, something that will achieve a result."

Thought-forms, like behavior since Adam, are things of good and evil; when the latter, they serve as awful examples:

The interesting brown-green indicates to the practised eye the expression of jealousy; and its curious shape shows the eagerness with which the man is watching its object. The remarkable resemblance to a snake symbolizes the extraordinarily fatuous attitude of the jealous person, keenly alert to discern signs, which he least of all desires to see.... The moment that he does see them, or imagines that he sees them, the form will change to the far more common one shown where the jealousy is already mingled with anger. A vague cloud is interspersed with definite flashes of anger ready to strike.

There are also pleasant sights in the colorful world of thought.

There are few more beautiful thought-forms than this. This is a thought-form of love and peace, protection and benediction, sent forth by one who has the power and has earned the right to bless. It may be reminiscent of childish guardian angels. These forms appear all unknown to the creator.

Of such is the wonderland of thought-forms! Directions for reaching it are scanty. Thought-form-seeing is an esoteric art. A book by Annie Besant and Charles W. Leadbeater contains an entire gallery of gay and sad thought-forms of all sorts and conditions of men, emotions, and situations. The reader is asked to accept the assurance that they are reported by a competent clairvoyant, and rendered in color by a competent artist from the clairvoyant's description. From the text one may learn that the laws of thought-forms are derived from the forms, and that the forms of thought-forms follow from the laws; thus forming a perfect circle of proof. The first law reads that

---

THOUGHT-FORMS

A: "A revolving cloud of pure affection, and except for its vagueness it represents very good feelings. The person from whom it emanates is happy and at peace with the world; thinking dreamily of some friend whose presence is a pleasure."

B: "The dull hard brown-gray of selfishness shows itself very decidedly among the carmine of love. . . . It would scarcely be possible that these two clouds should emanate from the same person in the same incarnation. Yet there is good in the man who generates this second cloud."

C: Even a first glance shows something definite, effective, capable, something that will achieve a result. This is intentionally generated.

D: "This is a thought-form of love and peace, protection and benediction, sent forth by one who has the power and has earned the right to bless." It may be reminiscent of childish guardian angels. These forms appear all unknown to the creator.

E: The brown-green indicates jealousy. Its curious shape—the remarkable resemblance to a snake—shows the eagerness with which the man is watching its object. The moment that he sees it, the form will change to the far more common one shown in

F: where the jealousy is already mingled with anger. A vague cloud is interspersed with definite flashes of anger ready to strike.

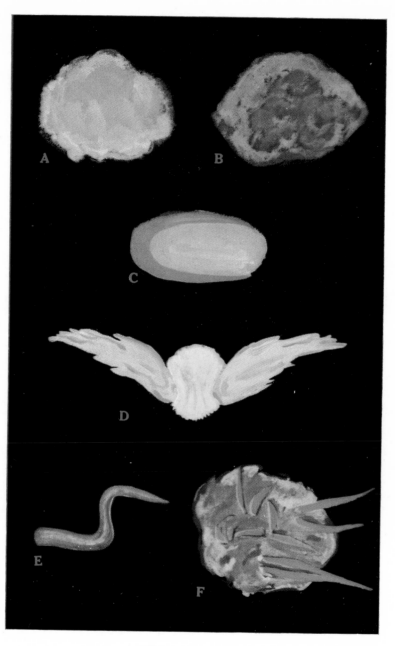

THOUGHT-FORMS

After Annie Besant and C. N. Leadbeater, *Thought-Forms*.
For explanation see page 216, opposite.

the *quality* of a thought-form determines its *color;* the
second that the *nature* of the thought is indicated by the
shape; the third that the *definiteness* of the thought—usually an emotion—shows in the *definiteness* of the contours.
The analogy of idea and form is obvious.

The illustrations seem to bear this out; but as they were
drawn to do so, there is no great marvel in their fitness. Is
there no way to prove the thought-forms? Can they be
photographed? Alas! they cannot. "A camera and plates
are not ideal instruments of astral research." Eagerly we
turn to "astral research" only to find that "by the laws of
astral matter, each definite thought produces a double
effect, a radiating vibration and a definite form." We seem
to be getting no "forrader."

Before the reader has recovered from the marvels of
thought-forms, his clairvoyant guide through the psychic
wonderland transports him upon a far more wonderful
excursion. Space has shrunk, and he sees the life on the
moon; time is turned backward on its flight of eons, and
he sees the human race in its distant stages of evolution.
Clairvoyance dissolves all that is dark or opaque or hidden, in a universal transparency. The astral vision of the
moon puts to shame the meager, lifeless details revealed
by mundane telescopes; it presents a more dramatic news-
reel.

Near what corresponds to the equator is a great city. It
looks like a cemetery with large white mounds for houses. The
poor people among the inhabitants sleep out of doors at night;
when it rains, they crawl under flat roofs, reminding one of
the dolmens which lead into chambers cut out of the solid
rock. The higher classes of the inhabitants live in the domed
houses. These higher types of Moon-men will become Lords
of the Moon. They are already quite civilized. In fact on close
observation one can see in one room a boy sitting at a table
writing in a script that is unfortunately unintelligible. The

climate there reminds one of choke-damp; but it obviously suits the moon inhabitants.

From some favorable point in cosmic space, we are now looking backward, endlessly backward. At one stage,

consciousness enters the bodies of small mammals, long in body but short in legs, a mixture of weasel, mongoose, and prairie dog. They have clumsy bodies that look unfinished, and have red eyes. After this stage of animal life comes another with creatures living in trees; they are double-jointed and have padded feet. The consciousness of these animals after the death of their last bodies on the globe, slept through the remainder of the Fourth Round and into the globes of the Fifth. On Globe D of the Fifth Race, they again take form as bodies, indeed as large monkeys leaping forty feet at a bound. Henceforth, in due course, these consciousnesses are specifically human.

Another and another transportation, and more wonderlands! Lost races and other races than those we know are revealed, other "planes" and "rounds" than those on which we live, other states of consciousness, other types and conditions of men. Nothing is withheld from astral vision. Thus is revealed *Deva* in the mystic state of *Devachan:*

Deva, holding out his arms over the people, now pours out through this color-form a wonderful stream of influence, a stream which reaches through their own corresponding color-forms precisely in proportion in which they have been successful in making their color-forms like the Deva's. The feeling which in an ordinary man is a smile, in the Deva causes an expansion and a brightening of the aura and also manifests itself in musical sound. A greeting from one Deva to another is a splendid chord of music; a conversation is a fugue.

We have passed into the stratosphere of thought-forms.

There is a further excursion, in its way the most wonderful of all, not to the infinitely distant but to the infinitesimally minute. We have become astral chemists. We see the atoms, record the shapes and groupings of each of the elements, count the particles and verify the formula. We gaze on what no ordinary eye has looked upon, no ordinary mind conceived. In one and another element, according to its group, we see whorls, spirals, spikes, dumb-bells, spheres, cubes, tetrahedons, funnels, cigars! And we note what the merely mundane chemist never suspected: that atoms have sex!

The male atoms from which force emerges are positive, and those through which force disappears are female or negative. The atom is a sphere, slightly flattened; and there is a depression in it at the point where the force flows, thus making a heart-like form. Where no line appears entering the depression, the force wells up from the fourth dimensional space. Each atom is surrounded by a field formed of atoms of four higher planes which surround it and interpenetrate it.

Astral chemistry is no unprogressive affair. It discovers new elements. "In addition, we found three chemical waifs, an unrecognized stranger between Hydrogen and Helium, which we have named *Occultum* for purposes of reference, and two varieties of one element which we named *Kalon* and *Metakalon*, between Xenon and Osmium."

These revelations were contributed to the world's knowledge in the early years of the present century, which none the less has pursued its stupid plodding way unmindful of the great enlightenment. But wonders do not cease, and one extravagance inspires another! Most recently appeared the first contribution to *astral art*. By the same theosophic route came portraits of our contemporaries, if we may speak so familiarly of the venerable Masters or Mahatmas who have lived through many incarnations. Their seclusion protects them from the camera and the artist's brush; by mystic means they have "impressed" their countenances upon a chosen adept. Risking the contamination of earthly affairs, they submit to the anonymous

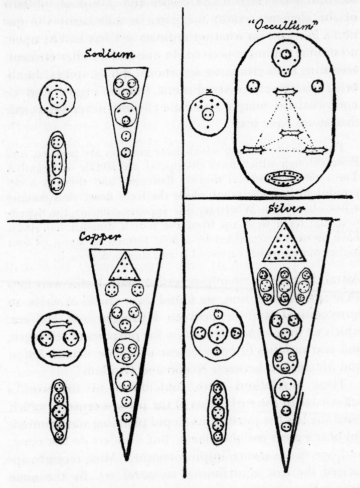

ATOMIC STRUCTURES ACCORDING TO ASTRAL CHEMISTRY

publicity of print. However, "to deflect attention from their appearance on the physical plane, they show themselves with reference to their previous incarnations."

The portraits include Master Koot Hoomi Lal Singh, familiar to this world as the author of countless letters to

Madame Blavatsky, his chief emissary. He is of Kashmir origin; studied at Oxford in 1850; was Pythagoras in one of his previous incarnations; resides at Shigatse; altogether a rather interesting personality. There is a Master Venetian with a Vandyke beard, who was Paul Veronese in another life. There is Saint Paul in preaching pose. There is Lord Maitrya, who was Christ in Palestine and Saint Patrick in Ireland. There is Master Serapis, a Greek by birth, who works with the Deva evolution, but whose dwelling place may not be revealed. There are Masters with turbans, and Masters featured like "movie" sheiks. "The combined notes of these nine Masters create a chord of harmonious sound in heaven, yet within the aura of the earth for its helping."

We return to earth with the arresting query, What shall we make of it all? For the reader hardly needs assurance that there are no thought-forms, that occult chemistry is a figment weakly modeled on stray scraps of fact, and "occultum" is a new element of the imagination. The portraits of reincarnated Masters have no other than a studio origin. The Moon-city and Lords of the Moon, the somersaulting apes and red-eyed, double-jointed mixtures of weasel, mongoose, and prairie-dog are weird, infantile animalic conceits, and the rest a shade more intelligent but equally mythical.

Apart from the fantastic embellishments suggesting an occultly minded Gulliver, the exhibits of thought-formers and their forms have only the modest value of contributing an extreme instance of *subjectivism*. Thought-forms are not subjective sensations like ringing in the ears, or the purple after-images that follow upon looking at the setting sun; though strangely enough, Mrs. Besant, knowing no physiology, cites the floating chains of rings seen through nearly closed eyes fixed on a gray sky—which are in fact shadows of particles within the vitreous humor—as the first stages of etheric vision. Thought-forms belong to an elaborated stage of subjectivism, in which the thought determines the form.

Crystal-gazing, the ancient scrying, depends upon a similar projection of the subjective vision upon an objective ground. What one sees—if one is adept—on the bright reflecting surface is the pictured imagery of the mind's construction. In all such experiences, you get back what you put in. Ignoring that fact makes the mystery, the apparent mystery of an objective reality.

The psychiatrist who listens to a patient who subjectively hears accusing voices and answers them, hears only the replies but not the accusation. The patient's mind is the author of both; but one would have the same difficulty in convincing him as the thought-former that such is the case. The disordered mind is the victim of imposed voices or pictures; the crystal-gazer and the thought-former deliberately seek them, and the latter with no other device than his vividly projecting imagination.

The process moves a stage farther toward an intellectual—or verbal—content only, with slight visual imagery, in composing the atomic patterns of imaginary chemical elements following loosely the text-book diagrams; it becomes entirely fancy-free in hallucinating the animals and habitations on the moon or the scenes of earlier evolutionary ages. Once launched on that enterprise, not even the sky, only the universe, is the limit.

Rationalizing attempts to save the face of the thought-former by positing a new order of vision. What it posits is just the universal folk-mind belief in second sight or super-vision. Clairvoyance was claimed in turn by mesmerists and spiritualists; it acquired a doctrinal touch when it was called *astral*, or *etheric*, or some other blessedly confusing and ennobling word.

ASTRAL PORTRAIT OF KOOT HOOMI

But Mr. Leadbeater is the unique inventor of ingenious varieties of imaginary super-vision, described in the language of actual optics:

There is a distinct difference between etheric sight and astral sight, and it is the latter which seems to correspond to the fourth dimension. The easiest way to understand the difference is to take an example. If you looked at a man with both the sights in turn, you would see the buttons at the back of his coat in both cases; only if you used etheric sight you would see them *through* him, and would see the shank-side as nearest to you; but if you looked astrally, you would see it not only like that, but just as if you were standing behind the man as well.

Or if that is not perfectly clear, then this may be:

If you look at the back of a watch etherically you see all the wheels through it, and the face *through them,* but backwards; if you look at it astrally, you see the face right way up and all the wheels lying separately, but nothing on the top of anything else.

The extreme thought-former invents not only the forms but the method of seeing them, and holds both as real as X-ray or ultra-violet photographs. Subjectivism can go no farther.

When partly fanciful and partly intelligible, thought-forming is just making pictures of analogies and metaphors—a trick we all have learned without taking the result literally. We paint the town *red* in gaiety, or see *red* in anger, or call anarchists *Reds,* with no temptation to believe these states of mind produce actual, visible colors. We call jealousy a "green-eyed monster," we "look daggers" when we scowl, without seeing zoölogical snakes or steel stilettos. Thoughts are thoughts, and things are things. The hooks over the heads of the gamblers at Monte Carlo are no more real than the Devil's horns and hoofs.

Thought-forming is also weak sentimentalizing. "The devotional thought of an unselfish heart is very lovely in color." Thought-forms acquire "a radiant and entrancing loveliness as the intellect becomes more highly evolved and is employed chiefly on pure and sublime topics." Discarding all factual baggage as sand-bags, the ballooning thought-former travels with no other license than the caprice of his none too sane imagination. The esoteric thought-former draws upon "consciousness in the Buddhic phase" to carry him into still more exalted heights, far from the madding crowd of sordid realities. Thought-forming belongs to the kingdom of weird wisdom, which prefers to abandon the restraints of rationality; it travels far indeed, but starts from the neglect of the simple principle of science—the distinction between thoughts and things.

PART V

CONGENIAL CONCLUSIONS

FOLK-MIND AND DOCTRINAL SURVIVALS

Learning makes the wise wiser, and the fool more foolish.—
JOHN RAY.

When the learned man errs, he errs with a learned error.—
ARABIC PROVERB.

There is no error to be named that has not its professors.
—LOCKE.

ARGUMENT

Congenial *conclusions are beliefs which would make life more interesting if true, and have an engaging air of plausibility. Since many of them originated in the older, cruder days of the vast un-understood, they usually go by the name of superstitions, both by reason of their weak logic and of their origin in outgrown ideas. I have introduced the term "congenial conclusion" to include both superstitions circulated by the folk-mind and allied beliefs in which the congeniality is that of a doctrine of more learned and respectable source. The "harmony of the spheres" is a classic congenial conclusion—hardly a superstition in the ordinary sense. To a mind properly attuned, it was gratifying to believe that the great cosmos is regulated by the same laws that make tones pleasant to our ears; that the Creator is a musician; or that God geometrizes. The notion that the circle is a perfect figure, and consequently that the planets, as works of a perfect Being, must move in circles, retarded the discovery of their true orbits by many centuries; it was a misleading congenial conclusion. By the same congeniality, it followed that one kind of perfection implies another, a weak analogy at best. The perfection of the circle lies in the property of returning upon itself; the perfection of 10 is that it is the sum of the first four numbers, and has other impressive properties. Every slight similarity of relation is drawn within the magic circle of cause. As congeniality travels on, it becomes more fanciful, its similarities more tenuous and remote; its plausibility is felt rather than proved. It is to this domain of belief that the present section is devoted. The minds of men always have been and are still filled with congenial conclusions, more or less tinctured—at times saturated—with superstition. As the racial ages of man advanced in comprehension, the content and the congeniality shift, but do not move far from their moorings in strong and, by the same token, congenial interests.*

The selection of appropriate instances offers large latitude of choice. "Unwisdom about the body" is a favorable hunting ground for congenial whimsies; it affords a rich field plowed again and again, and bearing successive crops of congenialities—plausibilities that pass for prescriptions of wisdom. The body is always with us: its symptoms in health and disease furnish an abiding subject of inquiry and experimentation, promptly reducing theories to recipes.

The two most human features of our anatomy, the head and the hand, command the interest, not of cure, but of interpretation. The system-makers make of it a pseudo-science, following the logic of congeniality. They attempt some justification by theory and prejudiced observation; they combine congenial error with misinterpretation of data. Physiognomy and palmistry come down through the ages with spurious and fanciful languages of head and hand; they show a strange power in recent times to renew their hold, despite advances of knowledge which render them flagrantly contradictory to science, as indeed they are also to one another. But their logical inconsistencies are submerged in the greater hold of their plausible congeniality, strengthened by the prestige of tradition, and garnished to modern taste. Anomalous though they are, these systems continue their appeal, and do so largely by their promise of prompt and decisive application. They form invaluable illustrations of the ways of belief, with all their tolerance for inherent contradictions. They involve excursions into varieties of theories, some dating from older and fanciful analogies, others the issues of relatively recent and less venial blunders. These elements are all fused and confused, but are readily accepted by the omnivorous, uncritical appetite for guidance in the reading of character and fate.

Their wide prevalence reflects the ready communication of a modern world, and likewise the efficiency of the technique of persuasion developed by modern advertising, inviting the invention of such terms as "bunkum" and "ballyhoo." We are again confronted by the versatile and energetic exploiter, and he in turn in modern temper suggests the further addition to our vocabulary of the word "racketeer." A powerful aid to his exploitation is the persistent hold of the congenial conclusion, aided and abetted by the weak sense of logic, which prevails despite the efforts of universal education. But there is more than survival in the modern vogue; there is adroit invention of any even more preposterous logic, as though increasing learning had brought greater expertness in logical perversity. Of this there could be no more egregious example than the absurdities of numerology, putting old mildewed wine into new misshapen bottles.

From first to last, the major lesson of this group of unwisdoms is the extreme susceptibility of the mind to believe congenially rather than logically; to accept beliefs that make life less rational, but more interesting.

CHAPTER XIX

UNWISDOM ABOUT THE BODY

AN INFORMATIVE volume by Dr. Cannon interprets the *Wisdom of the Body*. His thesis is the adaptation inherent in physiological processes. My title concerns the unwisdom of the inhabitant of the tenement of clay in his function as tenant. Despite its accessibility to observation, the body has been subject to varieties of strange speculation, exceeded only by that concerning its intangible partner, the soul. Ignorance accounts for much unwisdom; but even more, the ready acceptance of congenial conclusions. Unwisdom is a specific term for the blend of magic, superstition, and occultism which stands in the antecedents of every branch of knowledge, and yields but slowly to its only effective antidote—education. The annals of unwisdom about the body furnish rich illustrations of the ways of mind.

A powerful urge to knowledge of bodily function is disease: insistent pains and disabilities clamor for accounting as well as for relief. Unwisdom about the body and unwisdom about disease go hand in hand. The vagaries of medical practice are vividly portrayed in Dr. Haggard's *Devils, Drugs and Doctors*. For its proper completion, the title should be prefaced by *Doctrines;* for the doctor doctrinates even as he doctors. It is with doctrines that the unwisdom about the body begins, and in influence as remote as the cosmos and its elements. An instructive example of how the mind thought congenially before it learned to think scientifically appears in the procession of doctrines and practices concerning the human body and its medley of functions.

PRINCIPLES

Greek speculation regarding things in general began with the elements, and embraced in one concept the constitution of matter and of our bodily make-up. The elements were four—earth, air, fire, water. Fire was the *hot-dry* (light) element; earth the *cold-dry* (heavy); air the *hot-moist* (light); and water the *cold-moist* (heavy). Alexander of Tralles (550 A.D.) made the "duty of a physician to cool what is hot; to warm what is cold; to dry what is moist; to moisten what is dry." Chills and fever were clearly cases of "cold-wet" and "hot-dry." Similar thinking underlies the doctrine of the *temperaments* adopted by Hippocrates and continued by Galen. Temperaments depend upon the *humors* or humids of the body; the source of life is in the fluid flow. *Blood* is hot and moist, corresponding to air, and in cosmic relation has spring as its season; blood purifiers for spring fever are still advertised. The temperament of *blood* is the *sanguine,* which, though it means just *bloody* (sanguinary) as applied to a battle, means *hopeful* as applied to mind. Its direct opposite is the earth, which is cold and dry and finds its bodily correspondent in the *black bile;* its temperament is *melancholic* and its season the decline of autumn. Fire as an element is hot and dry, with summer as the hot-dry season, and in the body is represented by yellow bile. This, in excess, produces the *fiery* or *choleric* temperament of the hot-tempered individual. Water, cold and moist, is allied to phlegm, to the sluggish season of winter and the *phlegmatic* temperament. Thus are elements, seasons, constitution, and character brought into one survey.[1]

---

[1] Chaucer's diagnosis by Pertelote of Chanticleer's affrighting dream—an early instance of dream-analysis—referred it to the great superfluity of

This solution of the body's constitution and ills remained congenial for twenty centuries. Still more universal is the cosmic unwisdom—the relation of bodily symptoms and remedies to stars and planetary influence. In ancient days, medicine, in common with agriculture and other arts, was guided by astrology. Remedies, no differently than planting and reaping, were regulated by the phases of the moon; they were compounded and taken when the stars indicated favorable conjunctions. In 1581 a physician writes to his patient: "I cannot come to you Friday or Saturday, as the signs will then be in the heart, and Sunday, Monday and Tuesday in the stomach, during which time it will be no good dealing with you by ordinary physick until come Wednesday, sevenight at the nearest." Another physician lays down the law: "No part of a man's body ought to be touched with the Chirurgical instruments, or cauteries actual or potential, when the Sun or Moon or the Lord of the Ascension is in the same sign that ruleth that part of a man's body [to be operated on]." And another sets forth that "two days before the change of the Moon and a day after is ill to let blood." Ancient or modern, the practice is the same. In old Bagdad, on a day announced by the astrologers as propitious for bloodletting,[2] the gutters of that opulent city flowed red.

his red *coler,* causing dreams of fire, as melancholy causes dreams of bears. She advises digestives and laxatives to purge him of choler and melancholy, and reminds him—as his red comb so obviously indicates—that he is "coleric of complexion" and should beware of the "sun in his ascension."

In the sixteenth century, the Italian physician Jerome Cardan made the long journey to Scotland to treat the Bishop of St. Andrews, whose ailment his own physician had diagnosed as a "temperature and condition too moist and too cold, the flow of the humors coinciding with the conjunctions and oppositions of the moon." He promptly diagnosed that the Bishop's brain was too hot and too dry. He placed his patient on a cold and humid diet, yet had him sleep on a pillow of dry straw or seaweed, and had water dropped on his shaven crown.

2 Bloodletting may be of several origins. It was a favorite method of relieving "sanguine superfluity." The blood-sucking leech, when its habit

Astrological medicine went far beyond the regulation of favorable moments in bodily care and general venture. It parceled the entire anatomy among the signs of the zodiac and their protecting or threatening influences. This voluminous phase of unwisdom about the body is summarized in the zodiacal man, prominent in medical treatises for centuries and still current in Farmers' Almanacs. Its principle is thus interpreted: "Since Capricornus,

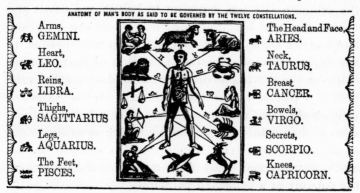

ANATOMY OF MAN'S BODY AS SAID TO BE GOVERNED BY THE TWELVE CONSTELLATIONS.

Arms, GEMINI.

Heart, LEO.

Reins, LIBRA.

Thighs, SAGITTARIUS

Legs, AQUARIUS.

The Feet, PISCES.

The Head and Face, ARIES.

Neck, TAURUS.

Breast CANCER.

Bowels, VIRGO.

Secrets, SCORPIO.

Knees, CAPRICORN.

THE ZODIACAL MAN

From a contemporary almanac.

which presided over the knees in the house of Saturn, and all crawling animals, are connected with the planet, the fat of snakes is an effective remedy against gout in the knees, especially on Saturday, the day of Saturn."

In addition to the elements and the stars, the third great principle of disease is the evil spirit; hence the Devil, who along with Drugs, comes into association with the Doctor. The "possession" origin of disease appears in the diagnosis as well as in the derivation of epilepsy—literally seizure—called by the Romans the *morbus sacer*—the sacred

was discovered, became the doctor's assistant; cupping was also in favor. The association of barber and surgeon survives in the red-and-white banded barber's pole, reminiscent of blood and bandages, pictured as the emblem of Surgeons' Guilds.

disease—under the belief that the epileptic was possessed by a god and inspired to prophecy. Dreams were similarly explained as the result of the occupation of the sleeper's body by an alien spirit, under the general notion that one mind can inhabit another. Demon-possession dominated the field and gave rise to witchcraft[3] and the witch-doctor. Pains and contortions were the inflictions of devils exulting in torments. The medical art was dis-possession, as the religious rite was exorcism to banish the devils and relieve the pain by "holy" or "magic" means; in primitive practice the medicine-man and the priest combine. In the stories of popular healers, as well as of licensed practitioners, the driving or drawing out of disease reflects the belief in disease as the infliction of a "spirit." Diseases continued to be "drawn out" long after a belief in "possession" had waned. A similar idea gave sanction to the laying on of hands, to the King's touch, to magnetic[4] action and tractation, and many other medical measures seeking the support of a congenial principle.

The most general term for the animating principle—the soul of things—that imparts vitality to the body and is likewise the opposite of the material and superior to it, is the *spirit*. Spirit-belief shaped the doctrine of possession. In the early tradition, the *daimon* included a protecting spirit, a guardian; later demons came to mean fiends. The spirit doctrine reappears in the *Animal Spirits*, which Descartes accepted from the then current belief that they actually flowed through the body; it was Descartes likewise who regarded the pineal gland as the seat of the soul, because it was the only single organ in the otherwise bilateral brain. The "soul" kept marching on in learned doctrines about the body long after its physiology was recognized. The spirit aspect of nature was more real than

[3] "The Devil in his Prime" considers this phase.
[4] "The Cult of the Magnet" is largely a tale of medical unwisdom.

the corporeal. Everything had its spirit when animism ruled as the favorite explanation of this life and the next. The spiritizing of bodily processes appears throughout the uncertain course of body lore.[5]

It is the motley combination of such diverse sources of influence under a magical-mythical type of explanation that characterizes the ancient, which in our retrospect is the superstitious, approach. The composite source is explicitly stated by Paracelsus when he prescribes that remedies shall contain six ingredients: two derived from the "planets," two from the "elements," and two from the "narcotics." The planets will conciliate and correct the medicine; the elements will enable the grade of the disease to be overcome; the drugs are needed in that the other forces are themselves too weak to produce the effect. The "elements" in many formulæ were replaced by the "spirits." The "drugs" grew in importance as the diagnoses became specialized and therapeutic reactions observed.

A collection of recipes from Saxon manuscripts of the fifth to the twelfth centuries—issued by the Master of the Rolls, London (1864) —bears the intriguing title of *Leechdoms, Wort-cunnings and Star-craft*. It reflects the character of a medical thesaurus developed under this state of opinion concerning the body. The leechdoms represent the doctor's specific and often magic contributions, replacing the Devil; the wort-cunnings are drugs; the star-craft is astrology. The progressive history of medicine records the steps by which an orderly rational view of bodily functions and disease replaced this chaotic confusion.

[5] An allied supposition of something mystic behind the physical appearance gave rise to the doctrine of *essences*, of which *quintessence*—the primordial nub of things, but literally the *fifth* essence beyond the *four* elements and the secret of power—is the verbal vestige. By similar survival in language, we still speak of the "spirits of ammonia" or the "essence of peppermint" and find no incongruity in using *spiritous* for distilled liquors and *spiritual* for religious concerns. Usage lingers long after the ideas that gave them currency have been discarded.

RECIPES

Leaving principles—to which we shall return—we may read in the exhibits of practice the variegated array of unwisdoms about the body and the fleshly and spiritual ills it is heir to. The process of *translation* from principle to practice is as puzzling to our otherwise focused and differently tempered minds as either the *premises* or the *conclusion*. We get a blurred impression of the operations of sympathy, transfer, correspondence, analogy, signs, signatures, charms, amulets, relics, somehow converted into rituals and remedies, and ever with the aid of a capricious imagination.

The procedures for retaining health and avoiding ills were not unreservedly medical; there was ever the efficacy of divine intervention and ecclesiastical ritual—combinations of prayers and poultices, of paternosters and powders, of relics and recipes. There were "holy" drinks as well as magic potions. Whether an ointment was a healing salve or a sacramental anointing may be uncertain. Nor is there any rigid distinction between remedies for ills and charms to work other desirable changes in human affairs, or to reveal what could not otherwise be ascertained.

As further puzzles to our rationalized understanding, there are many gaps in the "evidence" by which the properties that they were alleged to possess were ascribed to the drugs or objects selected and often obtained with great trouble and expense. All in all, it makes a hopeless tangle of credulous belief; and it may as well be cited as miscellaneously as the formulæ and their virtues seem to have been assembled and apportioned.

By the same warrant, since in temper the "argument" shifts so little in time and circumstance, the array may be drawn from all ages and places.

When you see a star fall, count quickly and you will be free from inflammation of the eyes for as many years as you can count while it falls. (Marcellus, 380 A.D.)

Medicine made from the *hyena*, if caught when the moon is in Gemini, cures bleared eyes, rheumatism, lumbago, ghosts, mad dogs. (Pliny)

For colic take the dung of a wolf with bits of bone in it if possible, shut it up in a pipe and wear during the paroxysm on the right arm or thigh or hip, taking care that it touches neither earth nor water. (Alexander of Tralles, 550 A.D.)

If a man take to his bed when the moon is in Aries, Saturn being in opposition, quadrature, or conjunction with it, especially if the moon is on the wane, the beginning of the disease will be by a chill. There will be heaviness of head and eyes and tonsils and mucus rising about the chest, and sobbings and nightly intensification of symptoms. (Saxon)

In case a woman is suddenly turned dumb, take pennyroyal and rub it to dust, and wind it up in wool. Lay this under the woman; it will soon be well with her. (Saxon)

For erysipelas, take a green yardstick or rod, and make the patient sit in the middle of the floor or house and place straw about him and make him say the words as in the text. (Saxon)

As soon as a man gets pain in the eyes, tie in unwrought flax as many knots as there are letters in his name, pronouncing them as you go, and tie it round his neck. If a man have a white spot, a cataract on his eye, catch a fox alive, cut his tongue out, let him go, dry his tongue and tie it up in a red rag and tie it around the man's neck. (Saxon)

If thine heart ache, take rib-wort and boil it in milk, drink it for nine mornings. It will soon be well with thee. (Saxon)

If a worm attacks your heart, cut up a large radish, mix with salt and eat on an empty stomach. Your heart worm fears nothing so much as a radish. (Oswaldt Babelthouer, physician to the Duke of Württemberg)

Against a warty eruption, take seven wafers such as a man offereth with and write these names on each wafer: Maximanus, Malchus, Johannes, Martensius, Domnesius, Constantius, Seraphim, and let a maiden hang it on his neck. (Saxon)

In case a man drink an insect, if it be of male kind, sing this lay in the right ear. If it be a female kind, sing it in the left ear. Sing the charm nine times in the ear, and recite a Paternoster once. (Saxon)

Heliotrope. If one gather it in August and wrap it up in a bay leaf with a wolf's tooth, no one can speak an angry word to the bearer. Put under the pillow, it will bring before the eyes a vision of one who has been robbed, a thief and all his belongings. If it be set up in a place of worship, none of the women present who have broken their marriage contract will be able to quit the place until it be removed. This last is tried and most true. (Albertus Magnus)

The heart of a hen placed on a woman's left breast when asleep will make her tell her secrets. [Pliny, who evidently tried it, adds that this is a portentous lie.]

In many of these "connections," though presented as prescriptions, there is little more than the fanciful bond between cause and effect or a sign and its reading, which gives currency to superstitions. The simpler unwisdoms about the body are plain superstitions; they form one chapter in the popular sign-language of occult meanings, with occasionally a shred of thin reason hanging to them. Weather-lore and dream-interpretation proceed by the same crooked logic. In body-lore they appear in popular beliefs. When your ear burns, it is a sign that some one is speaking of you—favorably if it is the right ear, and unfavorably if it is the left; when your nose itches, it is a sign that you will have a visitor; if you have a shudder down your spine, some one is walking over the spot of earth that shall be your grave; a blister on your tongue—here enters the moral tone—indicates that you have told a lie.

In the same temper is the interpretation of such a natural process as sneezing, which becomes an omen to be turned to good by saying *"Gesundheit!"* or "God bless you!" This harmless bit of unwisdom derives from the notion that a sneeze is an escape of your vital spirit or soul. Even Vesalius, the great anatomist, thought that the discharges through the nose emanated from the brain. Similar "good health" precautions and remedial practices survive on the basis of notions once acceptable to the people and no less to the learned mind. We could find still current in backward communities, or only a generation ago, the practice of having a child with whooping-cough cough into the mouth of a live fish—the principle of transfer; we could find the custom of lifting a ruptured child through the opening in a split tree—the principle of analogy; and a hundred other survivals of notions and practices which not so many generations ago were the seriously prescribed principles and remedies of the medical profession.

If ancient body-lore is unwise, it is so in the first instance by its too ambitious appeal to the great forces of the universe, upon which knowledge was lacking but speculation rife. Elements, stars, and spirits formed an impressive battery of causes to account for a crick in the back, a lazy colon, a convulsion, a tremor, or a general decline. It hitched the bodily wagon to quite too many stars, and neglected its simpler tracks on earth. The convention of accountings did not stop there; it became a veritable galaxy under the influence of an applied magic, shaping so capriciously the technique of operation. The practise of magic, whether its purpose be to read fate, to inflict evil or relieve a spell, to cure or prevent disease, to seek protection from a hostile world, develops rites and formulæ, and for disease prescriptions; it is the "mighty medicine" of the mind.

It is the unwisdom of the second instance—the crude concocting of remedies by fantastic analogies—that is responsible for the weirdness of prescriptions, for the motley paraphernalia—drugs, parts of animals, bits of minerals, and oddities of nature—that were displayed by the apothecary of Romeo's description and may be duplicated today in any Chinese druggist's shop. The rationale of the "drugs" contains a specific logic of unwisdom that pervades the primitive pharmacopeia. Drugs must be nasty and powerful, acting on the imagination through the taste; they must produce drastic effects—purging, bleeding, sweating—or they must be compounded of the rare and the precious, and impress by virtue of their value; or they must be unusual, bizarre, and a bit revolting. The ingredients of the older prescriptions are not unlike the ingredients of the witches' caldron; and the brew had no more rhyme or reason for the one purpose than for the other.

An instance from primitive medicine apparently influenced by contact with "civilization" will serve, as well as a more classic example. For an Indian warrior who was brought to camp after a most disastrous encounter with a grizzly bear, the doctor prescribed a medicine "made by boiling together a collection of miscellaneous weeds, a handful of chewing tobacco, the heads of four rattlesnakes, and a select assortment of worn-out moccasins. The decoction thus obtained was seasoned with a little crude petroleum and a large quantity of red pepper, and the patient was directed to take a pint of the mixture every half hour."

Gold and mummies and vipers and moss from the head of a murderer—called *usnea*—enter into prescriptions by one or another route, by a property or virtue "magically" derived. The "toad that has a precious jewel in its head" was by the same reputation dried and its essence used, like that of vipers, to preserve the precious beauty of the complexion. The *bezoar* was a powerful magic remedy; partly fabulous, it was, in some instances, the stone removed from a patient's kidney or bladder. Bits of rope that hanged a criminal were sold by the hangman to be used as remedies, the part touching his neck commanding the highest price; it was applied in treating chronic throat affections. These preparations represent not a lost art but a lost logic, a way of thinking, an unwisdom, that attracts our attention by its very illogicality, but was impressive reasoning when credulity ruled.

A prescription of Dr. William Salmon of London, in the year 1693, "accommodated to mean capacities" of her Majesty's subjects, summarizes the beliefs. It was presumably a quack remedy made to sell—and it sold.

Take of the "king of the metals" [gold], of powder of a Lion's heart, filings of a Unicorn's horn, ashes of the whole Chameleon, bark of witch hazel, earth worms, dried man's brains, bruisewort, Egyptian onions, in quantities indicated; mix and digest in Universal spirits with a warm digestion, from the change of the moon to the full, and pass through a fine strainer. It is not specially great for any one single distemper, but of much use and benefit in most cases wherein there is difficulty and embarrassment, or that which might be done, doth not so clearly appear manifest and open to the eye.

So varied a shot-gun prescription must hit something. Such "theriacs," as they were called, were in use until recent days. Into the bottle labeled *Theriac* went all the remainders of common drugs that might otherwise be wasted in the druggist's shop. The mixture had the approved medicinal flavor, and finds abundant descendants in patent medicines.

SYMPATHY AND SIGNATURES

Among the semblances of logic to save the prescriptions from becoming wholly arbitrary pronouncements, the doctrine of *sympathy* has a leading place. Giovanni Baptista Porta thus formulated it:

> By reason of the hidden secret of things, there is in all kinds of creatures a certain compassion as I may call it, which the Greeks called sympathy and antipathy, but we term it more familiarly their consent and their disagreement.

Porta finds proof in nature—in plant, animal, and mineral world alike. By the route of sympathies and antipathies, prescriptions were devised.

For plants

There is deadly hatred between the colewort and the vine. The vine with its tendrils clings to everything else, but shuns colewort as if told that her enemy were at hand. And if colewort is seething in the pot, if you put ever so little vine into it, it will neither boil nor keep its color. By the example of which experiment Androcides found out a remedy against wine, namely that coleworts are good against drunkenness. And this herb is at enmity with *Cyclamine* or sow-bread. If either of them be given it will dry up the other. So sow-bread increases drunkenness.

For animals

The wolf is afraid of the urchin; thence if we wash our mouths and throats with urchin's blood, it will make our voice shrill, even though before it were hoarse and dull like a wolf's voice.

The lamprey fights the basilisk, the most poisonous of serpents, but the cock frightens it; so the broth of a cock is a good remedy against the bites of serpents.

The ape of all things cannot abide a snail; now the ape is a drunken beast, for they are wont to take an ape by making him drunk; and a snail well washed is a remedy against drunkenness.

For plant and animal

A bull being tied to a fig tree waxes tame and gentle. So the stalk of a wild fig tree, if it be put to beef as it is boiling, makes it boil very quickly.

For plant and mineral

Garlic and loadstone are opposed. So a loadstone smeared with garlic will not draw iron, as Plutarch and Ptolomæus have written; but if no man had written, we might conjecture it to be so, for it [garlic] is good against vipers and mad dogs and poisonous waters.

For animal and mineral

There is the tale reported by Albertus Magnus that when a ring was drawn around a toad and an emerald, the emerald began to crack like a nut, and broke apart when the toad gazed at it. [It was expected that the toad would burst, provided that the gem "was in full vigor."]

All such notions turn vaguely upon signs and symptoms, loose analogies, false correspondences. General belief in sympathy developed (about 1640) the *Powder of Sympathy* of Sir Kenelm Digby, a distinguished courtier. The powder or salve, made of simple ingredients, was applied to the bloody clothing of a wounded duelist, and by that treatment the wound was healed. Such transfer of rites performed upon objects to affect persons abounds in black magic. In a seventeenth-century trial for witchcraft the accused had buried a glove of the victim, so that "as the glove did rot and waste," the liver of the victim would do likewise—the liver being somewhat leathery as the glove. The same argument applies to what is prescribed and what forbidden; eating the heart of a lion either to obtain courage or to ease heart ills, and avoiding the heart of a deer lest it make one timid, but eating its flesh to make one nimble of foot. By the same analogy the parts of animals were used in prescriptions corresponding to the parts of the human body affected.

A world-wide unwisdom is the prescription of drugs by resemblance, under the doctrine of *signatures*. As expressed in Coles' *Art of Simpling* (1656), God placed on herbs marks to indicate their uses; "malignant plants could be told by the sad or melancholic nature of their leaves, flowers or fruits." Euphrasia, or eye-bright, is "signatured" for eye trouble because of the eye-like spot on its corolla. The saxifrage (literally, rock-breaking), a plant that sends its roots over rocks and crumbles their surface, was prescribed for the stone; nettle tea for nettle rash; quaking grass for ague; pine-cones, resembling teeth, for toothache; and walnuts—with the hard shell resembling the skull and the kernel the convoluted brain—for head troubles. Or a resemblance in color would suffice: pomegranates, mulberries, and fruits with red juices were used for blood disorders, and yellow plants for jaundice. Bloodroot derives its name and use from the fact that when the stem is cut it exudes a sap as does a vein. For scarlet fever even the furniture was painted red; the surviving notion that red flannel is more protective than white has a similar origin.

Appearance in plant or animal was accepted as indicating purpose; toads or leaves with blights upon them were prescribed for warts; snails, suggesting the winding passages of the ear, for earache. It is still the Chinese practice to prescribe the roots of plants for foot troubles, the stems and middle parts for chest ailments, and the flowers and upper leaves for headaches. Sometimes it was by roundabout resemblance and even legend that properties were attributed to plants. Both the bracken fern, because a section of its roots looks like a *C*, for Christ, and the clover, its three leaves suggesting trinity, are good to drive away witches; and witch-hazel is used as a divining-rod and in remedies. Fern seeds make one invisible because the spores of ferns are themselves so nearly so. To the mandrake (man-dragon), by virtue of its resemblance to the human form, is ascribed a variety of qualities, including that of uttering a cry when torn from the ground.

There are "analogical" theories as well as analogical drugs. What may be called *iatrology*—the ideology behind medicine—would include such theories as possession, the temperaments, crises, the nature of disease generally. It would include a principle enunciated by Paracelsus, *like cures like,* which inspired the system developed by Samuel Hahnemann (1755-1843) and called by him *homeopathy.* For a time it flourished as a rival school, foisting the name *allopath* upon the "regular" profession.

Hahnemann was essentially a vagarist, holding among other eclectic beliefs that the "spiritual influence of a morbific agent" caused disease and the "spiritual operations of medicine" cured them. The principle that extreme dilutions—the high and low "potencies"—retain and even intensify the efficacy became the pillar of the school. The like-cures-like principle was interpreted as in accord with the growing practice of inoculation. Homeopathy comes into the picture as a strange projection from an older ideology into modern medicine.[6]

Into the false rationale of medical practices I cannot enter, nor review the pretenses and pretensions based upon the prevalent acceptance of unwisdoms, which constitute *quackery,* nor upon how they work, which is the subject of *cures.* This is a versatile and a profitable province. It is the wide prevalence of unwisdoms of all sorts and conditions that invites the invention of systems and cures, which gain a following by congeniality with accredited notions, and in latter days impose by assumptions of scientific discovery. Charlatanism, though it applies to all fields of knowledge, finds a peculiarly favorable field of operation in medicine, in the special genus of the quack. Vying with the interest in man's immortal soul, the management of his mortal body has shaped human thinking in most comprehensive manner, contributing equally to science and to superstition.

[6] The reference is to the *ideas* of the original homeopathy; the career of that movement, while retaining the name and a few distinctive practices, gradually adopted the advances of the medical art.

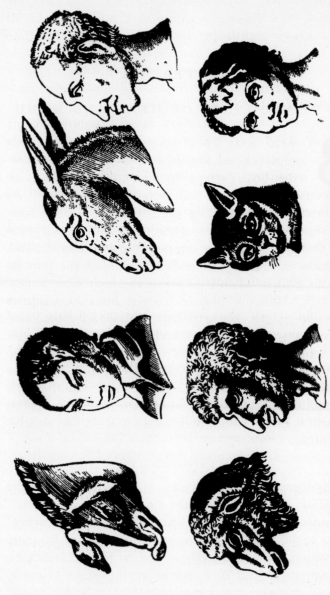

CHARACTER SIGNS IN ANIMAL RESEMBLANCES
From a sixteenth century work by Gianbattista della Porta.

Chapter XX

SIGNS AND LINES OF HEAD AND HAND

BY THE ROUTE of congenial conclusions body lore developed to a motley conglomerate of doctrine; bodily symptoms were accounted for by almost everything under the sun, including that orb itself. By a kindred order of thinking, the nobler parts of the body were regarded as an index of the mind within; and there arose character-reading by signs of head and lines of hand. Doubtless, outside the superstitious parts of the population, the grosser unwisdoms about the body have waned. But such wisdom as obtains has not been an adequate protection against quackeries and faith in advertised nostrums. Extravagant, baseless, and irresponsible, character cults continue by their appeal to congeniality of conclusion. In our exploiting days, they have taken a new lease of irrational life. It will add to the survey of the logic of congenial conclusions to consider the origins of notions that still flourish—for all their unwisdom—in our enlightened midst.

PHYSIOGNOMY

"Physiognomy" Bacon defines as "the discovery of the disposition of the mind in the lineaments of the body." Examined three hundred years later, the "discovery" proves to be largely assumption, supplemented by loose observation, superficial analysis, and far-fetched analogies. Physiognomy begins in a treatise attributed to Aristotle. He read character by *animal resemblance,* accepting the

247

congenial conclusion that human faces with animal-like features imply the corresponding traits. By that principle, men with a thick bulbous nose like a pig's will have the pig's lack of sensibility; a sharp-tipped nose like a dog's indicates the irritable disposition of a snarling, snapping canine; a large, round, blunt nose like a lion's indicates magnanimity; a slender, hooked nose like an eagle's is a sign of a noble though grasping nature. Since coarse-haired animals like the boar are courageous, and fine-haired ones like the rabbit and deer are timid, coarse hair in men becomes a sign of courage, and fine hair of timidity.

THE LEONINE JOHN JACOB ASTOR

From James W. Redfield, *Comparative Physiognomy, or, Resemblances between Men and Animals*, 1852.

As history, when imitative, repeats itself, let me anticipate that in the mid-nineteenth century the same notions are set forth in James W. Redfield's *Comparative Physiognomy*, which proceeds upon *Resemblances between Men and Animals*. His notion of resemblance is lenient, and in execution the artist aided and abetted his thesis.

John Jacob Astor is a lion. "A sordid look, we see, is compatible with the lion, otherwise there would be no pertinence in the allusion to 'the lion's share.' But there is no littleness in anything that he thinks or does." The Germans are lions, but when the "German descends from his proper characteristic, he approaches the hog." All Jews are facially goats. John Bull is not a figure of speech. The English are physiognomically bulls; the portrait of Hume the philosopher serves as an example, and to Redfield any typical Englishwoman resembles a cow. Erasmus is a boar and Daniel Webster a bear. Jenny Lind, the "Swedish Nightingale," is not that song-bird, but a lioness, her voice being "the counterpart of the most splendid bass." By the same principle, the Laplander and his reindeer, the Arab and his camel, look alike and are so represented. It brings the topic nearer home to find that such feeble and fanciful doctrines were acceptable to our grandfathers; and through all this zoölogizing of man runs a strain of moralistic lessons, indicating how mankind may acquire the noble and avoid the base qualities of animal creation.

Renaissance physiognomies, as the selection of illustrations shows, though reminiscent of Aristotle, went far beyond his simple if crude principles in reading character-traits from bodily features. The doctrine became systematized and sophisticated, and native structures confused with acquired characteristics. Coarse hair is made a sign of a rustic or thick-witted person, or of a brutal and overbearing one; fine hair a sign of gentility or of a feeble and timid nature. Noses, if they point down, belong to prying and curious persons who put their noses into everything; upturned noses are disdainful, untruthful, frivolous—on women's faces particularly. Mouths with thick lips are daring, reckless, lewd, and deceitful; even teeth are kindly or cruel. Foreheads are vain and salacious, or irascible and covetous; eyes are lazy, reckless, and voracious, or pacific, loyal, good-tempered, and intelligent—and even eyelashes may be proud and audacious. The "high brow," today a sign of the intellectual, was once oppositely interpreted:

HAIR OF A RUSTIC AND THICK-WITTED
PERSON AND BEARD OF A BRUTAL
AND OVERBEARING PERSON

NOSES OF A WEAK AND CURIOUS PER-
SON AND OF A VAINGLORIOUS PERSON

MOUTHS OF DARING, RECKLESS, LEWD,
AND UNTRUTHFUL MEN

TEETH OF AN UPRIGHT MAN AND A
CRUEL MAN

FOREHEADS OF IRASCIBLE, CRUEL, AND
COVETOUS MEN

EYES OF A CRAFTY MAN AND A
SIMPLE MAN

PHYSIOGNOMY OF THE SIXTEENTH CENTURY

The upper and lower pairs after Barthélemy Coclès, *Physiognomonia;*
the middle pairs after Jean d'Indagine, *Chiromance,* 1549.

Those with a high forehead are lazy and ignorant, and if it is fleshy and sleek, they are wrathful. Those who have little foreheads are bustling and foolish, as are they likewise who have them great and narrow. Those with long foreheads are docile and gentle and of good sense; those who have them as it were square and pleasant are magnanimous and strong.

Such "physiognomies" are easy-going compilations, posing shrewd guesses as established generalizations. They reflect the simple standards of belief of their day.

For the most part the styles in reading faces show little change in three centuries:

In Seventeenth-century Treatises

Body Sign	Mental Quality
Small eyebrows	lazy disposition
A wide space between eyes	quick apprehension
An angular chin	benevolence
A round dimpled chin	good nature
A pointed nose	passion
A long neck	gentleness
Hair and eyebrows of different color	questionable character
Furrows in the cheek	brutality
Small nostrils	timidity

In Twentieth-century Handbooks

Body Sign	Mental Quality
Gray eyes	calculation
Puckered eyebrows	jealousy
The ear high on the face	brain power
A large nose	cleverness
An oblique mouth	sarcasm
An upward sloping forehead	self-esteem
Falling hair	loss of mind
A dip in upper lip	concentration

Each is as capricious as the other; each has as much, which means as little, validity as the other. The progress of science has made clear that these indications have slight value, and may be added to the mountain heap of discarded notions.

A unique lead, belonging to the same period, is the *Celestial Physiognomy* of so distinguished a man as Jerome Cardan (1501-1575). In accord with the astrological notions of the day, he concluded that a man's character or a woman's fortune were written neither in the face nor in the hand, but in the *wrinkles of the forehead*. The system derives from astrology. Each wrinkle is dedicated to a planet; the mental traits associated in mythology with the god whose name the planet bears are transferred to the owner of the forehead! Cardan called this art *metoposcopy*, and created a gallery of wrinkles, which we gaze upon with skeptical curiosity; yet that, too, had its vogue. Fashionable ladies, aiming to be wise, carried about pocket editions of the *Celestial Physiognomy*, and forsook their genteel embroidery to read character in one another's foreheads. Such notions were in keeping with accredited beliefs of their time. When their fair successors of today, some of them college graduates, consult astrological physiognomists and palmists in luxurious offices, they become sisters under the skull of their seventeenth-century forebears.

The modern renaissance of physiognomy may be attributed to a worthy of the late eighteenth century, Johann Kaspar Lavater. He was clergyman, writer, reformer, orator, a man of distinction and incidentally a skilful draughtsman. His five-volume treatise is a sumptuous publication, beautifully illustrated. It was "designed to promote the knowledge and the love of mankind"; to manifest the glory of the Creator, since the human body was made in the image of God! Pages of the *Fragments on Physiognomy* read much like sermons, with scriptural citations as texts and the illustrations as moral lessons. Yet

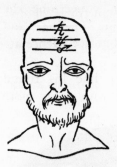

FOREHEAD MARKED WITH
THE LINES OF MARS,
JUPITER, AND
SATURN

FOREHEAD MARKED WITH
LINES INDICATING AN
UNPRINCIPLED
CHARACTER

FOREHEAD MARKED WITH
THE LINES OF
SEA-TRAVEL

WOMAN'S FOREHEAD
MARKED WITH LINES
INDICATING A VIO-
LENT DEATH

WOMAN'S FOREHEAD
MARKED WITH THE
LINES OF COM-
PASSION

WOMAN'S FOREHEAD
MARKED WITH THE
LINES OF FIERCE
VIRTUE

CHARACTER AND FATE IN THE LINES OF THE FOREHEAD

Examples of metoposcopy, from Jerome Cardan, *Celestial Physiognomy*.

in other sections there are attempts to consider the features as biological structures.

Lavater's method was his undoing: his complete faith in the value of impressions. A common-sense shrewdness he elevated to the dignity of "a universal physiognomical sense: those feelings which are produced at beholding certain countenances and the conjectures concerning the qualities of the mind," which they arouse. "Feelings" and "conjectures" are the stuff that dreams but not science are made of.

Lavater was a genial moralist who, like his friend Goethe, excursioned into science, but with a far more

G   F   E   A   B   C   D

THE PHYSIOGNOMICAL SENSE

"It is not by comparison that these faces produce different effects. The effect is instantaneous and antecedent to all reasoning. These faces do not please us equally. The central one (A) is more agreeable than the one to the right (B). The whole world would prefer the next (C) (the woman's head) to the last to the right (D). We should not expect the same degree of good sense, prudence, and wisdom of the three to the left—(E), (F), (G). If it was absolutely necessary to decide in favor of one of the three, the award would go to (F)." Johann Kaspar Lavater, *Fragments on Physiognomy*, 1775-78.

meager equipment; the result was a brilliant success in his own day, and a disaster ever after. Lavater was an addict, an adept, and advocate of the congenial conclusion; one is tempted to call him a *congenialist* by method and conviction. Anything that is pleasant, interesting, and up-lifting to believe is true; if one looks patiently and shrewdly, one will find confirmation.

Lavater's character-readings have little in the way of principle behind them. Pleasant commentary does not advance insight into the relation of "lineaments" and "disposition"; Physiognomizing *à la* Lavater is hardly more than an engaging diversion. Unwittingly he set the pattern for purveyors of readings at a price.

Lavater physiognomized thus:

> The subject is well fitted for a business career. The upper part of his face shows calculation and deep thinking. He is better fitted for geometry than poetry. He is sanguine but not firm enough to prevent pleasure from interfering with business.
>
> Firm, with good judgment. The bony formation shows constancy of purpose—a mind not easily shaken. His forehead is too concave, which lowers the superiority of his character. The physiognomy is appropriate for a lawyer or a judge.

Then as now, those thus delineated found these descriptions acceptable.

By elaborating upon detailed features, the "system" became increasingly arbitrary; there was no control, just the *ipse dixit* of an impressionist.

> The nose of this face is not that of an ordinary man ... neither are the eyes ordinary, especially the right one. Such eyes and such a nose seem to promise great services in the cause of religion and humanity. The left of the face by no means corresponds to the expectations which these have raised. Those gatherings above the nose, that mouth, the irregular underlying of the under lip mark an extreme restlessness, a debility of mind, an incapacity which is seeking to conceal itself under the vestige of knowledge and cunning.

Lavater filled pages and pages with portraits of eminent men, detecting in their features the known qualities of their personalities. By the same method he observed the signs of criminality in convicts; even in snakes he read "reprobate" qualities in their form, deceit in their color, and commented on the "naturalness with which we shrink from such a countenance." Upon so flimsy a basis, Lavater's Physiognomy achieved a reputation as an outstanding contribution of his time.

How amazing would all this be if true, and how marvelous that it should be discovered! But if we are inclined to extend our wonder to the fact that our grandfathers believed it, we may do well to postpone the reflection in the light of the parable of motes and beams. Yet there is a difference in the prestige which Lavater found among men of standing and the disrepute of such loose conclusions among reflective minds today.

While Lavater's Physiognomy was at the height of its popularity, the world was startled by the announcement of a wholly different solution of the sources of human traits in the *Phrenology* of Dr. Franz Joseph Gall. This was in no sense a "congenial conclusion," but a gross and unfortunate error of a scientific mind. The traits had no signs in features—Gall would have scoffed at any such lay notion; they were the operation of *organs* in the brain, visible on the skull. Gall called his system Organology. His associate, Dr. Spurzheim, gave it the name of Phrenology. It was a cranial [1] science, not a feature-reading art, but it happened to be a false one.

In the sequel, the locations of phrenology had an even greater obstructing influence than the delineations of Lavater. Though the two "systems" were mutually contradictory, uncritical followers, ready to read character by any royal road, fused and confused them. What they had in common—and that was sufficient for commercial purposes—was the promise of a minute analysis of mental traits indicated by outward signs, and an alleged scientific foundation. On these credentials they made their way all over the world in what Gilbert Seldes calls "The Stammer-

---

[1] It is so considered in "The Skull Science of Dr. Gall."

SAMPLES OF PHYSIOGNOMICAL READINGS
BY JOHANN KASPAR LAVATER

1. An openhearted judge. Sound judgment; free from prejudice; open to truth.

2. A visionary genius. Original but not profound. The nose discloses wit and sensuality. The contour shows a bold and enterprising character.

3. Benevolent, artistic. Natural goodness, chiefly in under part of face; upper indicates discernment for beauties of art.

4. Analytic discoverer. Most profound and penetrating head; spirit of research and analysis.

ing Century," a period of radical social experiments and new ventures in thought, and of charlatan solutions of personal problems. The phrenological wave was a far more inundating invasion than the physiognomical one; together they created a veritable Victorian epidemic of pseudo-science.

When these successive waves of character-reading had about spent their force, they reappeared in modern guise. They became parasitic to the new psychology that had come to its own through the establishment of the psychological laboratory and the understanding of human nature as a momentous problem in evolution. Psychology was to be applied; above all vocations were to be guided. This movement offered a ready temptation for commercial-minded practitioners, alias quacks. By rapid stages an ancient folly became a modern racket.

The keynote of modern "character-reading" is exploitation; it has something to sell. The salesman's wares combine the crudities of ancient days, the congenialities of Lavater, the errors of Gall, and are embellished with glittering extravagances not dreamt of in the parent philosophies. With a shameless disregard of truth and a brazen effrontery, it poses its conclusions in the garb of science. In the effort to outbid his rivals, every innovator announces new "discoveries" of the relations of lineaments and traits.

One "system" divides heads into *convex, concave,* and *plane.* This original geometric craniology goes by the slope of the forehead, continued along the ridge of the nose and reappearing in the chin. The owners of "convex" profiles are declared to be keen, alert, eager, aggressive, impatient, and penetrating; while the "concaves" are slow, patient, plodding, mild, and deficient in energy. Occupations suitable for convexites are distinguished from those fit for concavians; and marriage between them is discouraged. On this and similar spurious distinctions, a profitable career in advising employers was established; shrewd business men, whatever their features, have endorsed the scheme in glowing testimonials, testifying to its value in selecting employees.

Along with "concave" and "convex," consideration is given to "blondes" and "brunettes." "Blonde" traits are put down as positive, dynamic, speculative, changeable, quick; while "brunette" ones are negative, plodding, slow, thoughtful, imitative, and submissive. This congenial gospel has the advantage of a ready test that demonstrates its complete futility. When groups of university students were asked each to rate two blondes and two brunettes of their acquaintance in terms of these traits, the results showed that substantially as many brunettes had the "blonde" trait of positiveness as the blondes themselves; and the same number of "dynamic" persons were found in both groups. To be exact, the two groups scored eighty-one percent and eighty-four percent in the "blonde" test, and sixty-three percent and sixty-four percent in the "brunette" test. But character-readers do not make tests; they prefer rash statements! To them these conclusions are congenial in that they may be readily exploited among all sorts and conditions, shapes and colorings of men and women, who, in turn, find them congenial premises for self-knowledge.

There flourishes on hospitable American soil another "system," likewise numbering its adherents by the thousands, which has done little more than take over the phrenological traits of Gall and apply them, modified and augmented, to the face; upon that "analysis" it has prescribed vocations and all else to all who register for instruction. It announces that "far outstanding nose-tips are found in first-class engine-men, horticulturists, inspectors, and other callings requiring alert observation; while men and women with short nose-tips are superficial." Such phrenological locations as *intuition, individuality, calculation, synthesis,* and such aptitudes as *scrutiny, hospitality, zeal, secrecy, radiance,* are all indicated on one or another bit of facial tissue. The face becomes a pock-marked map of character, with every little tissue bursting with a meaning of its own. Yet it all poses as science, enlists customers and makes a living for its inventor to make academic psychologists envious.

For all of which doctrine and indefinitely more of the same order, there is, needless to say—yet it is important to say it so long as any and all systems find followers—not a grain of evidence, not an item of support. On the contrary, it is all flatly and crudely contradictory to all knowledge of the actual relation of features and traits. Below this grade of malpractice, there are the slums of character-reading, with no system to speak of, just a hodgepodge of statements which no person of sense would waste time in considering—meaningless compilations of misinformation:

A chin with a dimple or a cleft indicates a love of pleasure.
A large mouth means that the possessor is cold, severe, stern.
Vanity is shown by a short upper lip.
People whose ears stand out cannot conform to convention.
Three-cornered eyes are cynical, whimsical, and sometimes eccentric.
Eyes habitually half closed indicate secretiveness.
Broad feet and long toes belong to engineers, architects, and designers.
A flexible big toe means the separation of religion from life.
Pop-eyes show the faculty of memory.
The deep-set eye is the eye of reflection.
Very beautiful small teeth are usually possessed by stupid people.

To false facts are added blatantly false foundations and ridiculous applications:

It has been proved by observing thousands of cases that the extent of the upper forehead, other things considered, is an indication of the power to imagine and reflect.

These are inherent qualities, and the development of the muscle structure of the upper forehead gives evidence as to whether these powers have been controlled and developed into the working forces of creative thought, planning and reasoning.

The "muscle structure of the upper forehead" is no more characteristic than the muscle structure that enables one to wag the ears. A fool may frown more than a sage; and the so-called "upper forehead" is just part of the scalp that happens to be involved in facial expression. As for proof, the word in this connection has no meaning; it has been replaced by sales-talk.

"It would sound absurd if we were to say that nearly all reforms fail because the people who are the reformers have the wrong kind of ears, but the character analyst knows that it is true." He also knows that "a most cursory examination of the portraits of poets, educators, and essayists will show that they resemble *triangles* in head and body; while generals, pioneers, engineers, explorers, autoracers, and airmen are built on the *square;* and judges, financiers, organizers, and commercial kings are moulded on the *round.*"

The most inviting vehicle for the joy-rides of the character analyst is the ancient one of the temperaments remodeled to suit the modern taste. There are "thoracic," "skeletal," "cephalic," and "visceral" temperaments; "vital," "mental," and "harmonic" temperaments; and, latest and choicest, "chemical" temperaments. "The very first thing to find out about a person is his chemical temperament!" How the operation is performed is not revealed; the character analyst "intuits" it. Apparently the dominant chemical elements are different for the sexes.

The chemical analysis is judged by the shape of the face. The "Calciums" and "Silicons" have oblong faces; the "Potassiums" oval, and the "Carbons" circular, vital faces. The "Potassium" man brings chaos out of order; the "Phosphorus" type, in women, have soulful eyes, are delicate and refined, shrink from marriage, and are advised, for their characters' sake, to drink nice, yellow olive oil. The "Carbon" type is very negative; the "Hydrogen" woman is cold.

Clearly the up-to-date physiognomist with the license of freedom to print and the resources of ballyhoo at his command, far exceeds in unwisdom his ancient predecessors, whose leads he follows ignorant of their source. What was once misguided belief growing out of congenial conclusions has become a falsifying, mercenary profession—alias a racket. The psychologist may still retain the hope of making people wise enough to resist the lure of specious folly; along with other citizens, he must look to the constituted authorities to defeat the wiles of the dishonest.

PALMISTRY

Palmistry has a simpler genealogy than physiognomy; it begins as it ends in the same pseudo-science. Palmistry is an adopted daughter of astrology—the adoption by the daughter—and continues the family traits. In astrology the hour of birth is made decisive through planetary influence; the *horoscope* is the arbiter of fate. Palmistry makes a horoscope of the hand. The thrilling notion that the lines of the hand contain a character-revealing cipher would never occur to an anatomist, certainly not to one in modern days. As a fortune-telling art, it was called *cheiromancy*, or more generally *cheirognomy*. Columbus might have brought the system to America, for one of the earliest of printed books was on this subject; and the in-

SATURNIAN LINE   DOUBLE SATURNIAN LINE

SATURNIAN LINE STOPPING AT THE
MIDDLE LINE

DOUBLE SOLAR LINE BREAKING OFF
AT THE MIDDLE LINE

PALMISTRY OF THE SIXTEENTH CENTURY
From André Corvo, *L'Art de Chyromance, c.* 1545.

formation in the manuals circulating today is recognizably
the same.

The planets were assigned to the fingers; the forefinger
to Jupiter; the second finger to Saturn; the third, the ring
finger, to Apollo; the little finger to Mercury. If one asks
why, one must be content with weak analogies, flimsy connections, and arbitrary assertions. It may be no more than
that Jupiter is in mythology the commanding god, and the
forefinger the commanding finger of the hand; and Saturn
just came next in some mystic scale of importance. It is
better to check one's reason at the door on entering the
house of palmistry.

The human palm, with its fine network of lines, became the happy hunting-ground of cheiromantic venture.
The prominent vertical line running to the finger of
Saturn was called the *Line of Saturn,* later the *Line of
Fate.* In its course were read signs of such major destiny,
including tragedy, as Saturn governed. When the Line of
Fate was broad and straight, it indicated uniform prosperity; wavy, instability of fortune. If the line was double,
it was decidedly ill-omened, suggesting duplicity or a
double life. The mind that believes this in 1935 is still
thinking after the model of 1545!

The two transverse folds, actually determined by the
structure of the hand as a grasping organ, were called—
no one knows just when, why, or by whom—the *Line of
Heart* (upper) and the *Line of Head* (lower); the curved
line of the bending thumb originally the *Line of Venus,*
became the *Line of Life.* Once accepted, the scheme was
repeated again and again, as though repetition conferred
authority; and palmistry was launched upon a flourishing
career in human error and folly.

Cheirognomy mapped the lines, the mounds, and the
marks of the hand, and took some account of the general
shape of the hand and fingers. The palmist classifies hands

as elementary, belonging to crude, brutal, limited minds; conical or artistic; spatulate or active; pointed or psychic; and mixed, indicating a jack of all trades.

Soft hands are more affectionate, hard hands more capable of true love; a thin dry palm indicates timidity; a hollow palm indicates an empty life; when the fingers are long and stick together or "fall over one another," it indicates lying or stealing; conical hands are impulsive; spatulate hands make explorers and engineers; people with square hands are honest in business, and will give a square deal; knotty hands can solve knotty problems; the psychic hand is "rarely found in its purity today."

Thumbs and fingers reveal character. A clubbed thumb means a brutal person; murderers often have such thumbs. A firmly jointed thumb indicates a resisting nature; supple thumbs belong to easy-going people. Long fingers imply love of detail. If the fingers bend back like an arch, their owners are charming companions, lively, clever, but inquisitive. Crooked fingers indicate a crooked, twisted, and evil nature. A short forefinger denotes dislike of responsibility; too long fingers make one domineering; a short little finger indicates difficulty in speaking. Nails also reveal: short-nailed people have critical reasoning power; long-nailed people are calm; short red nails indicate irritability.

Even the spaces between the fingers have their indications. A wide space between the fore and middle finger means independence of thought; between the middle and ring finger, independence of circumstances; between the ring and little finger, independence of action. If the next space is wide, "no circumstances can confine you"; you just *must* crash your way to success.

But the center of interest is in the fine markings of the palm. In these dermatological patterns, the inventive and

irresponsible modern palmist, like his fellow-physiog-
nomist, makes new "discoveries." He finds a line of marriage, the markings of which indicate also the number and
sex of the children. If the "child-line" is broad and deep,
it's a boy! if narrow and fine, a girl! If the lines are straight,
the children will be strong and healthy; if faint and un-
even, sickly; if one line stands out, then one child will be
outstanding.

According to the modern palmist, the left hand shows
the hereditary tendencies, the right the result of experience. This, indeed, is one of the most generally accepted
"principles," accepted on no other warrant than that of a
congenial conclusion of the superstitious order. The right
hand will show improvement or arrest, health or disease,
and the future generally. Health, mentality, love-life, destiny are read in the stars, crosses, islands. The lines also
tell what you are to put your hand to; they afford voca-
tional guidance. For unprincipled principles, for statements of wild fancy as sober fact, for abuse of logic and
childish nonsense, the modern palmist is in no wise in-
ferior to the physiognomist.

If the Mound of Jupiter is prominent on your hand,
you are a Jupiterian, and in the language of conferring
degrees, you have all the rights and privileges thereunto
appertaining, likewise the dangers and defects. Jupiterian
and Saturnian children are different orders of beings and
should be differently educated.

When the Line of Marriage is broken up and linked
like a chain, the owner of such a line should be warned
not to marry at any time. One of the surest indications of
a happy marriage would be the possession of an influence
line running from the Mount of Luna and joining the
Line of Destiny, combined with one very distinct and outstanding line on the side of the hand under the finger
of Mercury.

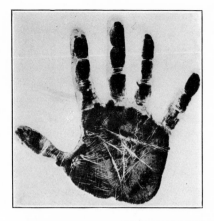
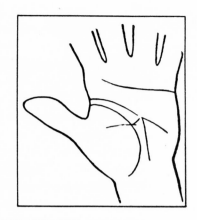

THE BROKEN LINE OF LIFE

Palm-print indicating that the person would die at the age of thirty-five, because the Line of Life, as indicated in the diagram, is broken in the middle.

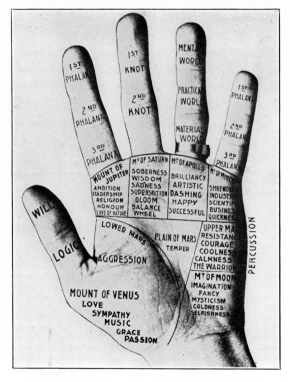

CHARACTER IN THE PROMINENCES OF THE HAND

And finally:

I found the Line of Health a most reliable and accurate indication of one's health and life. It is of course best that this line be entirely missing from the hand, for such absence indicates a very robust and healthy constitution.

The murderer for profit will have a most peculiar Line of Head.

In hopeless imbeciles, the Line of Head is made up entirely of islands and little hair-lines. In the vicious lunatic, the Line of Head is made up of short branches running in all directions.

When a child seems to be very irritable and temperamental, we should look at the palm to see if the Line of Head connected with the Line of Life runs across the hand downwards to the wrist, the Line of Life being at the same time delicate.

The most modernistic addition is the *life calendar* on the palm. What brain conceived it, I cannot say; the inventor may still be alive. His big idea was this: to divide the chief lines into segments corresponding to age-periods of ten, twenty, thirty years, etc. As seven is a potent and mystic number, the divisions in some manuals are by seven-year periods. The Line of Life is read downward, the Line of Fate upward; why—if there is a why—no one seems to know. Breaks or special marks in the lines—stars, crosses, islands—indicate specially important events—good fortunes or disasters. The *position* of the critical mark indicates *when* the fate will occur. Thus palmistry becomes more accurately predictive, the predictions more reliable if made after the event!

To give further appearance of scientific method, these precious creases are now recorded in palm-prints after the manner of identifying fingerprints. We are seriously informed that these dermatological trifles change their appearance when the owner meets with important changes in his life, quite apart from the natural changes which tissue undergoes with maturity. Indeed, one fanatical palmist proposes the examination of children's palms as

a guide to their education and a protection against un-
toward fate.

If we ask what these individually varying yet generally
conforming patterns mean, we are content to see in them
the result of the prehensile development from simian days
onward. While not in the least indicative of one's future,
they are reminiscent of one's remote anthropoid past. Thus
oppositely do wisdom and folly render their verdicts, meet
as strangers, and as strangers go their separate ways.

That such baseless notions as underlie physiognomy and
palmistry should have prevailed in uninformed days is
intelligible; that they should not only continue but develop into yet more irrational assumptions in enlightened
days is flagrantly incongruous. Such hospitality to older
credulities reveals a flaw in the educational process; the
harvest of misguided quests and misleading solutions cannot be accounted for by the drag of survival. We must
recognize a potent lure of wishful thinking to bring it
about that great numbers of neither unintelligent nor un-
educated persons take stock in the spurious findings and
vain pronouncements of the modern guild of character-
fakirs. This traffic in unreason is largely created to meet
the demand for easy solutions of personal problems. Of this
inclination, the exploiter takes advantage. The system im-
poses because the level of intelligence in such matters is
piteously low. The only effective antidote is to cultivate
a critical common sense. The psychologist acquires an
added importance as a protector of the human mind from
the exploitation of its wish-failings.

In accounting for the vogue of a practice deriving from
premises so blatantly false, the argument of *proof* cannot
be wholly ignored. That all these systems work after a
fashion scores against them far more than in their favor;

since they are mutually contradictory, they cannot all be true, and the presumption remains that they are all comprehensively false. No system, however worthless, fails entirely and always to apply: even reading fortunes by tea-leaves will not be invariably wrong. The readings apply because they are vague and ambiguous and general to the point of vapidity, and believers fit them to their own knowledge of themselves. They overlook the innumerable instances in which they fall wide of the mark, or the still more innumerable instances which are not tested or testable.

One dose of reason topples this flimsy support completely. It was applied in classic times when a skeptic asked whether all the soldiers who fell in the same battle had the same horoscope! If one were proof-minded, one would need only to observe the great variety of countenances in any representative group of whatever profession, and the great similarity of "hands" dealt by nature to all sorts and conditions of men. The argument, though stated in terms of fortune-telling, requires slight alteration when applied to erratic character-reading, despite the presence of an actual relation between physique and traits and the absence of any between planets and creases.

It may be illuminating to show where the ideas came from which are popularized as "analysis of the features" and of "the lines of the hand," determining fate and directing vocation; to make plain that belief in such damaged and decayed learning is no less anomalous than would be a man in chain armor driving a motor-car on Broadway. Improvements in intellectual standards of belief have hardly kept pace with those in physical transportation. Beliefs—congenial centuries ago, anomalous now—flourish with added extravagances. Twentieth-century knowledge has brought in its wake twentieth-century pseudo-science, thriving upon ignorance, and masquerading as wisdom.

Chapter XXI

NUMEROLOGY: OLD AND NEW

THE WORD "numerology" is a recent coinage—its paternity unregistered—not accepted, until within a year or two, by the dictionaries, and classified in library catalogues as *Symbolism of Numbers*. Where staid literary aids are silent, the popular press is eloquent in spreading this novel system of fortune-telling and character-reading, promulgating the potent number-values of names. Its popularity is amazing and far from creditable to the general intelligence. The mechanics of the system are borrowed from ancient sources. Professor E. T. Bell, mathematician, proposes to rescue the word and apply it to all systems of thought that attach mystic, symbolic, or superstitious meaning to numbers; his lead should be followed. Modern numerology would then become one preposterous variety of it, so closely approximating the frontier of the abnormal that the cult might well be called "numeropathy."

The ancient numerology has a respectable parentage. Pythagoras was its originator; he loved numbers both for what can be done with them and for their own sake. His romantic number-lore ascribed moral and esthetic qualities to numbers. Number *1* was masculine and the symbol of unity; number *2* was feminine and the symbol of discord; *10* was the perfect number as the sum of the sequence, 1, 2, 3, 4; even numbers carried favor, odd numbers were unfavorable. Plato dealt in mystical numbers, including the sumptuous and puzzling "nuptial" number, the derivation of which has only recently been solved. In folklore beliefs, numbers—especially their lucky or unlucky qualities—play a steady part, from ancient times to the present, and support the belief in their magic virtues or vices. Number 13 is the prize superstition—shunned on office floors, though displayed on the stripes of the American flag as representing the thirteen original States.

Numerology is not a folklore product but a learned system. Its older form is *gematria,* developed in the ancient Jewish Kaballah, elaborated in medieval rabbinical writings, and revived along with the twentieth-century fad. The Hebrew letters served also as numbers. *Aleph* (Greek *alpha*) was 1; *beth* (Greek *beta*), 2; and so on. Every word could be read as a number. If we followed the device, *c-a-b* as a word would be *cab,* as a number 312. By manipulating the number-equivalents of words, names and texts, gematria became a system or a game of cryptogram, fathoming hidden meaning. Thus, in the Book of Esther, the number-value of the letters of the Hebrew word for money —given to Haman to bait the Jews—is 165; the number-value of the Hebrew word for gallows is also 165. This, explain the gematriists, is why Haman was hanged! That connection—to us more amusing than convincing—is likewise the basis of modern numerology.

The pious gematriist was *not* a numeropractor. His purpose was to establish a moral-mystic meaning and to justify a text. To show the method, let me invent a profane example.

The number-value of $\underset{7+5+4+1+2+9+9+1}{G\ \ e\ \ m\ \ a\ \ t\ \ r\ \ i\ \ a}$ is 38, and that of $\underset{9+1+1+3+3+2+3+5+11}{i\ \ s\ \ a\ \ l\ \ l\ \ b\ \ u\ \ n\ \ k}$ is also 38. Thus is it proven that *gematria is all bunk!* However, with a different prejudice, one could substitute *B i b l e* for *b u n k ,* and still score 38, thus demonstrating that gematria is gospel truth.[1] This accommodating game permits the player to reach any score he desires, since he selects what is to be scored and reckons the score before he makes the selection.

Gematria is not dead, though it is a weak rival of numerology. The outstanding American representative of the cult is preparing a set of seven—the sacred number—volumes, of which three have appeared. Each consists of some five hundred pages of paragraphic texts, a crowded succession of demonstrations, of which a few samples will satisfy a satiable curiosity.

The seeker for truth puts to the gematrian sphinx the question:

$$W \quad h \quad a \quad t \quad i \quad s \quad D \quad e \quad a \quad t \quad h?$$
$$23 + 8 + 1 + 20 + 9 + 19 + 4 + 5 + 1 + 20 + 8$$

and she speaks in numbers: $= 118$. She, the sphinx (or she, the author) replies also both scripturally and numerically:

$$W \quad a \quad g \quad e \quad s \quad o \quad f \quad S \quad i \quad n,$$
$$23 + 1 + 7 + 5 + 19 + 15 + 6 + 19 + 9 + 14$$

which likewise tallies 118. Behold a miracle! The cryptic, cipheral truth that *the wages of sin is death!* Incidentally, the article "the" had to be omitted in the count, as it would have ruined the equation. If on another occasion it is needed to make the count, the truth seeker puts it in; so consolingly elastic are the rules.

Patiently, faithfully, with monastic devotion, day by day for fourteen numbered years, choosing texts, devising

---

[1] There are two ways of "counting" the letters. The one uses the full value of their position in the alphabet from 1 to 26; the other counts from 1 to 9, and then starts again. By the one, the 10th letter counts 10; by the other it counts 1, and so on. To this there are two exceptions: K, as the 11th or double-1 letter, counts 11; and V, as the double-2 letter counts 22. Gematriists follow the first method, though on occasion using the other. Numerologists follow the second as handier for reaching results. As the numerologists are in the popular majority, I have followed them in this example. You can prove anything you wish by either, if you take sufficient trouble, without the use of an adding machine or a high I.Q.

paraphrases, adding up alphabetical values, fitting, matching, dovetailing, until the phrases "add" alike, the author labors under the life-absorbing conviction that thus is truth revealed and God's wisdom made plain! What an amazing occupation for any human mind in this intellectually rich century!

The second volume of this *magnum opus* is devoted to the gematrial life of Jesus. It demonstrates such revelations as that *Jesus taught the People through the Numerical World,* which scores 539. The third volume is *Armageddon,* devoted to the Great War. "The outcome of the mighty conflict" was gematrially revealed in advance. The fact that *Hail Wilson Great Advocate of Peace* and *Executive of the Will of Jesus* both score 295 proves this point to gematrial satisfaction.

Gematriists are more than tabulating phrase-makers. They have a belief in "an omnific word," a cryptic message of divine wisdom. They define natural phenomena as "the reserves from which flow the causes of life intersected by numbers," whatever that may mean. A theosophical gematriist describes the ascent of man in two momentous volumes. "We take up the history of man's evolution at the point of the number 11, after he has passed the full period of effort (from 1 to 10) and has been born into earth life like a giant rising from his sleep, full of renewed vigor for the steep upward climb to conscious perfection, from the New Beginning of Number 11 to the ultimate attainment of Number 22."

The varieties of numeropaths are themselves numerous. They follow more or less closely or wildly the gematrial pattern of discovery. One adept "numerates" the illness of King George V, and finds in the harmony of the number-vibrations of the names of the King's physicians, especially in their initials—*H*ewitt, *H*owitt, *H*odgson, *H*umphrey Rolleston, *H*ugh Rigby, whose number-values are the

same as that of the royal patient—the causes of his recovery. Even the nurse, the valet, and the chauffeur who
accompanied the King to Bognor contributed to the cure
by the numerical fitness of their names. Of such is the
kingdom—or bedlam—of modernized gematria!

By this route we reach modern numerology. Gematriists
prove and *reveal;* numerologists *analyze* and *prescribe.*
Whereas the gematriist impersonally explores the universe
and interprets texts, the numerologist reads the personal
fate; he ultimates in the numeropractor.

Consider numerologically the oft-cited case of John Doe
vs. Richard Roe. The number-value of *J o h n D o e* is
$1 + 6 + 8 + 4 + 6 + 5 = 35$, which, divided by 9, leaves
8; that "8" is the precious result. The supreme modern
innovation responsible for the entire house of numbers,
flimsier than any house of cards, is this: that some unknown genius—or moron—decided that *an "8" is a special
type of person,* with a long list of characteristics, in which
all 8's agree by the destinies of numerological fate! That
is the corner-stone of numerology, and the most flagrant
absurdity yet cerebrated by the human brain.

Upon this foundation is built the entire fantastic super-
structure. In one text the traits are divided into three
aspects, distinguished as Constructive, Destructive and
Negative. By the use of an addled imagination and a dictionary, it was determined that an "8" such as is John Doe,
has these qualities:

If Constructive: Power, Authority, Success, Material Free-
dom, Judgment, Discrimination, Executive ability, Organiza-
tion, Leadership, Management, Practicality, Thoroughness,
Dependability, Self-reliance, Control, the Power to Succeed.
If Negative: Strain, Hardness, Materiality, Ambition for
Self and Money, Demand for Recognition, Intolerance, Worry,
Scheming, Love of Power, Carelessness, Impatience, Poor
Judgment, Misspent Energy.

If Destructive: Bullying, Abuse, Revenge, Oppressiveness, Injustice, Cruelty, Unscrupulousness.

Richard Roe proves to be a *"9."* Being a "9," he has another set of characteristics, duly enumerated. It is solemnly declared that "we are given the numbers"—by our ignorant parents; "we chose the aspects." John Doe may still make of himself the kind of an "8" that he thinks desirable. "Our numbers have the power to help us if we chose to live *constructive* lives." The negative side indicates defects, slumps, drifts, refusals. If one does the wrong thing, the numbers become destructive; or it may be that if the numbers become destructive, we degenerate.

The rest is all frills, but what frills! One who is described as "the first teacher of Numerology in the Western world" made the valuable contribution of adding the *vowels* of the name apart from the consonants, to discover "the vibration of the soul"! Consequently, John Doe's soul-vibration is indicated by the vowels *o-o-e:* $6 + 6 + 5 = 17$, which is again "8." So John's *soul-urge* goes marching on in harmony with his total self or *expression*. Lucky John! Richard Roe's "soul-urge" is expressed by his vowels *i-a-o-e:* $9 + 1 + 6 + 5 = 21$, which makes it a "3." The "soul-urge" of a "3" is "artistic, giving out joy and happiness, but never moping about failures in marriage or otherwise." He just tries again; "he loves pets, children, and flirtations"; he must "cultivate concentration and patience."

Another frill is your *Quiescent Self*, determined by the sum of your *consonants*. It is your "you at rest, what you really dream about when nobody is watching you." The revised Book of Numbers gives a table of nine varieties of "quiescents"! John Doe's consonantal self is a "9." By that token, this same hard-boiled executive is quiescently "one

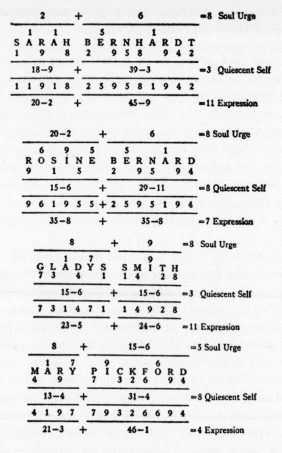

NUMEROLOGICAL MIRACLES IN CHANGES OF NAME

of the world's great artists, filled with a love of humanity, highly emotional."

A gala frill is attached to the "11's" and "22's." All blue-ribbon "11's" "seek to express their ideals. The light of divine fire is in their eyes." An "11" may be "an evangelist, or an inventor, or an actor—always an inspired one—or even "a psychologist." A perfect "22" is the innovator in practical affairs, and may be anything from a "buyer in large concerns" to a "public benefactor."

Next in numerological importance to your name is your birth date, which indicates your *Life Path*. For ex-President Hoover it is August 10, 1874: $8+1+2=11$, making him a distinguished "11." He must then seek his key word under "Realization, Inspiration and Consolation," and will find it to be *Revelation*. He is advised to "specialize in subjectivity, investigate mysticism and put it to its highest use." A rather difficult program, even for Mr. Hoover!

The numeropath's lot is not a happy one. He can take no step without considering what the number-fates have in store. The numerological almanac and time-table become rather complex. There is the "Universal Year" which affects all of us, which as I write, is a "7" year—"good financially, except when the previous one has spelled War." "The farmer should come into his own, for '7' loves the country." It is also favorable to "theories," "mining stocks," and "waterways"; existing affairs should be analyzed, and "there must be no branching out into new ventures."

As I write, it is May, a "5" month, which in the numerological calendar is not a month of blossoms, but will be marked by "universal projects" and "activity in the theaters." There is also a "Universal Day" which may also be a "5," such as July 4, 1776. "It needs no analysis to fit the spirit of this day with a '5.' The 'spirit of 1776' is really the vibration of '5.'" There is the *Personal Year*, which is calculated for James Joseph Walker by adding his birth month—6—to his birthday—1—and the Universal Year 1929, when he was elected mayor of New York, the result being "1"; from which "we may conclude that the vibration helped him to get something for himself," thus expressing his concern for number one.

Unchangeable is your birthday. If it is the thirteenth of the month, a "number of contradiction and some difficulty, creation, expansion, and restlessness behind the law of regularity and limitation"—how helpfully specific if one only knew what it meant!—you have one set of capacities, fortunes, and liabilities, specified in another table—in this instance of thirty-one panels for the days of the month. Your days are numbered, coming and going. By constant consultation of twenty or thirty different tables—each contradicting the rest—or with fates attached so vague as to mean anything or nothing, you can tell when to make deposits and when to draw them, when to shop or market, when to travel, when to stay at home. But the wisest course is to have a salaried numerologist as a constant companion.

This sample of inconsequence is derived from an undergraduate introduction to numerology. The advanced course deals with the "elements," the "subconscious," the "cycles and pinnacles," the "challenge," the "barriers," the "triads," as well as "Karmic lessons." These gadgets are devised by malpractice on number-relations and assignments of associated arbitrary qualities. Unless the styles change too rapidly, you may in a few years of concentrated study, with the help of favorable vibrations, become a number adept, provided you are still at large and have developed no more serious symptoms under the stress of cultivated irrationality. The ordinary—that is to say, the sane—mind stands aghast at this carnival of extravagance. Yet my excerpts but partially suggest the extent of the tomfoolery or chicanery of numeropractors; they need to be supplemented by some gems of principles and applications.

There is even a prenatal numerology:

Many instances also have been known of babies named before birth choosing their own birth dates—for easier going in later life. In these cases, unless the doctor and the mother are numerologists, they wonder at the premature or delayed arrival, as the case may be.

We are placed, chorded, colored, numbered, and named before we arrive on this scene of action and we cannot select our own vibrations, for each is part of the ineradicable label placed upon us by the Creator of all things.

Our own street and house numbers have a decided effect upon what we want to do or are trying to do. Try to relate your own Chart numbers to the numbers you are able to choose for yourself, and you can do and will do what you must do.

There is also child guidance in a numerological world. Consider the case of Eva Amy Downs:

She started life with two physical letters and one mental, as a *1* essence and a *5* Personal Year. The *E* (first vowel) would make her a very energetic baby and the *A* very active. After the reaction of the storms and tempers of her scattering and wilful 5-year, after January, 1921, when her Personal Year is *6*, we shall expect to find her more harmonious and amenable. . . . On her birthday in August she picks up an *M*—another earth-vibration—giving her a *4* Essence. Between her fifth and tenth years, her intuitional faculties will develop with amazing rapidity. . . . When she comes into the *A*, after her 9th birthday, she will make an important change—probably a change of residence.

She will begin her love affairs early—certainly by the time she is 16, for she will be influenced by a return of her dreams and live in the imagination (in *V*); will still be under the physical *M* (a marriage letter). . . . When she is nineteen she will probably marry—although any Numerologist would advise her against it—for she will be under a *Y* (*7*) and also a *7* Essence. . . . If you have already noted her principal numbers, you are not surprised to find her meeting many difficulties in life.

Thus unthinkingly did Father Downs and Mother Downs name their innocent offspring *Eva Amy,* and condition her for life.

Without this circumstantial account of the actual contents of the popular and pompous books on numerology, the uninformed reader would hardly credit the measure of their absurdity; especially would he hesitate if he has friends who take even a fractional share of stock in its speculative gyrations. How could a sensible mind subscribe to such preposterous notions? How could a person intelligent in general be so crassly unintelligent in particular? That they can and are is precisely what this chapter in the book of numbers demonstrates.

As for that recurrent lame defense, *proof*—the argument that it works—just consider the motley, ambiguous, and generous list of qualities assigned to the mythical being called an "8." How can they fail to apply vaguely to many of the vast army of "8's," especially as each "8" is his own judge of their application! As in each bracket there are nine orders of fates, and as there are about ninety million inhabitants in the United States old enough to be numerologized, there are about ten million "8's" and as many of each of the other numerological species. *All the proving is read into the readings;* and that is another lesson of this vast delusion. As your numerological tag is pure chance—and if the nine orders of fate were distinct, which they are not—the odds against your guessing right are heavy.

Taking a name nationally known, I find its number-equivalent to have these characteristics: Universal Love, Brotherhood, Charity, Compassion, The Higher Law, Artistic Genius, Selfless Service, and other noble qualities on the "constructive plane." I find listed for the *Soul-Urge* such qualities as "Wants to right and adjust all wrongs," "a sort of cosmic parent or guardian," "originated the saying 'There ought to be a law,'" "has no ambition to make a great name." In *Expression,* he is an artist in words or music; a welfare worker or clergyman. The gentleman's name is *Alphonse Capone!* His qualities are so generally esteemed that he is now being supported at the nation's expense.

One could publish a thousand of such readings that fail flagrantly without weakening the faith of those who believe in the rare virtues and prophetic value of numbers. The proof of the pudding is less in the eating than in the digesting; those inclined to swallow this variety of mental pabulum will insist that it is wholly to their taste and highly nutritious, besides, containing all the vitamines of the higher wisdom.

Numerology as a system is the subject of my theme; but I cannot overlook that numerology as a racket is the actual basis of its wide currency. The numeropractor is typically a psychological racketeer.[2] The physiognomists, astrologists, palmists, and handwriting readers were practising profitably—analyzing, advising, predicting. The numerologists became their rival—of the astrologists, particularly—by claiming that each of us is born and travels through life not under a star, but under a number. Their methods are the same, flattering every "8" or "9" or "11" by citing the distinguished persons who bear the same "number," and enlisting, like the patent medicine makers, the grateful testimonial: "My life was a continual maze of mistakes until you unfolded to me this system of numbers. Since I came to apply it all has changed, and I am today instead of the failure I was, a successful woman even in a worldly sense and a happy woman in my home life."

The numeropractors supply the demand which the numeropaths create. The majority of them may be sincerely deluded, finding in the alleged revelations the consolation of spiritual inspiration or security or vanity. The numeropath may be so blinded by number that he sees

2 Those who are interested in the schemes and methods of *Psychological Racketeering* will find them described in a book by that title by Dorothy H. Yates.

everything under that distorted gaze. He may write such a stultifying paragraph, mingling irrelevance and uplift, as this: "It was encouraging to note a resolution [of an Academy of Medicine] to standardize the nomenclature of diseases by the use of *numbers*.... Perhaps that is only a short step to teaching them all what the numbers mean; and then indeed we shall all be in sight of the Promised Land—where every man knows himself and either loves or tolerates his neighbor."

No one could live consistently or sanely in a numerological world. If on travel bent, he would select his destination not by the place of his business or pleasure, but by the favorable number of the train that is ready to leave the station; he would take a ticket for Schenectady or for Troy because of more congenial vibrations or easier spelling. A time-table or a telephone directory or a book of logarithms or a bank statement would be deliriously exciting reading. The numerologist is fortunately immune to the implications of the topsy-turvy world which he advocates, or we should have had to recognize a "numeropathic personality" in texts of psychiatry.

Numerology belongs to congenial conclusions. To Pythagoras it was just that, maintained on a noble, if misleading, plane. It is the same congeniality that led to his doctrine of the harmony of the spheres—an intrusion of romantic fitness into the cosmic scheme. In apparent support of the congenial wish which he mistook for the supreme wisdom, Pythagoras had a startling fact to go on: his discovery that musical intervals depend upon the simple relations of vibrations: 1 to 2 (octave), 2 to 3 (fifth) and 3 to 4 (third). For this and many another discovery he remains a great pioneer in science; his numerological vagaries retarded for ages the right view of the universe. This "numerological intoxication," this congenial idea that numbers have moral, esthetic, and occult qualities, is the heritage for which Pythagoras is remembered by the devotees of delusion. Pythagoras remains a master despite his incidental but portentous numerology.

The gematrial manipulation was a congenial sleight of mind in the rabbinical treadmill of textual commentary; that provided the rules of the game. It does not stand alone. The "number of the Beast," 666, in St. John gave rise to "beasting"—attaching an evil omen to one's pet enemy. The numerologists of the Reformation made the name of Leo X a "666"; the papists retorted by finding it in the name of Martin Luther. On the other hand, 6 became also one of the "perfect" numbers, in that it was $1+2+3$; that explains why Creation occupied just six days, with man, the lord of creation, made on the sixth, most honorable, day. In those days, the numerological habit of mind became a typical obstruction of rational thinking; but there was so much more unwisdom in the same temper that its total contribution to error was meager.

It remained for the twentieth-century apostles of muddled thinking to convert these products of an earlier mislead into a cultivated irrationality, and to do so by masquerading a superstitious character-reading in the garb of an equation. Congenial to what James called the "feminine-mystical mind," under the spell of numbers, is such sentimental gush as that "we must take our place in the Cosmic Orchestra, if we are to bring out the harmonies of the inner self"; that "22 is the *practical* idealist who has seen the vision of 11, and uses it for the benefit of mankind"; though owing to its rapid vibration, it "has been known to cause insanity in those not sufficiently balanced to handle it." Numerological uplift becomes a menace when on prescription bent, even to advising the change of one's name as a last refuge in times of stress. Modern numerology seems to prove that to a certain *genre* of intellect, irrationality is a most congenial pabulum—an opinion anticipated by George Eliot in her scathing comment that to some orders of minds the absurd is a perfectly juicy thistle.

Accepting Professor Bell's proposal, we may make "numerology" mean the doctrine of the symbolic and mystic virtues of numbers, originating in Pythagoras; thus numerology becomes one of the opposites of science. We may include under it the allied reference of potency of good or evil to numbers, such as "beasting," and under it place the gematrial development; and we find a place under this broad concept for the modern irresponsible innovations that have achieved so strange a hold upon uncritical minds. Pythagoras would certainly writhe in his grave were he aware of the degradations of his speculations upon the virtues of numbers.

PART VI

CULTS AND VAGARIES

STRANGE SOLUTIONS

Knowledge is choked by its own undergrowth.—ANON.

Error is prolific.—ERASMUS.

O Belief! How much you block our way.—MONTAIGNE.

When a man's knowledge is not in order, the more of it he has, the greater will be his confusion.—HERBERT SPENCER.

ARGUMENT

By THE ARGUMENT *of* Wish and Wisdom, *the foibles and errors of belief are proclaimed of the same flesh and blood as more orderly tissues of the mental organism. Schemes may be sound in intention and fallacious in execution; they may be ambitious ventures on a meager equipment; they may be navigations with a disordered compass; they may be quests vain, fanciful, irresponsible, suggesting a rift in the mental lute. Yet folly is part of the story of wisdom, error, of the search for truth. The study of how beliefs go wrong complements that of effective thinking by correct logic.*

This thesis justifies the inclusion of a variegated sheaf of vagaries, and of the cults to which they give rise when strange solutions find a following—and none so strange but that it does. This engaging borderland has ever been recognized, alike when genius steps over it through the ivory gate, and in the proximity of the uncertain frontier of eccentricity to the precincts of reason.

The fanatics in our midst are neither far nor few, and like the fabled eccentrics, the Jumblies, set out on the sea of speculation in a sieve of their own making. None the less they arrive at their point of destination, for it is none other than their point of departure. Supported by an intense conviction, they pursue their course, finding at every turn a confirmation of the one chosen idea of their devotion. The vagarist—a distant and often not so distant relative of the monomaniac—is typically a single-tracked mind.

Singleness of purpose and a life of devotion to one project —such as that of Darwin—has contributed notably to the advancement of knowledge. The value of the contribution is a resultant of many factors, with sound logic an invariable requisite. All vagarists are logically unsound, whatever their

287

compensating strengths or further unbalancing weaknesses. The case of phrenology is that of a wholly legitimate problem, framed by a scientifically trained intellect, carried out with a glaringly false logic. In result it was as disastrous—since theory was at once converted into practice—as though it were the arbitrary fancy of an irresponsible mind. Phrenology played into the hands of ignoramuses and charlatans.

In the next instance vagary is likewise of respectable origin and continues the laboratory prestige. The Jaeger cult flourished as a health provision of protective woolens; actually the underwear was derived from an oversoul, whose essence is odor, whose reality is established by experiments, but experiments as fantastic in plan as prejudiced in execution. In further descent from science to sciolism, we reach the vagary of Psychometry. Its originator was an eclectic, in the less as well as more respectable sense. Its quackery does not exclude delusion.

The concluding picture is an ensemble of eccentrics with the spotlight directed in turn upon the fanaticisms—the content of the vagary—and upon the fanatics—the personal traits of the leaders of the faiths. Again we realize that beliefs reflect psychology even as they parade as logic. The attraction of cosmic schemes to an enlarged ego is no other than the lure of importance conferred by the distinction of originality. The bliss of ignorance and the assurance that seems a perquisite of flagrantly inept logic complete the conviction of salvation by solutions that seem strange to travelers along common-sense highways. The world would doubtless be less interesting if deprived of its cults and vagaries; but the custodians of sanity may well insist that education shall supply the checks and balances of their control.

Chapter XXII

THE SKULL SCIENCE OF DR. GALL

THE CAREER of Franz Joseph Gall, founder of phrenology, is an appealing one: a leading anatomist of his day is remembered by his one great lapse from scientific grace. It is true that it was a long one and completely shaped his career; but he was a man of parts for a' that. The story of phrenology belongs to the general history of human error, and but indirectly to that of wish. It misses wisdom by reason of false assumptions developed into an ambitious but insubstantial system—a vain structure on hollow foundations. But it belongs to the annals of one-man vagaries which found a vast following, because, once under way, phrenology proceeded by the same loose logic and prejudiced observation that pervades irresponsible wish-systems taking the name of science in vain. Phrenology in its day became an influential rival of psychology; it also, without intention, gave the impetus to the deluge of fake character-reading which the nineteenth century inaugurated and the twentieth century disseminated with all the popularizing devices of a ballyhoo age.

Dr. Gall was a distinguished man of science. His great work on the *Anatomy and Physiology of the Nervous System* was the authoritative treatise of the day; and he was a young man when he wrote it. When he added to the title: *together with observations on the possibility of determining mental and moral qualities in men and animals by the contours of their heads,* he courted the usual disaster of serving two masters. A sober anatomist gave way to a a reckless phrenologist. It may be that the erratic streak was with him from the outset. We know that as early as 1796—at the age of 38—he introduced phrenological conclusions into his medical lectures. His colleagues shook their heads in dismay. From 1800 on, he was lecturing unofficially. His views were regarded as "subversive of religion and morality"; political and religious factions were involved. In 1807 his lectures were proscribed; he left Vienna under a cloud for Paris, where again he met the opposition of the medical profession; later he withdrew to London.

The advocacy of phrenology ruined Gall's scientific career. The older wholly misleading views of the relations of mind and brain—such as that the "soul" flowed in fluids of the ventricles within the brain or that spirits coursed in these channels—had been far superseded. The brain substance, particularly the outer layer or cortex, was recognized as somehow the organ of mind; which meant that these masses contained the effective controls of the sensory, the motor, the emotional, and the intellectual apparatus. Beyond this the details of their operations were just beginning to be understood.

The controversy of the day concerned the functions of the cerebrum, the big brain: whether it operated as a whole, or whether its areas were specifically apportioned— one area to sight, another to hearing, another to manipulation, another to speech. Flourens, the leading French physiologist, held to the "single function" idea; Gall to the specialization idea, which doctrine later became known as "localization." And no one at that time had more than an inkling of what went on in the brain in the varied mental operations; a correct view had to await the refined techniques of our own day.

In the early nineteenth century some experiments had been inaugurated. Gall seems to have been the first to note that an impairment of speech followed upon a lesion in the third convolution in the frontal lobe of the left hemisphere, though the discovery is usually referred to Broca at a later period. Experiments on pigeons had shown that the loss of function varied with the region of the pigeon's brain that was destroyed, though Flourens did not accept that finding. In the main principle Gall was right; in the application he was wrong—and disastrously so. Flourens agreed that the little brain, the cerebellum, had a specific function: that of controlling locomotion. The part of the skull at the back of the head covering it, and consequently the cerebellum itself, was in Gall's phrenology the seat of *amativeness*. Here was an irreconcilable clash; if the cerebellum regulated the love-affairs, it could not regulate the gait, and vice versa. So Gall asked "whether women, with a smaller cerebellum, walked and danced with less regularity, less art, less grace, than men?" In that argument he had ceased to think as a critical physiologist and had become a prepossessed phrenologist. The man of science was completely lost in the convinced propagandist.

Looking in upon his early lectures in Vienna, we find him considering a question which itself indicates the bias of his conclusions: why the skulls of monkeys and those of women show the same prominence.

In a favorable disposition of mind, during the delivery of one of my lectures, I was struck with the extreme love that these animals [monkeys] have for their offspring. Impatient of comparing immediately the crania of male animals in my collection with all those of females, I requested my class to leave me; and I found, in truth, that the same difference exists between the male and female of all animals, as existed between man and woman.

Thus was the cranial localization of "love of offspring" established! What is superficially the method of the laboratory is actually no more than a casual and prejudiced impression. One observes prominent qualities in one's friends; some are very generous, others decidedly ungenerous, some proud and vain, others modest. One notes the peculiarities in the shape of their skulls, and becomes convinced that the generous have a bulge on the skull where the stingy have a hollow, that the proud have an elevation in another part of the skull where the modest have a depression. And one has located the Organ of Generosity and the Organ of Pride! One might do as much with slight knowledge of anatomy, and be quite as right—which means quite as wrong.

Gall was not the originator of character-reading by the bodily features. That attempt has a continuous history from Aristotle down, under the name of *physiognomy*. This system received a notable revival at the hands of Lavater, who was not a man of science but a clergyman, a writer, an orator and a facile draughtsman. Gall had reached his conclusions independently, though he may have been influenced by the extraordinary vogue of Lavater's publications; these doubtless he regarded as falling beyond the pale of science altogether. The two have little in common, though in the sequel the extravagances of both systems were fused in an indiscriminate medley of baseless "signs" of human traits.[1] Lavater saw the sign of *firmness* in a square jaw, and of *wit* in a peculiar formation between the eyebrows; such notions Gall would have dismissed as guesswork. Lavater made slight attempt to explain the "signs"; he accepted them as a wise provision of the Creator. Gall, as an anatomist, referred mental traits to regions of the brain, not as *signs* but as *organs*. Lavater deliberately adopted the rôle of char-

[1] Physiognomy is considered in "Signs and Lines of Head and Hand."

acter-reader; Gall became one incidentally through the study of brain structures. Reading facial features became a fashionable occupation; but it never created the enormous vogue that was awaiting phrenology.

Gall's *Organology*—Spurzheim gave it the name "phrenology"—was based upon three assumptions, unfortunately all three hopelessly wrong. The first: that the shape of the brain, enveloped within the skull, is repeated in the minute variations on the outer bony surface of the skull itself; the second: that the brain-areas are definitely divided into minutely distinct functions. As sharply as Delaware is marked from Maryland on the map of the United States, are *tune* and *number* assumed to be mapped on the "united states" of the mind. The prominence of *tune* explains the musician, that of *number* the mathematician. That assumption involves still another and greater error: that talent is just a matter of the *size* of an organ; that the better musician simply has a bigger bump of *tune*. But the biggest assumption and the most momentous was the third: that the knowledge of how the mind's powers are composed could be determined by such crude, loose, and prejudiced observations.

In Gall's day, psychology had hardly begun; but enough was known to make plain what is much more so now: that the mental powers are *not* arranged on the arbitrary scheme which he announced upon shallow, flimsy evidence. How absurd to suppose that *memory,* which applies to a wide range of service, and *tune,* which is a very special quality, and *number,* which is a human device with which most people until educated dispense, are actually all provided for in the prophetic topography of the brain! Why stop there? Why not a bump for memory for faces, and another for names or dates? Why not an organ for the violin and another for the piano? Why not one for geometry and another for algebra? The skull could be tatooed with faculties until there was standing room only and not begin to exhaust the variety of employments to which we in our richly educated days put the original endowment of the brain; this endowment was quite the same in the caveman's skull, innocent of our complicated ways. No more unnatural scheme could be devised. In principle, phrenology is error thrice compounded; in application, it is absurdity multiplied and elaborated. A slight divergence in what to begin with was a legitimate physiological controversy, carried far enough in a false direction, led to one of the most comprehensive errors that befell modern thought.[2]

If phrenology had been true—but what an *if* that is!—any other psychology would have been superfluous; important human problems would have been quickly solved; and Gall would have been the greatest contributor to knowledge of all time. As it is, he has the doubtful honor of being the forefather of more false character-reading, more perverse notions concerning the mental make-up, than any other modern. Gall went far on false trails; his followers were still greater sinners. Lacking scientific training and spurred by a profitable charlatanism, they added

[2] The reader will gather that the most extravagant deductions from the tenets of phrenology were not made by Gall, though he went amazingly far and set the pattern for his irresponsible followers. Gall by intention and training was a man of science. When, in his beautiful anatomical plates of the brain's surface, he marked one little nodule of a convolution XIX, with key below telling that it marks "Memory for Numbers," and another XXVIII, "Veneration," which he located on his own brother, he was little aware of the utter incongruity between those indications and the result of his dissections. Yet other trained observers have attempted to reinstate his conclusions on the basis of all the elaborate findings of modern pathology, notably Dr. Bernard Hollander (*Mental Functions of the Brain*, 1901), while the list of good intellects that succumbed to the fallacies of phrenology is impressive. All of which shows that in so complex a problem it is easy to go wrong; and still more importantly that one can accumulate an impressive array of evidence for even so false a system. Logic is a delicate art; it is readily malpractised even by conscientious and skilled performers.

extravagance to extravagance. The doctrines came to be peddled by fakirs in booths at country fairs; though still here and there finding respectable advocates to attempt a reinstatement of the grand error. But for Dr. Gall, there would not have been so weird a skull-science. It stands as the product of a single-track mind.

Forgetting for the moment the subsequent degradation that befell Gall's system, let us briefly trace its career. Gall's phrenological interest seems to have started early. He observed that his schoolmates with good memories had prominent eye sockets, thus locating memory. At church, scanning the kneeling congregation, he noted that the most devout had a marked development at the crown of the head; at that point must be located the organ of *veneration*. His quarrelsome friends showed *combativeness* behind the ears; a bulge on the temple of a five-year-old musical prodigy located *tune; ideality* is in that part of the head which is touched by the fingers in the attitude of composition. The locations were assembled and systematized; they were summarized on those wonderful plaster casts, revered as gospel truth a few generations ago, now preserved as curious specimens in museums. The phrenological head may serve not as a wonderful and fearful map of the human faculties, but as a reminder of man's use and abuse of his power to think.

Dr. Gall's able lieutenant was Dr. Johann Caspar Spurzheim. The two traveled together over Europe giving demonstrations in asylums and prisons, reading in the skulls of the inmates the peculiarities that brought them to their doom. For insanity and crime were interpreted as the result of the *overdevelopment* of one or another of the *phreno-organs*. Crime diagnosis was simple; there was an organ of *murder* and an organ of *theft*. One prisoner showed the organs of *theft, murder,* and *benevolence* all

well developed. True to his organs, he robbed an old
woman and had the rope around her neck to strangle
her, when his "benevolence" came to the rescue and pre-
vented the fatality.

They phrenologized on the street. Gall met a beggar
with fine manners and a peculiar prominence on his head.
The beggar told him that he was the son of a rich man
too proud to work when adversity came. Gall recalled the
same bump on the bald head of an Austrian prince who
was always talking of his noble birth. Prince and pauper
suffered from an overdevelopment of *pride!*

But the favorite method of phrenologizing was to find
in Napoleon's head the marks of *ambition* and *cruelty,*
in Voltaire's head an excess of *wit,* in Washington's of
patriotism; and to contrast these noble and shapely vaults
with the lowly and misshapen ones of the weak-minded,
the ne'er-do-wells, and the miscreants. Such lessons in head
shapes were supposed to contribute to the cause of morality. The method was as simple as prophesying after the
event. But it won the crowd; for with this demonstration
of the truth of phrenology, people were ready to offer their
own heads for examination, and to be instructed how to
choose a wife or a partner or a pastor or a president, or
to be told in flattering terms their strong points and gently
cautioned as to their weak ones.

Phrenology was not content just to read "bumps" and
satisfy personal curiosity. It was to solve problems in every
field of human interest, to become the far-reaching *Science
of Man.* Gall was terribly serious about it, though his conclusions seem only amusing to us. Differences of race and
the endowments of animals as well as of individual
humans were phrenologically explained.

The foreheads of negroes are narrow, and their musical and
mathematical talents are in general very limited. The Chinese
are fond of colors, and have their eyebrows much vaulted.

According to Blumenbach, the heads of the Calmuks are depressed from above, but very large laterally, about the organ which gives the inclination to acquire; and this nation's propensity to steal is admitted.

Observe the narrow forehead of the dog, the ape, the badger, the horse, in comparison with the square forehead of man, and you will have the solution of the problem why these animals are neither musicians, nor painters, nor mathematicians.

In a skull preserved at Rome, relates Dr. Spurzheim, said to be that of Raphael, the organ of constructiveness is very large. Gall possessed a skull of a milliner of Vienna, who was very dexterous in changing the shape of her products, and who likewise had a large constructiveness. The skulls of animals that build and make burrows, such as the beaver and field-mouse and marmot, have also this region well marked. "Hence Phrenology can refer to similar organs the sublime conception of a Raphael, the petty products of a milliner and the natural habits of a field-mouse."

Gall was tireless in his pursuit. He collected over three hundred skulls of persons whose mental traits he knew; he had one hundred and twenty casts made from living persons, who presumably had their heads shaven for the purpose. He asked that "every kind of genius make me heir of his head. Then indeed I will answer for it with my own—we should see in ten years a splendid edifice for which at present I only collect materials." Instead of the temple of science of which Gall dreamed, the house of phrenology became a shelter for charlatans.

The fortunes of phrenology during the century since Gall's death make too long a story to tell briefly. One incident in it is notable as it turns upon the same order of error—finding what you look for—as was responsible for

Gall's ambitious structure. It concerns James Braid, who gave us the word *hypnotism*. There were many false notions regarding this peculiar mental state, particularly those of Mesmer [3]—another single-track mind—who referred the effects to "animal magnetism"—a high-sounding name for a force which does not exist. Braid showed that hypnosis was a variety of trance, artificially induced by strong suggestion in disposed subjects.

But Braid, under the influence of phrenological notions, actually carried out so bizarre an experiment as this:

I placed a cork endwise over the organ of *veneration* and bound it in this position by a bandage under the chin. The patient thus hypnotized at once assumed the attitude of adoration, arose from his seat, and knelt down as if engaged in prayer. On moving the cork forward, active *benevolence* was manifested, and on its being pushed back *veneration* again manifested itself.

By pressure the phrenological organs were played upon like stops on a musical organ. What an ingenious idea, but what a futile one! What actually happened was that the subjects got a hint of what was expected of them and —not perhaps without conscious deception—played up to the part. It is gratifying to add that Braid saw the error of his ways and admitted that he had been misled. But he never quite recovered his scientific prestige.

That the doctrines of Gall and Spurzheim met with strong opposition goes without saying. Men of science ridiculed their pretenses; people who kept their heads and did not submit them to be phrenologized recognized the source of the delusion. But prestige and pretense alike have their following; and it becomes intelligible why as these worthies traveled about and their fame spread, they were heralded by some as great leaders of science, by

[3] Mesmer's views are considered in "The Cult of the Magnet."

others called "a pair of vainglorious mountebanks." Nor must it be supposed that phrenology had no distinguished followers—it had many—nor that its influence has wholly died away. Attempts to renew the doctrines and bring them in line with modern findings have been made. But in the progressive story of what is now recognized as scientific psychology, phrenology is but a strange interlude and an amazing episode.

Phrenology was Americanized in 1832 when Dr. Spurzheim brought it to this country. He died four months after he landed. He bequeathed his skull to the Harvard Museum of Anatomy, where it now rests. He was followed by Alexander Combe of Edinburgh, who brought with him an extensive collection of casts, at which the curious gazed with wondrous awe.

This period inaugurated the procession of modern cults that thrive so luxuriantly on American soil. If the "Century of Progress" Exhibition of 1933, displaying a multitude of Aladdin's palaces of scientific marvels, had arranged a nook for an assembly of the fads and foibles of the beginning of that epoch and had placed side by side a parallel collection of the cults and systems that flourish today in the period of enlightenment, the contrast of a century would have been lost in the resemblance.[4]

It is interesting to record the humble origin of the promoting and commercializing of phrenology upon Ameri-

---

[4] It will be noted that psychometry (p. 312) likewise falls in this period. The great movement of American spiritualism began in 1848. The general belief in occult forces and hidden relations appears in the survival and revival of mesmerism and allied mysterious action. The "force" was called *Nervaura* by one propagandist, *etherium* by another; one cult took the name of *electro-biology*, another of *phrenopathy*. It was a free-for-all arena; pronouncement replaced proof, as it still does. It is with this group of extravagant doctrines that phrenology was associated. The great modern addition is in the technique of advertising and a closer parasitic attachment to the advances of science.

can soil. The scheme was hatched in the study-room of an Amherst student by name of Orson Squire Fowler, who charged his fellow-students—among them his classmate and convert, Henry Ward Beecher—the modest sum of two cents for a reading. Upon his graduation in 1834, the youth at once assumed the title of "Professor," and, armed with show-bills and a showman's talent, entered upon a life career. The phrenological house of Fowler and Wells in New York became a mecca of the cult. Dr. E. Douglas Branch includes the movement in the survey of *The Sentimental Years*—the period from 1836 to 1860. A flabby mentality was allied with soft emotion; and through it all runs the dominant moralizing proclivity characteristic of the American temper in that period and persisting far later—still a factor to be reckoned with in the hinterland of our expanded territory.

Fowler was a versatile enthusiast; he went in for hydropathy and uplift cults; he designed octagon houses to obtain an all-day sunshine—a fad that extended to the Middle West. But his stand-by was phrenology, which enterprise was continued by succeeding generations of Fowlers. Phrenology was destined to succeed and introduce the millennium when "all past and present fractional attempts to expound and improve humanity have signally failed." "So great is its moral power, that it will prostrate and ride over *whatever* religious doctrines, forms, or practices conflict with it. If even the Bible could be found to clash with it, then would the Bible go by the board."

A political adherent, convinced that all who had the bump of conscientiousness would vote for the right party, perorated thus: "Let the Genius of Freedom with Christianity on one side and Phrenology on the other, sit sublime in this her mighty continental home." Fowler's *Natural Theology and Moral Bearings of Phrenology* helped its vogue; but the head-readings at so much per

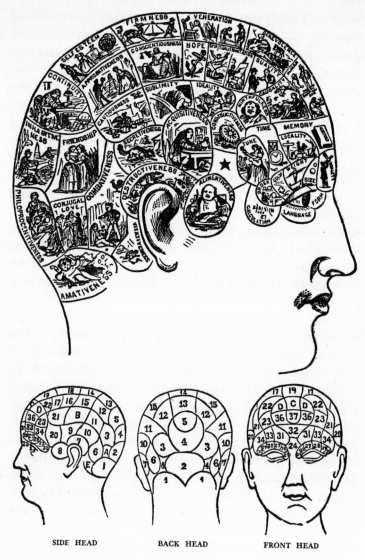

SIDE HEAD   BACK HEAD   FRONT HEAD

THE SYMBOLICAL PHRENOLOGICAL CHART
Illustrating the locations of the organs or faculties.

head, and the flood of literature profitably merchandized, filled the coffers. Each sitter purchased a little handbook which included a chart and a table of the organs provided with blank spaces in which he could enter "large," "medium," or "small," and depart satisfied that he held the key to his own endowment.

Phrenologizing à la Fowler introduced such comforting instances as the correction of a depression between *Firmness* and *Kindness* in an undevout subject (which should have been filled by *Devotion*), by a change in the manner of life. For lo and behold! After three years of life as "a praying man," the hollow on his head was replaced by a bulge—so amenable is the skull to discipline! Another of the Fowlers, after concluding a long lecture tour carrying phrenology all over the continent, found, by feeling his own bumps, that his *Eventuality, Language,* and *Comparison* had been enlarged.

It was this brand of phrenology that took New York by storm, and from there spread to all portions of our vast domain, already gaining its reputation as a "land of humbug," a favored hunting ground for the exploiters. It set a-going a wave of character-reading which has persisted ever since. Phrenology may still rank as the vagary of one mind that found the largest following. For it was not content to finger skulls and to diagnose faculties; it embraced the analysis of crime and the clue to mental disorders; it dictated education, gave the clue to anthropology, and included every department of the science of man. The commercial vogue of phrenology set the temper of modern cults.

Beginning in the noble calling of the laboratory, by successive stages phrenology descended to the slums, where you may see a phrenological chart displayed in a window in charge of a gaily dressed gipsy, who evades the law against fortune-telling by posing as a phrenologist, though she reads palms and not heads. The descendant of a learned anatomist is a frowsy and ignorant gipsy.[5]

[5] A hundred years after Gall's death, an ingenious American inventor actually reduced the recording of the original thirty-two organs to an electric device, called the Psychograph. It consists of 1,954 parts and cost $100,000 in the twenty-six years of labor spent upon its perfection. A helmet descends over the head and is pressed down until it is fitted to the contours of the skull, barring the irregularities of the hair. A motor sets a sheet of paper in motion which stops thirty-two times, when by a set of levers the registry is made of your place in the thirty-two qualities. For a fee of fifty cents, you receive a chart indicating whether your amativeness or alimentiveness, your combativeness or ideality or wit or tune is marked, average, or deficient. The truth of Gall's assumptions is assumed. It would almost appear as though the inventor were inspired by the dictum: Be sure you are wrong, then go ahead. But what an amazing expenditure of ingenuity on a baseless supposition one hundred years old and obsolete.

Chapter XXIII

WHY PROFESSOR JAEGER MADE WOOLENS

A WRITER looking for an intriguing title for a sprightly tale called his story *The Bishop's Jaegers* —"Jaegers" standing for woolen underwear. Did the author know, or the Bishop, the unique story, woven unseen and forgotten, in the texture of their favorite garments? The story of the Jaeger Sanitary Woolens forms an amazing chapter in the annals of scientific vagaries. It is recorded in a solemnly scientific, thoroughly Teutonic, two-volume work on the *Discovery of the Soul,* which excited an amused sensation in a limited circle when it was issued fifty years ago, and has rested in peaceful oblivion since.

Dr. Gustav Jaeger, professor of zoölogy, was a respected member of his profession who introduced Darwin to German readers. Jaeger announced a startling discovery. With a zealot's faith, he was convinced that for this a grateful world would remember him for all time. It deserves a line to itself:

The soul is Duft, *an odorous emanation. Smell senses the soul.*

What has recently become politely abbreviated to B.O. —with remedies for it offered by philanthropic advertisers —is in reality S.O.—soul-odor! This odor exhales from the skin, mouth, and nose, and "as I have proved by experiments, directly from the brain as well. If a portion of brain substance be pulverized in a mortar and a few drops of nitric acid be added, the same odor is obtained."

In pursuit of this idea, Professor Jaeger became a psychoösmologist—possibly the only member of that profession. His first principle is that all odors are either pleasant or unpleasant—*fragrances* or *ordures;* the second that the agreeable odors are beneficial, and the unpleasant ones noxious; the third and completing discovery is that *animal wool* is the one and only substance that *retains the beneficial odors or dufts*—the soul essence. But the *wool must be one hundred per cent pure!* Hence, *the Jaeger woolens!* The woolens live on; the theory that created them is forgotten. Such is fame!

How Professor Jaeger established his conclusions and applied them affords a convincing picture of the workings of a single-track mind. *Duft* is declared to be the essence of emotion; each emotion has its peculiar *duft.* There is *angst Stoff,* "fear stuff," a secretion or emanation that induces fear; also there is "anger stuff," which, like the lingering scent of the roses in a shattered vase, remains after the quarrel is over. Beware of anger-*duft!* It disturbs household peace. It was Dr. Jaeger's philanthropic idea to *retain the salutary dufts* clinging to the body, and to *expel or exclude the noxious ones.* Wool clothing was the completely protective armor. *Wear all wool and save your soul!*

The reader is entitled to sense the flavor of the doctrines in the original text:

I define the physical source of the emotions to be subtle essences bound up with and emanating from the albumen in the bodily tissues.... Only when a decomposition of albumen in the tissues occurs are they set free; they then become perceptible to the senses, especially to that of smell, and create in the body emotion or mood. The salutary principle makes emotions that are cheerful, enterprising, and courageous; the noxious principle produces gloom, depression, want of courage, and a distaste for food.

The salutary principle is fragrant; the noxious, tainted and offensive. If the subject of the test be of cheerful, pleasant mood, the scene will be agreeable and sweet; if sorrowful or in pain, disagreeable.

Upon these principles Professor Jaeger undertook to become a stylist for men and women. With Teutonic gallantry, he prescribed paternally for the gentler sex:

Women should wear all underclothes, stockings, even corsets, made of pure wool. A dress of pure wool, closing well around the throat and having a double woolen lining at the chest and downwards, should be the winter and summer wear of women, who would then participate in all the advantages which I have described, and of which they stand even in greater need than do men.

One precaution is essential: there must be no trace of cotton in the garments, lest the mood become less cheery, less equable. The soul's health must be guarded by night as well as by day. Even bed-sheets and mattresses must be all wool. The right *duft* protects from infection also. Salutary *duft* keeps off germs and parasites. Hence the Sanitary Stuttgart Woolens!

With academic consistency and disregard of esthetics, Dr. Jaeger launched the "reform" clothing. In its original one hundred per cent following, it created a docile cult in Germany. It established a branch in London, serving the wool-loving inhabitants of a damp climate, presumably with no ill effects upon their souls. The design as worn by men appears in the photograph of the discoverer of the soul-stuff. The Jaeger designs for the fair sex suggest designs against them, particularly to eyes accustomed to modern sheer and diaphanous fashions, which must leave the soul shamelessly unprotected. It was the underwear next to the skin, nearest the soul, that offered the most important protection. By later experiments with varieties

PROFESSOR GUSTAV JAEGER

In the all-wool costume he designed to retain the beneficent soul-odors.

of wool, Dr. Jaeger found that camel's wool was the most completely soul-preserving substance as yet known.

Let us not forget that all this was taken most seriously and that Dr. Jaeger, a German *Gelehrter,* appealed to experiments to confirm his conclusions. These were not limited to the laboratory, but included the family circle. Life in the Jaeger household could hardly have been a bed of roses. Trusting implicitly to the discrimination of his own sense of smell, Jaeger found human hair to be one of the choice depositories of the *personal odor-soul.* In the interests of science, he accumulated a collection of hair-nets which had been worn by women. Those were the days of braids and imposing sculptural tresses surmounting matronly heads. *Duft*-saturated hair-nets seemed providentially created for osmological experiments. The nasally alert doctor had noted that each age had its characteristic aroma. On so delicate a matter one must cite his own words: "If you smell the hair of a flapper, you will find the odor somewhat insipid and flat; or, as one of my women observers put it, the odor was like that of a 'rubber stopper'—not a bad observation."

The laboratory yielded a second great discovery. The instrument of research is the well-known Hipp chronoscope. This electric timepiece measures in hundredths-of-a-second, intervals of time as short as that elapsing between the firing of a pistol and the start of a runner. Such "reaction-times" Dr. Jaeger measured on himself. He found that his normal time was *76/100 of a second;* with this as standard, the crucial experiment begins! For one minute he sniffs at his wife's hair-net, being careful to tell us that she never uses perfume. Again he measures his own reaction-time. It has fallen to *68/100 of a second!* By so much has his soul been inspired and his nerve-impulse been quickened by the "sympathetic" odor. The same result was observed upon his son-in-law using the hair-net of

his wife; from which experiment Dr. Jaeger concluded
that the second generation of Jaegers were likewise a sympathetic couple. Thus did laboratory science validate
marital bliss!

This method of psychoösmological research was called
nerve analysis, or *neuranalysis.* With this supplementary
instrument of investigation, the soul-science of smell proceeded to novel and somewhat spicy demonstrations. He
took a hair from the head of a professional singer, a young
woman of eighteen, and placed it in water; he then diluted
this liquid to the *fifteenth homeopathic potency* and put a
few drops of this solution of the hair-*duft* into a glass of
water or beer, which in the interests of science he drank.
The effect was magical. Dr. Jaeger's voice became purer,
freer, clearer. While ordinarily he could only reach "G"
when in best form, he could now attain that note easily
and even sing one note higher. Such is the experimental
psychology underlying the Jaeger woolens!

Jaeger made a further remarkable discovery: that those
who sleep in camel's hair garments and also wear them by
day, experience a lesser need for nourishment; in some
cases this release from the need of food goes so far as
to create a desire to fast. Camel emanations were pronounced advantageous for reducing. If we recall the ab-
stemiousness of the camel, and how long the ship of the
desert can go without water, and how patient the creature
is, and consider further the constant nibbling and grazing
habits of the sheep, the reason of these effects is clear. The
principle is this:

When the duft of an organism is absorbed by eating the flesh
or by wearing the hide, hair, or feathers as clothing; or by
using the fat of the animal for cosmetic purposes; or by lingering long in the atmosphere of such animals; or by consuming the homeopathically diluted extract from the hair or

feathers; or the customary use of ashes of burnt feathers or hair; then the organism thus absorbing the duft acquires not the entire set of qualities characteristic of the animal absorbed, but its traits are more or less inclined in that direction.

We thus return by way of the laboratory to crudely superstitious, folk-minded notions. But to Herr Doktor Jaeger it was all science. He knew of an actor who suited his diet to his rôles. When about to play a tyrant, he ate pork; when about to play a lover, he ate *hammelbraten,* mutton.

This eclectic account by no means includes all of Dr. Jaeger's smell vagaries. One is too choice to omit. He "humanized" foodstuffs. Wine may be "humanized" by mixing it with a dilute tincture of hair-*duft,* preferably from the head of an attractive young woman. You then drink the humanized wine with exhilarating effect. If your ordinary alcoholic limit is three glasses, you can now drink five glasses, and still keep sober and merry.

The essence of "humanized" food was called *anthropin.* It was actually prepared and sold to the wool-clothed citizens of Stuttgart, to the still greater benefit of their health. You can also use your own *self-anthropin.* Devoted Frau Jaeger had kept a lock of her husband's hair, snipped when he was a lusty youth of twenty-seven. When, twenty-five years later, Dr. Jaeger sniffed this precious memento, thus inhaling the "strong soul" of his youth, his reaction-time was shortened! Clearly the experimental method is wonderful!

It may be well to explain the error of these minute measurements. The results, seemingly objective, are actually entirely subjective. The chronoscope is a temperamental instrument, and used as Jaeger used it, taking his own reaction-time, has a very large "error" of operation. The quicker reaction is made when you *try* to be quick and *know* what you have been inhaling. There were no control experiments, when the subject did not know whether it was the proper maiden's hair-*duft* or the exciting drug he had been sniffing—for Jaeger also tested the soul qualities of drugs by their odor. The game of finding what you expect may be played with laboratory instruments with perfect satisfaction, if the experimenter sets the conditions and keeps the score.

Dr. Jaeger insists that he is "not airing mere speculation evolved from his inner consciousness while sitting at his desk"; he is experimenting. What he forgot was that all his results were vitiated by a foregone conclusion which also devised the experiments themselves. The product was just as subjective as though he had "hallucinated" the entire book. He was throughout a subject of the kingdom of wish. Had the instruments been placed in another room and the readings been made by another observer with the subjects unaware of what was the essence which they were sniffing, there would have been no results whatever. It was all an uncontrolled and subjective procedure; exercising effort and attention would produce the insignificant differences on which large conclusions were based. Neuralysis is just a high-sounding name for an unreliable method; the notion that instruments do not lie is as false as that statistics do not. There is a manipulating mind that shapes the results.

The *duft*-soul is a universal principle. Plants share it. Dr. Jaeger proposed to revolutionize agriculture. That the soil has a *duft*-soul is proved by the use of manure. Psychoösmology demonstrated that the notion that heredity is conveyed by what was later called the germ-plasm is false. Heredity is transmitted by similar soul-stuffs; their qualities run in families. The same principle explains muscle-reading. It is not the slight involuntary movements of the subject, but the *duft* of the subject's mind, that affects the *duft*-soul of the mind-reader. The applications of the principle are many. German men like German food best, because it is cooked by women; and women enjoy French food best, because the *chefs* are men: this by virtue of the osmological law of heterosexual or cross stimulation. The food carries the soul-*duft* of sex-attraction: the source of "it" had been found. Jaeger's mission was to relieve the smell-blindness of the human race, and to reform the world accordingly.

What can we make of the case of Dr. Jaeger? The psychiatrist would call his mind paranoid, not an out-and-out paranoiac, such as form the aristocracy of the insane asylums, but of the same rationalizing inclination. He brought to what he considered a scientific problem the resources of a zoölogist, applied in paranoid fashion. He presents an extreme case of the fanatic devotion of a theorist deluded by his experiments to find what he looked for. The history of wayward thinking would have lost a precious document had Gustav Jaeger not written the *Discovery of the Soul,* of which the specialty shops were the commercial descendants. The case of Dr. Jaeger is exceptional because, apart from the first generation of ardent Jaegerites, the product of a theory survived long after the theory itself was forgotten. Gustav Jaeger's soul, whether *duft* or not, kept marching on long after his body lay moldering in the grave.

Chapter XXIV

PSYCHOMETRY: A MODERN
PHILOSOPHER'S STONE

THE SUPREME search in medieval days was for the philosopher's stone: the universal solvent. If found, it would turn baser metals into gold, yield the elixir of life, penetrate the secret of all things. The assumption of its existence was a grand wish, staged as wisdom. That was long ago. Since then philosophers have come into closer touch with science, and their quests have become more modest and more logically planned. Remotely in this tradition is a grandiose project in modern days, suggesting less a gem of philosophy than a "goldbrick." It was called *psychometry*.

Its bustling founder and promoter was Joseph Rhodes Buchanan, self-appointed "professor" in several medical schools of the eclectic variety, unlike Cæsar's wife, not above suspicion. He devoted a long, self-advertised life to strange doctrines and questionable practices with lucrative perquisites. He was the author of a *System of Anthropology, a Therapeutic Sarcognomy,* and most importantly, of a *Manual of Psychometry,* subtitled *The Dawn of a New Civilization.*

In his "investigations" he was ably assisted by his wife; in grateful acknowledgment her photograph appears as the frontispiece of the manual, with the announcement of "psychometric readings" supplied to all comers at two dollars, and "elaborate opinions" at five dollars. Psychometry was an exploiting scheme; but there may have been some measure of self-delusion. "Dr." Buchanan was a professional vagarist—and an irregular practitioner—living by his wits, and occasionally in trouble with the authorities. But he played the scientific game and placed *psychometry* on the erratic map of pseudo-science, where it remains to this day.

The idea was not new; it is possible that in his browsing among the older writers on mesmerism, Buchanan came across the very feats which started him on his career. He may have come across the word "psychometry" as applied by the Egyptians to the weighing of souls, and appropriated it as suggesting something exact and imposing. The notion of a personal influence clinging to an object, for good or ill, and carrying a reminiscence of a fate, recurs in many a myth and tradition. Be that as it may, Buchanan has the dubious honor of developing the practice of psychometrizing: reconstructing a scene or a person from an object placed upon the forehead of a "sensitive." He combined with it a portfolio of quasi-medical ideas. The "discovery" was made in 1842 in New York, and was formally announced in 1849 in Cincinnati, in Buchanan's *Journal of Man*.

The first observations were rather simple. "Persons of acute sensibility" derived a peculiar impression of taste when pieces of metal were placed in their hands; they could thus tell one metal from another. They could tell sugar, salt, pepper, or acids, getting the taste through mere contact. The "peculiar influence" passed up the arm to the head and there induced the feeling of sweetness, acidity, pungency, or whatever may be appropriate. The experiment is more successful in persons of "a nervo-sanguineous temperament," who are "of mental cultivation and refinement," with "a general predominance of the moral and intellectual organs"; which, more simply stated, means a vivid imagination. The result was more pronounced when Dr. Buchanan placed his fingers on the metal, or sugar or salt, through the "passage of nervous influence or nervaura, from my own constitution through the substance." Testimonials followed. A group of "forty-three gentlemen, members of the eclectic Medical Institute of Cincinnati," subscribe their names to the statement that when drugs wrapped in paper—contents unknown—were placed in their hands, they obtained the characteristic effect—such as burning, nausea, flushing, excitement, depression, somnolence—the drugs being capsicum, opium, lobelia, ipecac, belladonna, stramonium.

This limited field of action was greatly extended by a discovery of the same ambitious order in the same eventful year, 1842. It read that an autograph placed on the forehead of a sensitive subject would reveal the entire appearance, life history, and character traits of the writer. Psychometrizing autographs became a popular psychic indoor sport among Dr. Buchanan's followers. "Any one who can obtain interesting autographs and who has a circle of intelligent acquaintances, is fully prepared for a course of philosophical experiments." No other qualifications were required, with the exception of suggestibility and credulity. Psychometrizing by autographs produced exciting results.

A letter "written by a gentleman of strong character and ardent emotions immediately after the death of his wife," when placed in the hands of the wife of Dr. C., "though entirely skeptical as to such experiments," converted this sympathetic lady into a psychometric Niobe; she burst into tears. Mrs. G., "a lady of vigorous mind," though at first irresponsive, soon "fell into a melancholy vein and was thinking sadly of the utter worthlessness of earthly pleasures."

THE SIMPLE TECHNIQUE OF PSYCHOMETRY

The object in contact with the psychometrist arouses images revealing its origin, nature, or history.

The autographs of the popular political heroes of the day served for favorite experiments. The handwriting of General Stonewall Jackson was placed in the hands of Mr. K. "Every time I touch it, I feel more and more resolution. I feel as John Adams did when he exclaimed: 'Live or die; survive or perish.' . . . It seems from some foreign furious spirit, or from such a man as General Jackson."

At a private meeting of a neurological society in Boston, an unknown autograph was placed in the hands of the Rev. Mr. K. "who indulged habitually in glowing language." "I feel the influence of a great man. He is the glory of any age. This letter makes me feel as though I had an audience before me." Wonderful to relate, it was written by Daniel Webster!

Dr. Buchanan himself served as a subject. When a signature of Washington was applied like a plaster to his forehead, "it made a difference in my manner of lecturing the evening following the experiment. I was disposed to speak in a calm and very phlegmatic manner, quite different from my usual mode."

A scrap of blank paper, in which a letter of Carlyle's had been wrapped, induced in a psychometrist a complete analysis of Carlyle's career, including "a good wife," "not genial in his family," with "a vein of sarcasm." The date of Carlyle's death was placed too early. But one should not "expect mathematical accuracy, when there was nothing to guide the impression but the influence imparted by contact to blank paper. Such influences are not imaginary, though they elude all other senses."

When two letters, one from Charles Dickens and the other from an unknown writer were placed in the psychometrist's hand, each was given the other's character. The explanation was not that the letters got into the wrong envelopes, but that the two letters had been in contact, so that each psychometrically influenced the other.

Anticipating that Dr. Buchanan in his eclectic tolerance was also a phrenologist, it is interesting to note that the same letter of General Jackson influenced a lady of marked anti-slavery trends to feel "an intense excitement in the region of *Firmness* in her own head, and to feel as if her face, which was round and full, had become hard and elongated, her cheeks hollow, and her whole temperament changed to the energetic iron tone of General Jackson's."

Such highly charged objects as autographs should not be handled indiscriminately. "This physical sympathy occurs regularly in such experiments, whether observed or not. Hence the precautions against using the manuscript of those in bad health are often important."

"Dr." Buchanan was not on good terms with the conservative medical profession. When, by way of exception, he submitted his claims, the commission which "might easily on the first day of their appointment have ascertained beyond a doubt the truth of a discovery which revolutionizes medical theories," through their "verdant ignorance" and "Jesuitical influence" blocked the path. "The two actors in this manœuvre are now in a world in which they are made conscious of their errors." He found the same "dogmatic routine of thought and action" opposing the peculiar form of homeopathy which he advocated, whereby "the same vial of medicine may act in perpetuity," thus providing "an unlimited amount of saccharated potentiality more genial and appropriate in therapeutics than the original body." Such "spiritual saccharates," and the theory that contagious diseases were psychometrically transmitted, found greater favor among the spiritualists and occultists who embraced the new dispensation. It is related that in 1878 Madame Blavatsky gave Buchanan a letter—presumably her own—and was told that its impression was that of "a bold religious and philosophic leader."

By this route *sarcognomy* was discovered, which action arises because "the soul occupying the brain as the master occupies the mansion" leaves it "when invited by a congenial season of pleasure" and occupies "the body to the apparent neglect of the brain." "Even without this descent into the body" the telegraphic connection establishes a sufficient sympathy between the brain and the torso; the phrenological locations are repeated in the trunk where "heroism" appears in the left shoulder, "ambition" in the area of the biceps, "amiability" in the region of the right breast, with "intellect" in the sternum. These locations are determined not as in phrenology by the areas, but by sensations aroused in these parts when they are "psychometrically" stimulated by objects associated with persons possessing those qualities in marked degree. That divergence of diagnosis, however, does not interfere with the truth of Gall's ambitious system; it was merely inadequate. Dr. Buchanan discovered one hundred and sixty-six faculties instead of Gall's paltry thirty-two. Thus rapidly and wonderfully does science advance under the inspiration of a simple, but unfortunately subjective, method by which the frailties of the human mind as an instrument of thought are construed as a profound and objective revelation. Whenever the mind's disabilities are accepted as its most cherished abilities, a vagarist is in the making.

The imposition of such a theory upon credulous subjects composes the other half of the tale. It is the familiar case of suggestion; and it takes very little and rather subtle suggestion, much of it half conscious, to convey to a subject anxious to score a success what is the nature of the substance he is to taste or the qualities of the writer of the autograph he is to impersonate. In each case the success is helped along by looks and marks of approval when right, and of negation when wrong. The technique of apparent verification is familiar; any critical investigation would have exploded the theory in no time. But it was an engaging idea; through the showmanship of Dr. Buchanan, it gave the participants the pleasant feeling of taking part in "a philosophical experiment" and contributing to the greatest discovery of all times—a modern philosopher's stone.

There were other psychometrists who followed Buchanan's clue. His most important convert was William Denton, geologist, who developed an original application. In this he was ably assisted by his psychometric wife, in very truth the better half. Geology as ordinarily pursued required laborious field excursions and tedious study of formations and testing of hypotheses. All this was rendered superfluous overnight when it was found that a specimen of rock or fossil placed upon Mrs. Denton's head would at once arouse a full description of the state of the earth eons back, when the specimen was formed. All nature, Mr. Denton lucidly explains, has at one time sat for its photograph; the negative is there in the form of vibrations or emanations or influences; all one needs is to find a properly sensitized human brain that will respond to these vestiges and "take a peep backward to Devonian times." Geologizing by psychometry made science human and interesting. The geologist places on his wife's head a fossil tooth, or a bird-track in stone, or a pebble scratched by a boulder, or a bit of gold-bearing quartz. The psychometrist does the rest. "The life history of its time passed before the gaze of the sensitive like a grand panoramic view." A piece of lava from the volcano of Kilauea aroused a tropical scene; she saw flames, smoke, heard the rumbling sounds and all the disturbances of an eruption. The carboniferous period is sketched. The entire biography of a boulder is recorded. The several glacial epochs are passed in review. Chapter by chapter, the story of geology was psychically revealed. While in all the psychic explorations

Mrs. Denton's eyes looked down, when a meteoric stone was placed on her head, she instantly looked up and described the "celestial showers whence the specimens came." "When properly cultivated, what an advantage psychometry will be to the miner and to the world. Digging for metals will be as certain as the reaping of the ripened grain."

In *The Soul of Things* the geologically curious or credulous may read it. Yet strangely enough, the stubborn and conservative United States Government still maintains an expensive Geological Survey, and ignores the aid of psychometry!

It is just as easy to biologize as to geologize by this universal and agreeable form of revelation. The horn of a chamois which once roamed over the Alps evoked a mountain scene and the story of how horns were grown. A piece of whalebone placed on the head induced alarming sensations. "I feel I am a monster. My jaws are large enough to take down a house at a gulp." Even the Denton child, a boy of ten, when a piece of ivory was placed upon his head by his father, described the entire elephant and the animal's drinking through his trunk.

But the greatest freedom is afforded by archeology and history. One need only place a relic on the psychometrist's head, and listen to the story of ancient times. A brick from the baths of Caracalla, a stone from the temple of Serapis, a bit of fresco from Cicero's house, a charred fragment from Pompeii, a religious relic from an ancient cathedral, even a piece of red damask that hung over the chair of the Speaker of the House of Representatives in Washington when the city was taken by the British in 1814—all aroused correct and elaborate versions of the historical scenes in which these objects had figured.

How useless all our historical records, and how superfluous the labors of our bookworm historians! For prehistoric times may be cited the revelations of a belated psychometrist, by name of Emma Bullene, who as recently as 1905 published a *Psychic History of the Cliff Dwellers.* She hails from Denver and was both seer and recorder. By placing arrow-heads, stone axes, pottery, weavings, upon her sensitive head, she enjoyed and recorded her retroactive experiences. She watched the cliff dwellers build, attended their ceremonies, conversed with the men and women of the tribes. She heard from them the accounts of their migrations, their relations to the Norse invaders of America, to the Aztecs and Toltecs, and to the modern descendants of the Pueblo. This beautiful story of a forgotten people she modestly dedicated to "the progressive thought of the nineteenth century.". . . "This science will forever banish dead history from the human mind."

Dr. Buchanan lived to be an old man. He republished in 1885 the discoveries he had first announced in 1842. By that time the scheme of psychometry had grown and his extravagance of statement with it. He was convinced, like many a propagandist, that there was a conspiracy against the recognition of his exalted claims. He was ever adding to its applications. "The psychometric talent of Mrs. Hayden was very successfully employed by the president of the Globe Life Insurance Company, in protecting the company against losses in insurance of lives, until forbidden by the bigoted stupidity of the Board, a fact which contributed largely to the ultimate wreck of the company." The practice of law will be revised. A psychometrist can detect the guilt or innocence of a criminal, and by his own impressions restore the scene of the crime. Detectives and witnesses are unnecessary. Mrs. Buchanan constantly psychometrized criminals on trial; the verdicts proved her correct. "Yet I have never indulged in the sensationalism of publishing such opinions." Politics will be similarly

benefited when public men are psychometrized; by that
means Cleveland was indicated as the proper man for
President. But the great domain of universal knowledge is
last as first the proper study of psychometrical mankind.
"The past is entombed in the present"; the psychometrist
is the psychic excavator.

The philosopher's stone had indeed been found; it was
not psychometry, but the self-deceiving imagination. It
requires little imagination of a sober kind to realize that
Mrs. Denton by constant association with her husband had
obtained enough knowledge of geology, however scrappy
and amateurish, to put together a fair story on a slender
hint. It is always stated that she did not know or could
not guess the nature of the specimen which she was asked
to psychometrize; one may have grave doubts. And when
in doubt or when she went wrong, Mr. Denton supplied a
series of leading questions called "conversations." As in
the game of "Twenty Questions," in which the guesser
is informed whether he is "warm" or "cold", a hint to the
shrewd is sufficient. Had Mr. Denton, presumably sincere
and disinterested, entrusted the experiments to some one
else, *The Soul of Things* might have remained unwritten
and geologizing remained an orthodox pursuit.

To its discoverer psychometry was far more than an
instrument; it was a universal solvent, heralded—in manner
suggestive of his contemporary, P. T. Barnum—in *The
Dawn of a New Civilization*.

As a science and philosophy, Psychometry shows the nature,
the scope, and the *modus operandi* of those divine powers in
man, and the anatomical mechanism through which they are
manifested; while as an art it shows the method of utilizing
these psychic faculties in the investigation of character, disease, physiology, biography, history, paleontology, philosophy,
anthropology, medicine, geology, astronomy, theology, and
supernal life and destiny. Granting, as this volume will show,
that Psychometry gives us the command of all these sciences,

it is apparent that the introduction of Psychometry must prove the dawn of a new era in science, philosophy, and social progress, more important as to human enlightenment and elevation than all the arts and sciences heretofore known to the skilful and learned; for if all libraries, manufactories, and repositories of the arts in the world at present were suddenly destroyed by fire, leaving only in human minds a full knowledge of Psychometry, all might be restored in one generation and far nobler institutions of learning, of practical arts, of social order, and of religion would arise from the ashes, purified and relieved from a vast amount of falsehood—an inheritance from ancient ignorance.

Rooted vaguely in the conviction of immortality, that the dead live, and the past continues, the cherished belief is now and again removed from the realm of faith by some pseudo-scientific mind, and clothed in the garb of learning. When the evidence of experiment is sought, the procedure is so loosely conducted that the mislead of suggestion is added to the prepossession of wish. When to these favoring factors of delusion is added the possibility of exploitation and a profitable cult, psychometry—like many another psychic folly, which may become a racket—rises and falls but to rise again in other form, so long as vagarists find followers and fakirs dupes to accept disguised wish as precious wisdom and dross as gold.

Chapter XXV

ECCENTRIC THEOREMS: A CLINIC
OF IRRATIONALITY

THE THESIS of *Wish and Wisdom* extends the proper study of mankind to the improprieties in the use of his intelligence—to man rational and irrational alike. A psychologist interested in the erratic mind might readily, in any large assembly, conduct a clinic of eccentric beliefs. A census of eccentricity among the thinking population would doubtless reveal a great variety of occupations as well as sorts and conditions of men. My survey is dependent upon the members of the guild who take to print. Their outstanding trait is their gravitation toward ambitious schemes. A ready confidence and an active imagination serve to disguise their meager equipment. With no secure experience on earth, they hitch their home-made wagons to uncharted stars. They propose novel solutions of problems of large magnitude: the nature of the cosmos and man's place in it; the fundamentals of matter; the structures of life; the origins of races; the scope of mind. These eclectic cosmologists and physicists and biologists and anthropologists and psychologists form a bizarre procession; yet they have their place, along with other thinkers, in the total story of cerebration, if for no other reason than to illustrate how the mind can abuse the prerogative of thought.

"Eccentric" is a bare word to indicate the texture of such minds and the startling quality of the beliefs they cogitate and embrace. It suggests only an irregular orbit of thought and a departure from accredited opinions. The eccentric mind represents a distinctive *genre;* it disdains ordinary knowledge, or recognizes it only to replace it by the newly emblazoned truth. Proving others wrong adds to the glamour of being right—discovering what the great ones failed to find. In procedure, the eccentric mind takes to wings, sighting the conclusion from afar. Soaring with the imagination is swifter and more thrilling than tramping with a heavy pack of facts. One type of eccentric starts with the assurance that inspiration, revelation, a sudden captivation by a conclusion, yields a gospel of discovery far more authentic than the grubby texts of science. Others go through a preliminary marshaling of facts which are not so, or are contorted out of semblance to their real nature. Each is a self-anointed prophet of a new truth.

I begin with cosmologists, and they begin with the world and the theories of its creation. There are so many of them that I must treat them curtly. An old-time flavor attaches to Burnet's *Sacred Theory of the Earth* (1726). Burnet informs us, incidentally, that the Flood occurred just 3,983 years before he was born.

Previous to the flood the earth was a paradise, without any inequality of seasons; its surface was very different in Form and Fabric from the present Earth; there was no Sea then, no Mountains, nor Rocks, nor broken Caves; 'twas all one continued and regular mass, smooth, simple and compleat, as the first Works of Nature used to be. . . .

The Heat of the Sun also weakens more and more the Arch of the Earth, sucking out the Moisture that was the Cement of its parts, chapping it in sundry Places. And at length, when the appointed time was come, that All-Wise Providence had design'd for the Punishment of a sinful World, the whole Fabrick brake, and the Frame of the Earth was torn in Pieces, as by an Earthquake . . . and the Parts that stood above the

Waters are the Mountains and Precipices that we see and admire today.

With the same assurance of a certified vision, one Hampden declares the earth to be a motionless plane with the North Pole as the center; one Carpenter gives a hundred remarkable reasons why the earth is not round, with a challenge to the scientists of America to disprove them; one Symmes regards the earth as hollow and habitable within, with openings at the poles, which he offers to explore for the consideration of the "patronage of this and the new worlds"; while Symmes Jr. explains how the interior is lighted and that it probably forms the home of the lost tribes of Israel; and one Teed announces, on equally conclusive evidence, that the earth is a "stationary concave cell . . . with people, sun, moon, planets, and stars on the inside," the whole constituting an "alchemico-organic structure, a gigantic Electro-Magnetic Battery."

Complete and authentic is the pronouncement of George Woodward Warder, author of the *Cities of the Sun,* who in due time expects to communicate with them, as by the "natural law of economy of space and power," there are "no dead worlds, no dead atoms in nature."

I claim that man is the product of planetary forces and the planets are the hatcheries of human souls, and the suns the places of their growth to perfection. Soul, an atom of Deity, by means of electric energy, controls its mortal body. I contend that sun rays, while not hot, furnish the electric power and the Earth heats itself. . . . Rays are wireless electricity from the sun's photosphere or corona, which is converted into electric light, heat, and all vital force. This vital force is generated in the dense atmosphere near the surface, since electric rays come from the photosphere, shot by the laws of electric repulsion from the sun and drawn by electric attraction to the earth, where coming in contact with the earth's opposite electric polarity and the resistance of its atmosphere, these electric sun-currents burst into new found light. . . .

After looking the whole Universe over most carefully, I have fixed upon the sun as the most rational place for the personal headquarters and abode of God.

I could go on indefinitely. There is an erratic cosmology of a comet, which reads thus:

A comet has by nature an assertive, pregenital, generating power of its own, and thus sprang into existence in spite of and without God's assistance; it possesses a self-concentrated, vital energy, capable of defying even God in its effort to be born. Thus there are two all-powerful powers behind the great system of the Universe; the Dictator and his Electric Dynamo, God and His Comet.

There is a cosmologist who has discovered the primary force of the universe which he calls "galom," and offers a prize of a thousand dollars for any one who will refute "galomatism"; he published a *Nirvanology,* which contains the science of extinction; he has discovered the location of the spirit world in the Tail of the Earth; he has written on the errors of Sir Isaac Newton, on Ghostology and has discovered that the law of inverse proportionality rules the world.

Of the weird wisdom of such cosmologists there is no end; its beginning is in the cerebration, somewhat askew, of an eccentric mind.

In the adjoining alcove are to be found the cosmic physicists. In this galaxy belong the Smith brothers—not those of cough-drop fame, but twins by birth and profession: the Reverends John H. and William W. Smith, authors of *The Magnetic Astronomy of the Bible,* who jointly and twinly made two momentous discoveries—"the two unknown silent forces": the *source of the magnetic power* which afforded the *key to the tides.* They were travelers as well as thinkers, and made endless observations conscientiously while at sea on a voyage to Brazil, announcing the results to church conventions upon their return.

Electricity is the outer manifestation of magnetism. The mechanisms of the spheres are such that by heat, moisture, motion, and friction, they produce an electromagnetic power that brings to us the tides, the magnetic currents, and the earth's electricity. When that is at the maximum, the tides are large.

The basic discovery is the force of *repulsion*. Over the signature of William appears this modest biographical parallel:

First: Newton discovered the Attractive force;
           Smith discovered the Repulsive force.
Second: Newton discovered the Centripetal force;
           Smith discovered the Centrifugal force.
Third: Newton discovered the Negative force;
           Smith discovered the Positive force.

By these coincident forces, we can explain the Newtonian Theory of Attraction, but by no other hypothesis. These three links complete the positive magnetic chain, as we adopt the Positive Magnetic force, which is the ultimate force in Celestial Mechanics.

In further appreciation of their momentous discoveries, the Smith brothers graciously conclude: "And now in the centennial year of the landing of Columbus, and the year of the World Fair in Chicago, and in honor of that landing, we dedicate this work to the Columbian Exhibition of 1893."

It might be supposed that since the data of anatomy and physiology are as plain as the nose on your face, they would be immune to the operations of the fantasying mind; but such is not the case. The hidden processes within the body likewise provide grist for the eccentric's mill. *Physiology by analogy* replaces physiology by observation, and composes a fantasia of our mysterious insides. A choice volume bears the innocuous title: *The Human Body and its Connection with Man.* Its author is James

John Garth Wilkinson, of the Royal College of Surgeons, London, and its date, 1851. It is dedicated to his friend Henry James, Sr. Of the "cerebral globe" and its folds and convolutions, Wilkinson thus discourses:

The mind's revealings are here represented in moving spirals; and the subtle insinuations of thought, whose path lies through all things, issues with power from the form of the cerebral screws. They print their shape and make themselves room in the hard inside of the skull, and are the most irresistible agents in the human world.

While the doctrine of animal spirits was decidely out of date when Wilkinson wrote, he clung to it as picturesque, but fused it with the emphasis on fluids, "the highest animal juices, being the cream of the body," which, were it not so fantastic, might approach our very different notions of glandular secretions.

The existence of an animal spirit has great historical probability attached to it. . . . The triumphs of this age are peculiarly due to the introduction of the mind to the empire of the fluids. The steam engine and its nervous system, steam; the railway and its locomotive fluids, the train; the wire and its electric spirit, show the practical benefits of the subordination of the solid to the fluid. And in human progress, what are quickness, conception, and imagination but the fluids of the mind? . . . Indeed, I see not that there is any known sphere of things whose analogies do not cry aloud for the existence of a fluid brain governing the solid, and like it, organized, though on a more living plan. . . . Thus must a nerve-spirit be admitted; for not otherwise can the science of the brain be in fraternity with the other arts and sciences.

The rhapsody of circulation and respiration reads thus: "The body conspiring with the mind through the friendly intervention of the lungs"; yet sharing that exalted function with the heart, which "we aver, takes the central and most living blood; this it does by the love laws and justice of physics."

The heart shows all signs of loving the blood which is the fearful and recognized symbol and casket of human life, for it grasps at the blood eighty times every minute; with quadrumanous hands it clutches the passing life-stream.

The arterial lungs are the puberty of the blood, coming from the dreams or the imaginations, with whose hints and inventions the air is full. The left auricle is the marriage bed where the tension of the bursting life is continually taken down and renewed continually. Accordingly, this auricle or bed is the most hidden of the chambers, decently curtained away from the rest, and least to be felt from the outside.

There is a further "distinction between the private or venous and the public or arterial side of the heart. Hence the public chambers or left side of the heart retire from view to transact the private business of the feelings."

There are four hundred original pages, with ever unexpected quirks and turns where the corresponding chapters in the ordinary texts in physiology are monotonously similar. Analogizing, dramatizing, and moralizing, the eccentric mind proceeds, undaunted by the silence of the laboratory, upon such picturesque relations.

Eccentric "Psychology" is in some respects the maddest guest at the eccentrics' tea-party, which by comparison makes Alice's incoherent assembly look like a convention of rationalists. The eccentric psychologist posits a second self and "second sight" to reach it: a double, astral or phantom. To such a psychist "the physical world is the world of illusion; the non-physical is the world of realities"; his exalted study "brings no contact of the soul with vulgar matter."

Fairly unstable substance he seems inclined to recognize, for he records that "the body of the jelly fish is almost pure astral matter," and even ghosts seem to make terms with the chemical elements. "A genuine phantom can be established and preserved by the precipitation of fine forms of carbon on the image laid down in the brain." "Matter has its spirit and spirit its matter. Each is as axiomatic as the other." "There is not a phantom extant which has not its double in tangible things. When the body decays the wraith disintegrates; when the tree falls, its shadow falls with it. Yet we have adequate evidence that this is not the case with humanity, or at least when persons of fame and distinction are concerned."

A prominent phantomologist was Dr. Adolphe D'Assier, author of *Posthumous Humanity* (1887). He is careful to explain that so far from being a spiritist he is a positivist, dealing in molecules and gases and fluids.

Shorn of all supernatural explanation, the post-mortuary personality appears in its real aspect; and one can trace the origin of phantoms, their physical and moral state, and the destiny reserved for them....

The lethargic sleep is the first necessary condition for producing the Double, which is borrowed from the most tenuous molecules of the human body. In passing through walls, the phantom causes the molecules to pass singly, which becomes very easy, thanks to the elastic nature of the gaseous elements which constitute it. By the law of organic compensation, the phantom is developed at the expense of the body.

Thus is confirmed the existence of a plexus of fluidiform capillaries connecting the phantom with the body from which it emanates. An invisible vascular plexus snaps, and the phantom goes; but throughout life he is always with us as an internal replica.

Ghosts testify to "profound sadness and a feeling of impotence and eternal isolation." They shun the light of day because

the light vibrations of an almost infinite rapidity to which they are exposed would soon alter the fluidic tissues of the phantom by dispersing the molecules of it, did it not retire by day into the tomb or other obscure retreat.

But phantoms are mortal; ghosts can be laid.

The molecules of the phantom's tissues disintegrating from each other, there comes a day when it has no further consciousness of itself. In slow agony, it becomes weak. Tumultuous at first, it grows less and less so, as the shade suffers from cosmic agents, until definite annihilation occurs.

But while young and lusty, ghosts produce mechanical effects as great as if they were of large bulk, as their noisy habits testify. In lieu of stones, ghosts throw their duplicates which have the same effect and obey a rigid formula: its life force at the moment of fall is equal to half its bulk multiplied by the square of its velocity.

It is only through the vicarious sacrifice of our ghostly ancestors that we are able to live.

The accumulation of specters of the different tribes of the terrestrial fauna, heaped at the surface of the globe since the first geological epochs, would render the air irrespirable. We could not move in a dense atmosphere of ghosts.

As a fitting finale, I have reserved the contribution of the Baron Ludwig de Guldenstubbé, author of *Pneumatologie Positive et Experimentale* (Paris, 1857). Entering eagerly into the spiritualist revival of 1849, the Baron wished to secure "the most irrefragable and brutally convincing proof of spirit identity," and without the use of a medium. Placing paper and pencil in a locked box, he waited patiently for results; and at last, on August 13, 1856, was rewarded with a scrawl. Finding both the pencil and the box unnecessary, he simplified his technique by placing slips on statues in the sculpture-halls of the Louvre, on the royal tombs at St. Denis and in the cemeteries of Paris. Apparently the spirits, sensing immortality, took the bait. When collected, there were *écritures directes de l'outre tombe*—direct signatures from beyond the grave. His friends—barons, generals, doctors, aristocrats, and literati—vouched for their genuineness. He received long intimate letters from the beyond, as well as autographs and cipher scrawls. They range from Egyptian hieroglyphs to the graphic relics of Plato, Euripides, Isocrates, Cicero, Virgil, Caesar, Juvenal, St. Paul, Abelard, Héloïse, St. Genevieve, the Kings of France to Louis XVIII, and the Queens to Marie Antoinette. There are such circumstantial documents as letters in German from his own parents; and such esoteric ones as writings endowed with magical power, for when placed on the chest of a patient, the document cured his bronchitis.

By what manner of self-deception the Baron obtained these documents, I cannot guess; he gives too slight a clue. His orthodox faith appears in the citation on the title-page of the direct writing on two tablets given to Moses by God. This is his precedent; if the Deity, why not the spirits of the Great Beyond, and why not their sculptured counterparts? And if in olden days, why not now? That the signatures emanate somehow from the Baron's conscious or subconscious cerebration is indicated by the telling circumstance that the first message was in Esthonian, apparently his native language. At all events, the Baron's extraordinary experiments have not been repeated. There was no general vogue of leaving slips on statues and tombs; or if there was, the *billets* remained as silent as the Sphinx. Like that enigmatic lady, de Guldenstubbé carried the secret to *l'outre tombe*. Perhaps a slip placed on his grave would solve the mystery.

The diagnosis of this diversified clinical material is suggested by the temper of the beliefs and the arguments used in their support. The several patients present common as well as individual symptoms; they belong to one psychopathic genus. This order of mental product received a baptism when David Starr Jordan dubbed it *The Higher Foolishness,* borrowing the phrase from Zangwill; he also

SIGNATURES FROM BEYOND THE GRAVE

Paul the Apostle of Jesus Christ ("Paulos Apostolos Iesou Christou"), Plato ("Platon"), Octavianus Augustus, Mar[cus] T[ullius] Cicero, P[etrus] Abælardus, Maria Antoinette. After Baron Ludwig de Guldenstubbé.

called it *Sciosophy,* the science of ignorance, citing the precious words of Giordano Bruno, martyr to science in 1600: *Ignorance is the most delightful science in the world, because it is acquired without pain and keeps the mind from melancholy.*

The same dominant wish-habit of the eccentric mind Professor Morton Wheeler calls "hallucinating." The devotees of the higher foolishness do not quite fabricate out of whole cloth or hallucinate out of thin air. They have a loose acquaintance with an ill-assorted body of facts, feebly understood. They rationalize after the manner of their kind; they observe; they even experiment, but always with the same complete prepossession that deprives the arguments of even the semblance of logic. The result is a grotesquerie of deluded prepossession, a weakly rationalized, mainly self-hallucinated projection of fancy presented as facts, of wish proffered as wisdom.

What is impressive is the prolific abundance of extreme "thobbing," "higher foolishness," and scheme-making, thesis-proving "hallucinating." An intensive morning spent among the alcoves of eccentricity, taking down one volume after another, leaves one with the dismal reflection that the total shelf-miles containing the records of error, folly, eccentricity, and irrationality might compare in mass with the total of sane, worthy, and progressive contributions. Undisciplined cerebration and the invention of printing, the urge to solve and the *cacoethes scribendi,* have much to answer for in the output of the amazing creature self-righteously dubbed *homo sapiens.*

Admittedly my examples are extreme. They are conspicuous instances of how the mind goes wrong, of what happens when thinking becomes toxic or gets out of hand. As for motive, we may accept the psychoanalytic diagnosis. Eccentrics follow the Freudian urge to pleasure in dream thinking as opposed to reality thinking, which latter is a stern and arduous occupation. Eccentricity is a flight and an escape; it may be a compensatory device, a defense-mechanism, offsetting the capacity to think rigidly by an indulgence in imaginative discovery. Proceeding further in the same direction, the diagnosis overlaps the authentic cases of delusion that dwell in asylums beyond the ivory gate. A touch of irrationality makes the world akin.

PART VII

RATIONALIZATION

FLAUNTING REASON'S BANNER

Irrationally held truths may be more harmful than reasoned errors.—T. H. HUXLEY.

Men feel the need of reasoning and show it by throwing a veil over their instincts and emotions.—PARETO.

Words are of course the most potent drugs used by mankind. —KIPLING.

ARGUMENT

RATIONALIZATION *is assigning good reasons for poor conduct or for weak thinking. In argument it is a defense of a dubious conviction by claiming for it a scientific support; less formally, it is "finding arguments for going on believing as we already do." When the fox found the grapes out of his reach sour, he was rationalizing at a simple human level. Self-excuse leads to the disguising of motives by throwing over them the cloak of virtue or reason. Defensive rationalizing makes partial hypocrites of all but the worthiest of us, who still cherish or pretend to what the elect attain.*

The pursuit of truth is affected by the personal equation of one's commitments. In matters of belief, rationalization is a serpent of even more subtle mien and persuasive tongue than in excusing conduct. Arguments and adherents are of a nature all compact. Turning to the annals of science for illustrations most pertinent to Wish *and* Wisdom, *we find varieties of thobbing—one might almost write throbbing—of a reasoning mind cherishing the prestige of science and following the pattern of experiment, yet by subconscious intrusion disclosing an unacknowledged loyalty to a differently tempered persuasion.*

The plot is ever the same; the story is all in the execution. It may have a laboratory setting, with physical and chemical apparatus as stage properties; but the source either of the findings or conclusions or both is in the mind of the experimenter. The first instance in the selected group is the foremost. It comes from a chapter of physics and chemistry, fairly recent but largely forgotten. The story of "Od" fills almost providentially in every detail the requirements for demonstrating the rationalizing ways of wishful wisdom on science bent. A chemist of standing—with practical achievements to his credit, forms the legitimate hypothesis that he has discovered a new force; but he turns for proof to the subjective impressions of "sensitives"—persons reputed to possess senses denied to the rest of us. He names it Od; he determines its properties minutely, but at every stage by reliance upon the verdicts of suggestible neurotics. It is a strange picture: a scientist observing a strict protocol, charting his observations as though he were taking readings on a spectroscope or a galvanometer, and actually holding the hand of a Fräulein patient who reports degrees of warmth or moisture, by which the chemical elements are classified in new orders! Years are devoted to the observations, and there emerges an odized world.

By comparison, the N-ray is but a minor incidental lapse in mistaking a subjective impression for an objective discovery. It is noteworthy in that it occurred in the alert refinement of a modern laboratory, whose watchword is caution. It contributes a telling lesson to show that even the wisest may be deceived.

A sharply contrasted atmosphere of belief is that which gives vogue to theories of auras and vibrations. In this extravagant thought-venture, experiments of a kind abound; but the experimenting mind is full of vain imaginings and fanciful notions. It creates a new world, reached by way of a grotesque parody of scientific method.

The concluding example illustrates both types of rationalizing procedure. The theory is remote and derives from folk-belief, and is further associated with the discredited ways of miracle-mongers; but it is presented with all the prestige of the laboratory and of such diverse techniques as those of biology and engineering. The lure of transcendence and the ambition to discover new worlds combine—the same attraction that has led many an eccentric mind to erratic extravagance of belief. Ectoplasm is unique by reason of its associations and by its ambitious claim of revising the entire decalogue of science. From sour grapes to the reshaping of the cosmos, the story of rationalization runs.

Chapter XXVI

FROM "OD" TO N-RAYS

THE STORY OF "OD"

REPEATEDLY in the chronicles of *Wish and Wisdom* appears the double source of human error: the folklore stream of popular acceptance and the contributions of learned or would-be learned minds. Both rationalize; both seek to justify belief by fact and principle, and are alike inventive and deluded in the process. There are idols of the laboratory as well as of the market-place. The doctrinal mind is more adept in rationalization than the folk-mind. Each rationalizes according to his lights. The tale of *Od* concerns a flight into theory resulting in an assemblage of strange experiments, leading to stranger assumptions. It is a flagrant example of an imposing structure built on subjective sand, proclaimed to be objective rock. The fanatically rationalizing mind insists that its cherished "discovery" *must* be so, and proceeds by travestied methods of science to find it so.

Die Odische Lohe—odic force, stream, emanation,—is an almost forgotten episode, even among students of chemistry and physics, where it originated; they seem content to bequeath the story to the psychologist. The champion of *Od* was Baron Karl von Reichenbach, chemist, metallurgist, industrialist, a man of distinction, member of the Prussian Academy of Sciences, professor extraordinarius, discoverer of a series of paraffines. His *Researches*

(1845) appeared in a special volume of an authoritative journal: *Annalen der Chemie und Physik*. In it was announced the discovery of a totally new, hitherto unknown physical force. The methods of demonstration were even more remarkable than the conclusions. The entire evidence rested upon the reports of peculiarly constituted human "sensitives." They alone could see or feel the "effects of the new force, which could not otherwise be registered."

For twenty years and more, *Od* was a battle-ground. Reichenbach directed his armentarium of facts against the conservative professors, who scoffed at his results. In 1862 he at last obtained a hearing in Berlin; and this is what he presented to a Committee of seven experts: A bit of iron, hidden under the loose folds of a tablecloth, was located by the "sensitive" by the feel of the "outflowing current"; a ball of wool held for some minutes in the Baron's "negative" right hand was distinguished from a ball of wool that had been held in his "positive" left hand; a glass of "negative" water was distinguished by its pleasant taste from the unpleasant taste of "positive" water; a roll of paper—an odically neutral substance—when projected through a screen was correctly pronounced "positive" or "negative" according to its charge. Needless to say, the Baron assured the Committee that the subjects did not know in which hand the substance had been held, or whether and how it had been "odized." The examiners were not impressed.

The Baron found the atmosphere of Berlin *ungemütlich*. He bemoans the fact that whereas in his own congenial Vienna he had no difficulty in finding sensitives everywhere—among the gentry and military ranks, in medical and academic circles, among laborers and the humbler occupations—he found hardly any in the odic desert of Berlin. He attributed the failure to the climate. Indeed when Professor Dove, the physicist, brought his own magnets to the tests, in which the current was reversible and under control, the few sensitives Baron von Reichenbach was able to find failed completely to tell *positive* from *negative,* or whether the current was on or off. Reichenbach explained that the "magnetic" current reacted upon the "odic" current, to the confusion of the demonstrators.

Over their seven signatures, the Committee resolved "that the demonstrations of Baron von Reichenbach have in no wise established what they were intended to show, and give no proof of a new natural force." The Baron was in no wise daunted. He dedicated his next volume, a stinging rejoinder, to the seven wise men of Berlin—*den Gelehrten Berline Sieben.*

How the Baron reached his conviction that there was *Od* is not related—a characteristic omission. It is as though he said: Let there be *Od,* and there was *Od—Od* everywhere, as will appear. His starting point seems to have been the Aurora Borealis, in some respects an electrical phenomenon. This suggested that human subjects might be able to see in the dark similar effulgent, streaming, luminous, colored radiations. Doubtless he explained to his sensitives what was expected, and they met his expectations, to his delighted surprise.

Like many of his predecessors in ambitious speculation, the Baron had recourse to the magnet, with its opposite poles exemplifying a mystic attraction and repulsion. He soon found that non-magnetic substances produced effects likewise opposite in character, and best of all *crystals.* Presented with one axis toward the subject, the crystal felt *cool;* with the direction reversed, the sensitives perceived a *lukewarm and unpleasant* sensation. So the result was referred not to ordinary magnetism, but to some yet undiscovered force, which was also somehow inherent in magnets.

By this method, a rich mine of research was opened; "Psychic" chemistry was beautifully simple, swift, and conclusive. One after another of the chemical elements and compounds was presented to the sensitives, and their feelings recorded. A table of odically positive, odically

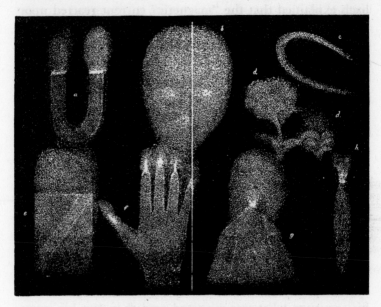

EMANATIONS OF OD

As seen and described by Reichenbach's sensitives.

negative, and odically neutral substances was prepared in short order. Thus lead, zinc, ivory, dolomite, sugar, were *inert,* while the diamond, mica, garnet, feldspar, topaz, were odically *active.* The evidence for these revolutionary results was no more than the feelings of the sensitives of warmth, of an agreeable radiation, of tingling, and the glimmer of faint streams of colored lights in the dark.

And the subjects? For the most part, they were neurotic young women. Miss R., aged 29, as a child fell out of a window and since then had nervous attacks accompanied

by somnambulism, her condition "passing into lunacy."
Miss N., aged 33, was subject to attacks of catalepsy, in
which condition she possessed the highest degree of sensitiveness, seeing a larger flame over the negative pole of a
magnet and a smaller one over the positive—this in the
latitude of Vienna. Miss L., subject to hysterical attacks,
observed the same odic cool sensation while gazing at the
firmament. Another neurotic contributed the discovery
that a glass of water subject to *Od* had a flat taste. In fact,
lunatics (in this instance a vague term for neurotics) and
those subject to somnambulism (a telltale symptom of
hysteria) "are uniformly sensitive." Such was substantially
the entire evidence. Later, when *Od* became the vogue,
subjects were readily found among normal persons. At no
time was there objective evidence, the claim being that
no instrument was sensitive enough to register the odic
force.

The extensions of the odic doctrine constitute the most
remarkable chapters in Reichenbach's "researches." *Od*
explained what was previously obscure or discredited. It
explained Mesmer's "animal magnetism." Mesmer found
that his equally hysterical subjects could be thrown into a
crisis by drinking the water over which he had made
"magnetic" passes. This was really *Od*. It explained the
divining-rod. It was odic force that tipped the rod in the
hands of sensitives. One of Reichenbach's subjects felt
the peculiar odic effect at a certain spot in her kitchen,
which proved to be just over the watermain.

Od explained ghosts. On a dark night, the Baron took
his sensitive to a cemetery, commending her courage in
undertaking the eerie venture in the interest of science.
There she saw the luminous odic light moving mysteriously from grave to grave. Indeed, on one highly odic
grave she stood enveloped in a flame four feet high.

"Most ghost stories will now find their natural explanation."

Od particularly explained phenomena in "terrestrial
magnetism"; for the odic force shifts with the points of the
compass. A certain Herr Schuh had the habit of awaking
after a few hours of sleep, and could not fall asleep again
until he reversed his position, placing his pillow where
his feet had been. Reichenbach cured the insomnia by
directing Herr Schuh to sleep with his head to the south
and his feet to the north. He found another subject who
slept comfortably only when he placed his body in the
magnetic meridian.

The doctrine of *Od* maintains that we and all our organs
are polarized transversely; digestion as well as brain action
is affected by one's position, which in turn varies with the
location on the planet. In the southern hemisphere people
will prefer to sleep on the left side—not as in northern
latitudes, on the right side—because "the north surface of
the earth is odically positive." Our occupations are
affected by *Od*. A musician felt uncomfortable while playing the piano in Reichenbach's drawing-room; when the
instrument was rightly oriented, she performed brilliantly
and with great satisfaction. And even our devotions! The
common fatigue and restlessness, which may reach the
point of fainting, that occurs in churches is not the result
of long tedious sermons, but is due to the placing of the
altar at the east end, thus exposing the backs of the wor-
shipers to the west—an odically unfavorable position.

The Baron obeyed loyally the laboratory code as he
interpreted it. Dealing with a physical force, he must
observe the conditions of scientific experiment; this precaution he combined with complete abandon to the subjective impressions of his sensitives. Choosing a bright
sunlit day, he placed one end of a long copper wire in the
hands of an invalid reclining on a couch; he projected

the other end through the window into the sunlight. As the distant end touched a copper plate, the sensitive emitted a cry of pleasure. Thus was proved the presence of *Od* in sunlight; but it seemed to be even stronger in moonlight. Another sensitive, while gazing at the Milky Way, had an odic sense of coolness, while Saturn, Jupiter, and Venus seemed to her warm. "This agrees beautifully with the former results in the case of the sun and the moon." There are even plottings of the firmament with variations in odic reaction of the regions at different times of day and night. At 9 P.M. the N. and N.W. were cooler; at 4 A.M. the N. and N.E. segments of the skies.

While experimenting, the Baron maintained a strict regimen of rest and diet and refrained from touching metals all day. Then at evening he held the hand of his sensitive while she reported hour by hour the variations of odic force transmitted through the Baron's hand; all of which is charted in curves, as professionally as the record of an experiment in thermodynamics. There was "positive" energy in the Baron's left hand and "negative" energy in his right; moreover, to the sensitive, the Baron's head felt cool on the right hemisphere and warm on the left. The curves indicate how it is that in response to odic variation, we come to rest at night and eat and work by day.

Idiosyncrasies and aversions are not accidental; they are all determined by *Od*. Some persons have a strong aversion to yellow and are fond of blue; in fact on moving a rod over the spectrum, one subject found the rod over *blue* exhilarating, but over *orange* nauseating; some cannot bear the touch of "German silver" in knives and forks but delight in pure silver. Some cannot bear to have a person standing in back of them, and there are parents who feel ill at ease in giving their children a "piggy-back" ride. The custom of seating our partners to the right is in

conformity with odic directions; some persons have a passion for salad, and others a disinclination for sugar; some
—even comely girls—feel uneasy in looking at their reflection in a mirror. All of which effects, by devious routes of
argument, are attributed to the action of *Od* upon sensitives who are even more delicately responsive than the
leaves of the mimosa plant.

Od is physical and chemical and biological and cosmic;
there is *magnetod* and *crystalod, thermod* and *photod,* and
biod—indeed *pantod. Od* completes the universe of forces.
But most remarkably, the sensitive replaces the test-tube:
"Is it not surprising in the highest degree that a simple
unschooled girl by the mere feeling of her fingers alone is
able in one hour to classify all the elements of nature into
a series, the constitution of which has cost the most learned
scientists more than half a century of tireless industry and
utmost expenditure of mental acumen!" It certainly is!
But more surprising that a scientifically trained mind
should be willing on the basis of this most elusive of all
testimony to reconstruct the universe. Hysteria and scientific research, suggestion and tabulated observations, are
as incompatible as oil and water; *Od* is an emulsion of
wish and wisdom. The true *Od—psychod—*Reichenbach
failed to find, or ignored.

The diagnosis of the "case" of *Od* turns upon three data:
first and dominant is the conviction that there is an undiscovered force; second is the rationalized search for it, its
properties to be determined by physical and chemical
research; third is the reliance upon peculiarly constituted
sensitives to demonstrate it. The first is pure assumption;
the second is the approved procedure, *if* rightly carried
out; the third is a fateful error. There the shoemaker
left his last. The legitimate researches in chemistry and
mineralogy which gave Reichenbach his standing could
be repeated by other qualified experts in their laboratories.

The methods by which *Od* was established belong to a wholly different realm. The physicist blundering blindly into the psychologist's territory courted disaster. The story of *Od* is too valuable to be forgotten. As an Odyssey—the pun is venial—of suggestion, it has an enduring value. It illustrates as does no other modern episode the extent to which a rationalizing mind under a prepossession may go in building a monumental research upon the fallibility of the human senses.

The instance is so extreme that it raises the question whether a sane mind could be guilty of such a comprehensive confusion. The plausible diagnosis is that *Od* began as a legitimate speculation of a normal mind, and became the fixed idea of a mind that gradually lost its balance, with senile involution in the final stages. By that circumstance it loses none of its pertinence as a tragedy in rationalization.

THE ERROR OF N-RAYS

History repeats itself with a difference, yet conforms to the French saying: the more it changes, the more it remains the same. Fifty years later, a parallel to the episode of *Od* recurs in that of the N-rays. The half-century between was rich in discoveries, and established the supremacy of the laboratory. The same simple ignoring of the psychology of suggestion applies to *Od* and N-rays. But the N-ray remains strictly within the stage of the laboratory and the refinement of its methods. There are no neurotic sensitives, no fantastic—though there are unwarranted—flights into theory; there are only misled scientists, with human, all too human, failings. And there is among the experts a critical caution in acceptance. The N-ray error turns upon a slight lapse in observation, but assumes the dimensions of a fictitious chapter in physics.

In 1902 M. Blondlot, a physicist of distinction, then

and later the recipient of important prizes in physics, announced a new ray, called N-ray in honor of its place of discovery, Nancy, strangely enough the home of suggestion, of Liebault, pioneer of hypnotic theory, and of Coué of more recent fame. In 1896 Roentgen startled the world by the discovery of the X-ray, and created a receptive mood for the acceptance of other unknown rays. It was while working with X-rays that Blondlot observed an effect of another order. He found that the brightness of a small surface made phosphorescent by a coating of calcium sulphide increased when a beam of light refracted through a prism fell upon it. Upon this slender basis the existence of another order of ray was predicated. A variety of similar effects were added in confirmation: a tiny electric spark became brighter, a blue flame from a gas jet became whiter. These effects occurred only in a dark room; they developed slowly and then slowly faded away. Some observers could not detect them at all.

Sensing the fallibility of this evidence, M. Blondlot argues that "the slightness of the effect and the delicacy of the operation must not deter us from a study which puts us in possession of radiations hitherto unknown."

Convinced that the N-rays were real, he proceeded to determine their properties. He found that gold heightens the glow. "Aluminum, wood, dry or wet paper, and paraffine do not enjoy the property of storing N-rays." A tool made in the eighteenth century, an heirloom in the Blondlot family, emitted N-rays; so did a knife found in a Gallo-Roman tomb—but only the blade, not the handle—thus showing that N-rays could remain active for twelve centuries. They are contained in sun rays. Bits of stone exposed in sunlight until 4 P.M. spontaneously emitted N-rays; vegetable earth does not, because the "thinnest layer of moisture arrests the rays." The blade of a chisel is N-ray-active, but becomes inactive when the temper is taken out of the steel. As M. Blondlot concludes: the N-rays "are reflected and polarized, and possess well defined wave-lengths which I have measured."

The error of N-rays derives from the low visibility and the inevitable fluctuations of retinal sensibility in the dark. *Dans la nuit tous les chats sont gris* does not hold when prepossession is at work. It is precisely in the dark that the creatures of fancy become luminous. The subjective play of color and fluctuation in brightness in the feebly stimulated retina is well known to students of vision. Without realizing that they pointed to an origin in the retina itself, M. Blondlot empirically discovered the conditions favorable to receiving them. He directs that one focus the eyes a little to the side of the phosphorescent strip, and a bit out of focus—much as an impressionist painter regards his canvas. When he further advises absolute silence and refraining from smoking, the stage-setting of expectant attention is complete.

The N-ray controversy was sharp while it lasted. A score of physicists confirmed the effects and even added to them, finding N-ray reactions in compressed rubber, in ice near zero, in ivory and celluloid. One discovered a "physiological" reaction, the N-ray effect varying as the screen was placed over the heart or the neck; another that the streak varied in glow when the brain was active. It was even proposed that the test be used for the diagnosis of disease. But the majority of physicists in repeating the experiment failed to observe the effect at all, and pointed out the technical errors in the observation. Some of them went to Nancy, where the N-ray had become a local cult, and became even more skeptical when they realized the loose conditions of the experiments. One of them, Professor Wood, of Baltimore, surreptitiously removed the prism essential to the effect, which none the less continued to be reported by the observer at the other end of the tube.

M. Faure drew the moral that all physicists should be trained in psychology.

The half-century that separated *Od* from N-rays represents far more than a tremendous advance in the technique of physics; it inaugurates, as did no previous period, the advent of psychology into the circle of the sciences. The possibility of subjective intrusion, previously recognized—notably by Chevreuil and Faraday in the "turning tables," contemporary with *Od*—had become an established tenet, with all the cumulative demonstrations of the ready play of suggestion. *Od* appeared in the pre-psychological era; that accounts for its temporary vogue. The N-ray confronted the established position of psychology; its refutation was prompt and decisive. Presumably, so far as laboratory science is concerned, we shall never see its like again. But in the layman's world, where beliefs travel upon less exacting credentials, errors sponsored by rationalization, seeking the confirmations of science, will continue to appear sporadically under shifting waves of interest.

CHAPTER XXVII

AURAS AND VIBRATIONS

THE PREPOSSESSED mind on rationalizing bent evolves elaborate constructions upon unrealities as readily and eagerly as though dealing with data as solid as the rock of ages, and with laws as certain as those of gravitation itself. In *Od* a cherished theory creates facts abundant out of vain imaginings; in N-rays a fact that is other than it seems creates a theory with a fatal flaw. *Auras and Vibrations* illustrate yet another variety of wishful wisdom, in which fact and theory are equally fictitious—both the issue of a common prepossession.

In origin the aura, like many another folk-belief, has a religious setting of which the halo is a rendering. It is an appearance of the soul that attaches to the body. The theosophists resurrected the aura for the modern world; though not they alone, for spiritualistic mediums report auras. But predominantly the aura is taken over from the oriental wisdom-cults; how authentically or intelligently is uncertain. We are told that the growing tide of our debasing absorption in material concerns has dulled and obliterated the sense for finer spiritual entities, including the perception of auras. We are accordingly dependent upon gifted clairvoyants for their revelation, which extends from the Far East to the Far West.

The thought leaders have passed from the proof of reason to the proof of clear vision; and experiments conducted by the inner perceptions now form a scientific basis for a practical

353

knowledge of transcendental yet natural laws. The London band of highly gifted and accurately trained seers reveal to us invisible, objectified thought-forms,[1] and describe from actual observation the nature and evolution of atoms; while here at the Gates of the Setting Sun, other students endowed with a rare combination of keen inner insight and a scientific habit of mind, give to the world the results of their work on the Human Auras, and that of plants, tracing the auric correlation with principles and forces so clearly that all may understand.

This is not a faith or a dispensation, but a demonstration, unfortunately not demonstrable to the common herd of ordinary scientists. The pronouncement goes forth that thus things are, and the seers proceed to find them so.

All objects exhale from their periphery a sort of vapor or cloud, constituting as it were, their own localized atmosphere, which is more and more extended and complicated as we pass to more complex organisms, from minerals up to man.

Even artificial objects made by man emit auric manifestations, since they are formed of material molecules, which, as such, possess their inherent auras.

As defined by Madame Blavatsky,

the aura is a subtle, invisible essence of fluid that emanates from human and animal bodies and even things; it is a psychic effluvium partaking of both the mind and the body, as it is the electro-vital and at the same time electro-mental aura, called in Theosophy the akasic or magnetic.

To a profane mind the quest of the aura suggests the *Hunting of the Snark,* an expedition materially equipped to capture a plausibly fabulated creature which might, however, prove to be a boojum—an evanescent and elusive variety of the fabulous order. There is a "Pranic Aura" and its innumerable Tatwic changes, and the Karmic Aura

---

[1] See page 214 *ff.* Thought-forms and auras, though mutually contradictory, seem to abide in astral harmony.

with its emotional flashes, ever varying, yet actually visible
to the astral senses and devachanic perception. There is the
"chromatic kaleidoscope of Karma"; but few proceed beyond the Karmic Aura. Beyond this, with a yellow edge,
are the "Lower Manas," and yet beyond them the "Higher
Manas," and shooting through them "ranges of geometrical
figures, clouds of glorious light," a "mist of golden dust";
and "through all the preceding, the mysterious zone of the
Sacred Auric Egg"—the completing envelope; and "this is
only a rough sketch, a mere specimen of classification."
Even in lithographic replicas the auras are astounding.

Confronted with the complete colorful, variegated, vi-
brating, luminous layers of the human aura of theosophy,
Solomon, in all his glory and wisdom, would perforce admit that never was he arrayed as one of these. There is
"the magnetic aura" which Mr. Sinnett, a devotee, is
pleased to call Jivic, which is "the influence under which
the lines of the Electric Health Aura remain radial in
position when the health is good." "Besides keeping the
lines of the Health Aura combed and straight," (and who
would not be ashamed to be seen even invisibly with an
unkempt aura?) "this emanation seems to the operative
as a protection against the attack of disease germs."

To believers these visions come from the realm of the
higher verities; to the uninitiate, they hail from the region
of "the higher foolishness." Yet it is all presented as though
revealed under a microscope, or precipitated in a test tube.
The same ecstatic seer who looks forward to salvation by
aura, when "all hypocrisy and crime will be vain, when
man will be able to see every other man just as he really
is," humbly inspects the auras of a rose leaf or a fig leaf
or a violet or geranium and draws them faithfully as revealed to his super-vision. To the common eye they have
mystifying resemblance to the perforated edging of shelf-
paper or the conventional designs of paper doilies. Such

is the esoteric aura, apparently a comforting belief, seeking yet evading recognition amid the busy haunts of men.

There are, however, more practical auraists. One of them is W. J. Kilner, author of *The Human Atmosphere, or The Aura Made Visible by the Aid of Chemical Screens* (1911), who conducts an auric clinic. He repeats the usual affirmation: "Hardly one person in ten thousand is aware that he or she is surrounded by a haze intimately connected with the body, whether asleep or awake, whether hot or cold, which although invisible under ordinary circumstances, can be seen when conditions are favorable."

Mr. Kilner is not dependent upon rare or uncertain clairvoyant vision. By the grace of chemistry, the aura is to be made demonstrably visible. His signal contribution is the discovery of a screen treated by a solution which he named *Spectauranine,* and upon the advice of a friend disclosed to be dicyanine. But our hopes are raised only to be shattered. Seeing auras through screens—such as are used in color photography—requires special conditions, and their continued use is said to be injurious to the eyes. With his own eyes once sensitized, or restimulated by a brief glance through the screen, Mr. Kilner found that he could see the auras just as well with the naked eye. Thus free to describe the auras as he sees them, he exercises the privilege to the full. What he actually sees, I cannot tell; and a chemist to whom I appealed for information shares my ignorance.

He finds "an inner, narrow, transparent aura" following the contours of the body, "which is very often obliterated by the second portion of the aura"—the Etheric Double; he delineates an inner aura and an outer aura. By their variations, he judges health and diagnoses disease. He examines his subjects or patients *au naturel* from the front and in profile, drawing the auras carefully, as would a sculptor sketch his model. Of a strong, even-tempered, healthy woman of thirty, he records: "Her aura is blue and is one of the finest we have seen, being as she faces the observer egg-shaped"; the outer aura quite twelve inches from the body has even an ultra aura beyond that. "Among women the ovoid shape of the outer aura is evidently the highest form, and the more the aura approxi-

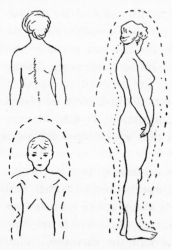

AURAS IN HEALTH AND DISEASE

After W. J. Kilner, *The Human Atmosphere.*

mates to this shape, the more perfect it is." An hysterical dressmaker, aged twenty-two, showed an auric ray emanating from the right lower ribs, about six inches long, which passed completely through the inner aura and lost itself in the outer. A patient afflicted with shingles shows a sharp indentation in the aura at the hip. A similar alteration is present in sciatica. "There is not the slightest doubt that the aura is affected locally when there is some local disorder of the nerves."

The aura as seen by Mr. Kilner has marked sex char-

acteristics. It changes in girls at puberty; they then develop a "transitional" aura before it assumes the matured
womanly form. The changes of the aura in pregnancy are
delineated, the aura itself an indication of the condition.
The aura locates tumors, indicates enlarged adenoids, and
becomes an impressive diagnosis in *immateria medica*. A
remarkable fact is the effect upon the aura of the action
of the *will*: will vigorously, and the aura changes; stop
willing and it returns to repose. In one experiment the
subject willed the bulge in the aura to appear over an
unknown place on the thorax; the result was partially
successful, and would have been completely so but for
fatigue.

All is set down as objectively as would be the findings
of an X-ray examination. It was, in fact, Roentgen's discovery in 1896 that encouraged the auraists to find corroboration for their "discoveries." Whatever their claims
and professions, auraists drift into the occult, from which
they have in temper never emerged. Reminiscent of *Od*,
they see auras at the poles of a horseshoe magnet. For all
his chemical screens, Kilner sees no differently than did
the odic sensitives or the theosophic clairvoyants.

A major prophet among the auraists, with whom perhaps I should have begun, is Dr. Hippolyte Baraduc, who
in a large volume, *L'Ame Humaine* (1897) announced that
he had captured all varieties of human auras on photographic plates exposed by contact without a camera. From
these the laws of auric formation are deduced; he likewise
used auric diagnosis in his medical practice. There is a
simplified statement of the text (1911); but even this is
beyond me. The photographs look like fogged or slightly
and irregularly light-struck plates. How these impressions
were produced I do not know; but the ways of photography, though they begin in strong light, are completed
in darkness. They show no resemblance to what the clair-

voyants depict in glowing colors, nor to what the auraists, who peer through screens, describe.

The champions of the aura, though they make no use of Dr. Baraduc's results, announce jubilantly to all skeptics that the aura has been photographed. The photograph was the culminating stage of what Dr. Baraduc calls the "brutal fact" of the physical demonstrability of the "human soul." Accepting the existence of "an invisible fluid" whose laws are duly formulated, he sought experimental conformation. His standard apparatus was a special form of galvanometric electroscope which he devised. When the human hands approach the instrument, the needle is deflected to the right or left, by attraction and repulsion, positive and negative, according to the psychic constitution of the subjects, who were usually neurotics. To Dr. Baraduc this experiment demonstrated the soul; it leaves his "brutal" and his "spiritual" facts dubious in the lay reader's mind. What may be the instrumental error of observation is likewise not clear.

Another independent auraist is Dr. G. S. White of Los Angeles, who has had the auraic gift since boyhood. He was brought up in a region of brilliant northern lights; in the aurora he found the patterns for the human auras which he so readily projected, samples of which he reproduces in color; brilliant, symbolic, but well within the compass of a meager talent. At the age of fifteen he earned his board and the opportunity to study medicine by acting as an auraic diagnostician for a practitioner—of what variety is not specified. Dr. White's picture-book contains sketches of his patients radiating auric rays. The female form is rendered in black outline, the auric emanations printed in red. But animals also have auras. He pictures a cat quietly purring with a quiescent aura, which at once breaks out into a violent discharge at the approach of a dog; he shows a pair of cooing mated pigeons whose auras merge, while those of an unmated pair are found to radiate oppositely.

The illustrations of his "experiments" combine the feminine allure with the panoply of the laboratory. In one picture, a healthy female is presented as would be an artist's model, seated on a glass-top table; glass discs are placed under the table-legs to ensure complete insulation. A metal standard carrying a ball is grounded by means of a wire attached to a gas-pipe. The auric rays proceed from the right breast to the insulated metal ball but without reaching it; while the auric rays from the left breast reach the uninsulated ball at once. The rays are more active when the left hand of a male is pointed at the breast. "The demonstration is made to show how the auric ray conforms to physical laws in all respects."

Another of the black and red figures shows "an extremely vivacious female," aged twenty, grounded to metal by an aluminum hook attached to her waist by a metal band. Although grounded, she was so charged with magnetic energy or vital force that the auric rays not only reached promptly to the left hand of a male who was not grounded, but they emanated in a "shower from her whole body." There are similar drawings of twin sisters, whose auras merge harmoniously and vigorously from the breast of one to the breast of the other. In contrast are the auras of two women of opposite temperaments; in which case the auras break out in a bulge in mid-air where they collide. A female immersed in a fresh-water bath shows an active aura; while one in salt water—salt being antagonistic to the auric rays—appears sans everything, with no aura at all.

As he proceeds from one demonstration to another, Dr. White is in an increasing state of surprise that these auras should appear in the proper places and prove the proper point. Since he is completely free to draw his red auric lines wherever he chooses, being the sole witness, the non-auric observer is not impressed by the confirmation. His surprise takes the form of wondering whether this auric practitioner is deceiving himself or arranging a game to deceive others. When he reads of the "Bio-Dynamic-Chromatic method of diagnosis," he senses the malodorous atmosphere of exploitation. The aura as a mystic doctrine or a symbol of sanctity has traveled far in its voyage, from Far East to Far West, to become the spurious basis of questionable practice in eclectic medicine.

In following the devious trail of wish posing as wisdom I have for the most part left it before it led into the underworld where exploiters prey upon the credulous. At one point [2] or another I have entered the territory. I must do so again in considering the "vibrationists." They form no distinctive cult, but appear in many cults, ranging from serious searchers for spiritual welfare to brazenly advertising charlatans. *Vibration* is a word to conjure with, to impress the unlearned with the badge of learning, to obscure pretense and to veil ignorance.

Vibrations appear, though with a minor emphasis, in the Besant formulations of theosophy. The astral plane "is ever answering to vibrations caused by thoughts, feelings, desires," and is thrown into a commotion by any of these. It is in another variety of psycho-religious philosophy dealing with the "power of mind over matter" that the vibration finds a congenial place; it is used to rationalize the material reality of thought.

The general trend of science is favorable to the enthronement of vibration. Waves of many kinds, conveyed through various media, and of various lengths, have come to the fore. Our age of marvel is set in a world of vibrations. Heat, light, sound, electricity, magnetism, are all re-

[2] See "Signs and Lines of Head and Hand," and "Numerology."

ducible to waves. Ultra-violet, infra-red, X-ray, Herzian, radio-active, cosmic rays, and many another wonder of the modern laboratory appear as additions to the repertory of waves. Each of these discoveries has been drafted into service as an analogy for rays, waves, and vibrations such as no instrument other than the human imagination discloses on sea, land, or sky. If so much of the universe is vibratory with waves, why not thought-waves and esoteric waves, and Health and Success vibrations? The exploiter's reply is a "College of Fine Forces"—and fair fees—where their use is taught. Most of all is the vibration an answer to the daily prayer of the one hundred per cent American for Success! "Join the Success Circle. . . . The Center of that Circle is my omnipotent WORD. Daily I speak it. Its vibrations radiate more and more powerfully day by day. . . . As the sun sends out vibrations, so my WORD radiates Success to 10,000 lives as easily as to one."

A "soul communion time-table" for your longitude enables you to meet and absorb the healing or prosperity vibrations as they pass. Get "in tune with the Infinite," and with your local station! Unwittingly Marconi gave a new impetus to the vibrationists of all callings and complexions; for once again and triumphantly has their faith in unseen vibrations been justified. Not the woods, but the market-places of exploiting cults, are full of them. From the "evil eye" to magnetism, attractive and malicious, to absent treatment and "New Thought," the vibrationists abound in the psychic jungle which is no sooner cleared for purposes of civilization than it grows up again. Parasitic upon the advances of science, the diagnosticians of auras and venders of vibrations ply their cults; the confiding public is the victim.

Rhythm, another law of life appearing in heart-beat and respiration, energy and recovery, ebb and flow, strengthens the analogy for the vibrationists. Rhythmic breathing and vital currents demonstrate vibrations; "everything is what it is by its rate of vibration." The Law of Vibration in Business makes booms and depressions. If one knows how, one may "vibrate the God Center," or "raise one's mental vibrations to a higher plane, so as to attract friends, power and financial success." In the dominant search for soul mates and affinities, the guiding principle is harmonious vibrations. Sex is vibratory no less than Success.

The guilds of vibrationists are many and competitive, marching under a hundred banners. In allied cults the vibration is the leading stock in trade, most of all for the numerologists. Hours, days, months, and years, no less than names, bring a vibration that makes or mars. "What is Music *but Vibration?* What is the Hum of the Factory *but Vibration?* What is the Hurry of the Business Office *but Vibration?* What is Everything in Life? *It Is Vibration.*" This is not an argument but an advertisement issued by *Vibration Studies* and offered to you to the vibratory tune of one dollar.

It is of slight purpose for the rationalists to set forth that it is not in our vibrations but in ourselves that we are underlings or overlords; for the vibration is too precious a combination of the mystic and the scientific to be abandoned for the trivial reason that there are no such vibrations. In these days of ingenious devices for raising revenue, a tax on the illicit use of the word "vibration" might be helpful.

"Psychic" vibrations do not monopolize the field. The curative effects of physical vibrations—with a possible mental counterpart—are also exploited. Colors vibrate; consequently what we wear, and the color scheme of our surroundings, affect the intimate welfare of our being. But the outstanding "vibratory" exploiter was Dr. Albert Abrams of the "electrotonic vibrations." Dr. Abrams was eclectic and versatile. He began with "spondylotherapy";

he added one gadget after another. The vibrations—which were also oscillations and direct percussions—played only one instrument in his grand orchestral quackery. The apparatus, called a dynamizer, was sold sealed to practitioners upon their promise not to open it; it brought rich royalties. The alleged vibratory power furnished a theoretical basis for the elaborate treatment. Dr. Abrams' most original discovery was the demonstration of the differential diagnosis of Catholic, Methodist, Seventh-Day Adventist, Theosophist, Protestant, and Jew by the areas of dullness on chest and abdomen; this clinical gem was found by the technique of percussion.

But the vibration played first fiddle; the importance of vibration-frequency in the newer physics gave the "osciloclast" a seemingly up-to-date authority, though it involved no more than the old notion that every disease has a distinctive vibration-rate. By setting the apparatus in tune with the disease, a cure would be effected. Professor Millikan, the distinguished investigator of the cosmic rays, describes the Abrams apparatus as the kind of machine which a ten-year-old might build to fool an eight-year-old. Yet on the combined power of an imposing apparatus and a vibrational theory, and shrewd advertising, this "system" momentarily disturbed the medical poise of two continents, and made millions for its inventor. Truly vibration is a word to conjure with.

The story of auras and vibrations is primarily that of a cultist doctrine making a bid for the rationalizing sanction of science; it wants to have its esoteric cake and eat it too. It is not like that of *Od* and N-rays, primarily an error in a scientific quest. Auras and vibrations carry consolation, insight and uplift. Their renaissance belongs to "The Stammering Century," which name Gilbert Seldes attaches to the nineteenth-century period of transition. It was a

time of abandonment of older beliefs and the rise of salva-
tional cults and 'isms, reaching for a scientific sanction,
but not expertly articulate. Innovations in creeds, erratic
psychology, daring experiments in communal living, are
among its expressions. In this general seething unrest, a
modernized Theosophy and the uniquely successful,
strangely irrational rationalization of Christian Science,
have their place. These two creeds—far outnumbering in
their following all other neo-religions—were promulgated
by two extraordinary women of as glaring a contrast in
appearance, ancestry, tradition, technique, and personality
as the *varium et mutabile semper* of femininity can supply.
Their realms of influence overlapped, each finding its
clientele in the receptive American temperament. An imaginary meeting of the two would be a theme for a Shavian
extravaganza. These wisdom-cults disseminated a favorable
atmosphere for the esoteric, the rationalized and modernized. It is on this wave of super-material reality that auras
and vibrations floated into popularity. The common theme
of all these enlightenments is the enthronement of a new
revelation, a super-truth of new thought that denies and
defies science even as it covets its sanctions.

Uplift and exploitation are but one of the pairs of
strange bedfellows that esoterics makes. In following such
careers, the interest is divided between the credulity of
the followers and the technique of the leaders. It is perhaps because the rationalizations of science had destroyed
so many illusions, that a more thrilling and personally significant doctrine was welcomed as a new vindication, by
original methods, of a persistent faith in things unseen—
more real than the commonly, vulgarly visible world. The
exploitation followed. The prismatic auras of clairvoyance
may be largely self-deception; but chemical screens and
photographs and sealed apparatus to produce electrotonic
vibrations, point to a subtle or a flagrant will to deceive

as well as to believe. Apparently vibrations may be capitalized in a mail-order business, without wholly losing the uplift quality of a higher possession. The trail of esoteric glory ends in a tawdry tale. The wish to rationalize the irrational accounts for the beginning of many an episode in the erratic ways of belief; the availability for profitable exploitation accounts for its sequel.

Chapter XXVIII

ECTOPLASM AND PSYCHIC STRUCTURES

ECTOPLASM

ECTOPLASM is an imposing word and has an imposing sponsor: Professor Charles Richet, distinguished physiologist, recipient of a Nobel prize. It suggests a laboratory origin, something arrived at by way of a test-tube or a microscope. Its actual birthplace is far less respectable: a curtained cabinet in a séance room. The appearance which invited the term goes back to at least two generations of spirit manifestations emerging in the dark in the form of human hands, faces, and complete figures, showing some semblance of life. They were called materializations. The mass of uncritical believers in their genuineness—which meant non-fraudulent source—bothered little about the process of their formation. To them what they saw or heard were just spirits, or spirit fragments, resuming their former shape for purposes of identification.

Not until a biologist was convinced that mediums command supernormal powers was there any temptation to rationalize the process as "ectoplasm," fully made or in the making. Analogous to, but unlike, protoplasm—the primary cellular living tissue—this plasm was supposed to be formed or ejected outside the body, though connected with it. Whatever its source, it led to the mystic beyond. The mediums presented the appearance; the interpretations were made by one and another scientifically trained

367

observer who took the appearances seriously, but failed to employ his scientific habits of mind in accounting for them.

Professor Richet records:

As early as 1895, in the course of my experiments with Eusapia,[1] I had verified that simultaneously with telekinetic movements of objects, there appeared barely visible and half-formed stumps like adventitious limbs, so to say, or efflorescences, for which I proposed the name of ectoplasm, a name now universally adopted. In numerous cases what look like rigid rods have been seen proceeding from Eusapia's body. I have often felt on touching her dress a resistant and mobile but formless object, while her hands and feet were being held unmistakably.

The medium who made ectoplasm famous and whom ectoplasm made famous was known as Eva C., née Marthe Béraud. Her Paris patroness, Madame Bisson, called her Rose Dupont; her Munich patron, Baron von Schrenk-Notzing, renamed her Eva C., reluctantly admitting her identity with Marthe, the somewhat discredited medium of the Villa Carmen in Algiers, where the story began a decade after Eusapia mystified a few scientists in Naples. It is as the star of the ectoplasmic theory of Richet that Marthe-Rose-Eva became an international personage and problem.

The present theme is the theory of ectoplasm as a belief, not primarily the spirit-craft of Eva C. that called it forth. Ectoplasm is a remarkable example of the attempt to rationalize in scientific terms a belief which has its remote origin in the wish psychology of the folk-mind, but has traveled far from that source. From haunting ghosts and poltergeists to elaborate apparatus and photographs is a long step in the technique of psychic marvels; whether it reflects an advance in rationality is another matter.

[1] Eusapia Paladino, whose career is described in "Paladino's Table."

The illustrations record the appearances upon which the theory was formed, or, it may be, that were devised by the medium to fit the theory. As usual, the enlightening first step in a marvel is glossed over. The critical moment remains unrecorded: when, how, why, what the train of thought which led Professor Richet to propose ectoplasm. It may be that he indicated in the presence of Eva C. that "materializations" might have a "biological" source; that the suggestion was a challenge and the frothy substance the answer. It may be that Eva C., discovering that she had the power of regurgitation, had the original idea of offering it as a mystifying phenomenon, and found it accepted and an explanation built upon it which startled the world. What Eva C. knows she shows no disposition to tell; she is content to have her sponsors speak.

Ectoplasm is presented as organized cellular matter in the first stages of the production of a living being. Accompanying its formation from the body of the medium are violent muscular actions, groans, and gasps, as if in childbirth, and thus called "mediumistic labor." The theory is expressed in the terms of biology and even embryology; but the data are stumps, rods, limbs, efflorescence, mobile clouds—reminiscent of Hamlet's "much like a camel or a whale."

Materialization is a development of a completed form after a first stage of coarse and rudimentary lineaments formed from the cloudy substance...moist, gelatinous and seemingly luminous extensions, which tend towards organization without immediately attaining it.... Two phases can be distinguished—a rudimentary phase, a sort of rough draft, and a phase of building up. With other mediums the organized forms may probably appear immediately, without being preceded by the indistinct, cloudy faces.

Strangely enough for a biologically creative energy, the ectoplasmic process can also fashion clothes. "The garments are usually veils and draperies, white, like muslin, or cloud-like." At times—but under lax conditions, particularly when Madame Bisson was alone with the medium and the cameras—there appeared flat faces as if drawn on crinkled tissue or paper; and under still other conditions, full-length phantom-like flat forms duly appareled in modern dress. The modernistic ectoplasmic stage-effect, while losing some of the personal appeal of the old-time materializations, is far more impressive to the scientific mind. By recourse to ectoplasm one may believe in marvels and save one's face.

The glory and repertory of ectoplasm under the artistry of Eva C. and her imitators is presented in hundreds of photographs. Whatever it may be as a stuff, as a theory it created a super-world. A gauze produced a cosmos. Upon it Professor Richet erected a *metapsychics,* transcending all physics and biology and psychology. "Nothing is touched that belongs to the classic treasury of science"; but that treasure becomes dross. The world of science knows only protoplasm organized through eons of development; a high-powered medium develops ectoplasm in a single séance. Ectoplasm makes the most amazing assumptions of an amazing world, which Professor Richet accepts as complacently as a change in diet.

The *metapsychics* of Richet consists of three divisions, of which ectoplasm is the central one. The other members of the meta-trinity are *telekinesis,* which is the power to move and affect objects at a distance or without contact, beginning with table-moving, proceeding to apports, levitations, and plastic molds; and *cryptesthesia,* which is telepathy, second sight, and the revelation of knowledge by other means than the channels of the senses. These phenomena are of a different order than ectoplasm, but involve the same order of misinterpretation. The mind

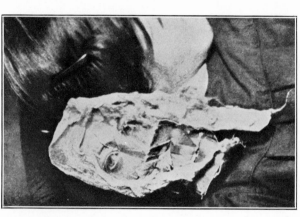

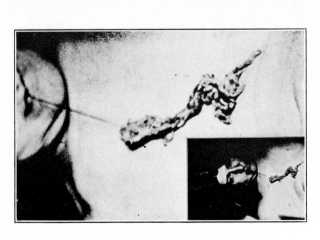

THE WONDERS OF ECTOPLASM

Left, Madame Bisson's earliest photograph of ectoplasm materialized by Eva C.; center, Eva C. with draped face evolved from ectoplasm; right, Father de Heredia demonstrating how ectoplasm could be concealed in a false finger and in a comb, both of which objects appear in photographs of Eva C.'s materializations.

hospitable to one is so to all, by reason of similar psychological inclinations, and allied logical lapses.

The stupendous contrast between the facts and the theory of their explanation makes the logical problem of ectoplasm. The same state of mind that accepts the one devises the other. To become a metapsychist, one must be first blinded to the nature of fact, and the defect extend from vision to judgment. The anesthetizing of the logical powers appears in the argument as well as in the observations.

It would seem that the materialization of garments discredits somewhat the hypothesis that a deceased human being should materialize. *Prima facie* it was unlikely that a body dissolved by putrefaction or disintegrated by cremation should be reconstructed—and any explanation we can give can hardly escape being ridiculous.... Instead of claiming that unknown powers pertaining to deceased humanity are capable of producing these phenomena, it is better to admit that we are dealing with facts as yet inexplicable, and await further elucidation. But there is no reason to deny a fact because it is inexplicable. As regards the substance of materializations, our ignorance is painful. Some facts ... would seem to imply that this substance can outlast a materialization. Katie gave Crookes a lock of her hair. I kept the hair that Phygia permitted me to cut from her head. Mme. d'Espérance allowed sitters to cut off pieces of the drapery surrounding her.... The materialization of hands is absolutely certain and likewise faces and whole bodies, though hands alone have been seen much more often.... What does seem to be proved (and it is a relief to find a positive fact in the midst of so much uncertainty), is that the ectoplasms in most cases emerge from the body of the medium; hence the word *ecto*-plasm.... Gelatinous projections come from the mouth or the shoulders of Marthe. I saw the arm of Bien Boa formed in this way. At first it resembled a thin, rigid rod covered with drapery. Little by little this rod thickened under the drapery and became a stretched-out arm. The same phenomenon was very clearly observable with Eusapia. A kind of supplementary arm seemed to come from her body. Once I saw a long, stiff rod proceed from her side, which after great extension had a hand at its extremity...a living hand, warm and jointed, absolutely like a human hand.

Certainly if "fact" means that something appeared on the basis of which these descriptions were written, there is no quarrel and no point to the statement; for these were not hallucinations. But what is the fact! The fact that ectoplasm is gauze or bladder or phosphorescence, and the bits of drapery and hair just the ordinary specimens; or the fact that refusing to see them as such, the observer made of them mysterious tissues and living limbs miraculously produced? Facts and theories retain their right relations when the logical powers are working rightly, but not otherwise. When that process is markedly disturbed, all sorts of distortions occur in arriving at cause and effect. The hospitality of Richet's mind to metapsychics is responsible for the ectoplasmic *fact-interpretation* which he accepts though the heavens of science fall; he believes that they have fallen in order to admit Eva C. and her ectoplasmic emanations.

PSYCHIC STRUCTURES

The *ectoplasm* of a biologist finds a parallel in the *psychic structures* of an engineer; the story of Richet and Eva C. in Paris is repeated in that of Dr. Crawford and Kathleen Golligher in Belfast. The Irish performance is simple. The medium is seated at a table supposedly beyond her reach, and the table rises; that is all. The explanation is most complex. The Crawford theory holds that a *psychic structure*—psychic because not composed of ordinary matter—lifts the table by one of two mechanical principles: as a *cantilever* for light operations, as a *strut* for heavier ones. In both cases the psychic structures emanate from below the knee of the medium. The cantilever extension grows out and forward until it comes under the table, then exerts an upward force. The strut takes a brace on the floor and then turns upward. At the close of the performance the structures are absorbed into the medium's body. The tests are planned as experiments in mechanics. There are scales, measurements, platforms, electroscopes, manometers, spring-balances, weighing of subjects, measuring areas of surfaces and distances, plotting diagrams,

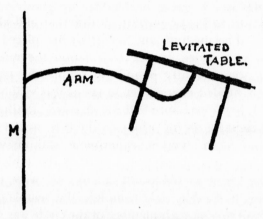

A PSYCHIC CANTILEVER

deducing equations. It is a Jacob and Esau affair: the hands are of the laboratory, but the voice that of the spirit séance.

The psychic structures depend for their energy on the vitality of the medium and of the Golligher family circle. Dr. Crawford calls the invisible agencies with which he communicates by raps "operators"; he regards them as "human beings who have passed into the Beyond." As an engineer he calculates the "psychic parallelogram of forces" involved in lifting the table; as a spiritist he follows the direction of the "operators" in keeping the space under the table dark, lest the "aura from the hand neutralize the psychic force." The calculations show that the medium is "in reality a psychic pump with a complete pressure system." There is the usual assurance that "every phenomenon is absolutely genuine to the minutest detail."

The details are enlightening. If the table is not properly placed, the operators adjust it. The psychic structures can take the forms of *rods* which by raps, with a code for *yes* and *no,* approve the arrangements and confirm the theories. Thus is a spirit séance rationalized as an engineering laboratory.

There are 128 experiments, all different and all much the same. The medium and her chair are placed on the platform of a scales. In one observation the medium—a slight person—lost fifty pounds to supply the structures with their needed energy; yet so far as was visible in the dim light, her appearance had not changed. (Shifting part of her weight by resting a foot on the floor would explain the miracle.) In another experiment she mysteriously gained in weight about the weight of the table. (This would be the expected result if any one were weighed supporting the table.) To complete the semblance of a precise experiment, each member of the circle was weighed before and after the manifestations; it was found that each had lost a few ounces. (An ordinary scale is not accurate enough to detect such slight changes.) And with it all are "direct voices" through "tin trumpets" and the paraphernalia of an orthodox spirit séance held in the dark.

All this went on for years, and is recorded in a series of learned volumes. To make the evidence more convincing, the "operators" were persuaded to place a box filled with clay in the dark space under the table and impress the structure upon the clay. It was an exciting moment. The first actual impression of a psychic structure was about to be seen by mortal eyes! What would it look like? *It was amazingly like the sole-print of a woman's shoe!*

But the reader must not be hasty in his judgment. Remember, we are in the hall of engineering miracles! Actually it was this: "The impression is really due to one of the largest rods thrown out from the medium's body; but to a careless eye, or to an eye which has not seen any other impression taken at the circle, looks more or less like the mark of the sole of a lady's shoe." There are even little holes somewhat resembling the stitch-marks on a shoe-sole and marks of grit that are apt to collect on mundane shoes. But this confusing "resemblance is only superficial"; the ends of the psychic rods when touched feel soft, and not hard as is leather.

The *psychic structural* imitation of stockings was even more confusing. The explanation reads:

When the medium wears stockings, nearly every psychic impression is lined with stocking marks.... The actual psychic structure is covered by a film of matter, which film is formed of psychic matter oozing round about the little holes in the stocking fabric. It is at first in a semi-liquid state, and it collects and partly sets on an outer covering of the stocking. It is of a glutinous, fibrous nature and takes almost the exact form of the stocking fabric. It is pulled off the stocking by the operators and is then built round the end of the psychic structure, which when placed in a dish of clay, naturally leaves an imprint similar to a stocking.

The type of matter created in the séances is first *X-matter*, which must be converted into *Y-matter*, before it can lift tables. The X-matter can go through wire meshes but not through burlap. The little hollow tubes which project through the wire meshes are stiffened by gas. If you thrust your hand under the table when the forces are at work, you get a cold, clammy, and reptilian sensation. The uncritical meddling with this part of space is apt to be physically injurious to the medium.

Toward the end, having become acquainted with ectoplasm, Dr. Crawford adopted that term.

I have discovered that plasma has the property of adhering strongly to a substance such as powdered carmine; and that if the carmine is placed in its path, it will leave a colored streak. It was thus found the plasma moved up and down the medium's legs, about as one leg might do in pushing a cloth against the other. The psychic structure thus becomes a plasmic column, which the photograph reveals with all the deceptive realism of a piece of muslin. It becomes plain that once plasma is formed, the operators can do with it what they like.

In the enjoyment of this complete liberty, we may leave them.

The story ends, but ends with a tragedy. For in July, 1930, in the midst of these photographic revelations of the structures, and after arranging to lecture upon them in the United States, Dr. Crawford committed suicide. He recognized his approaching breakdown. In a letter he says, "My psychic work was all done before the collapse and is the most perfect work I have done in my life. Everything connected with it is absolutely correct, and will bear every scrutiny. It was done when my brain was working perfectly, and it could not be responsible for what has occurred."

In the following year Mrs. Crawford invited Mr. D'Albe, a trained scientist, but a subscriber to the reality of Eva C.'s ectoplasm, to verify the experiments. A favorable report was expected. Mr. D'Albe's suspicions were soon aroused; he saw the medium's foot lift up a small stool placed under the table and made a sketch of it. He received permission to use an X-ray plate under the table, but only once. When the plate so plainly revealed the plaid pattern of the medium's stockings, the operators rapped out: *"No more tonight."* "They thought it best to adjourn before taking more risks." He comments: "If you insist on conducting the experiments in your own way, you obtain no phenomena, and are warned that the sittings will close. This habit of thought becomes impervious even to fairly obvious evidence of artificiality."

Doubtless Mr. D'Albe would agree with the summary of another critic that *"the cantilever which worked the experiments in Crawford's book was the leg of that Irish medium."* Sir Bryan Donkin, M.D., calls attention to "the superabundant exposure of the massive credulity and total defect of logical power displayed by Dr. Crawford," who gives "the most pathetic picture of a willing victim of pernicious deception."

It becomes clear in the sequel, as appears plainly in Dr. Crawford's books, that the initial and abiding belief in "the reality of psychic phenomena" was a faith in spirit survival and communication. He believed as a spiritualist; he rationalized as an engineer. The spirit-belief played havoc with his methods and his formulæ. Spirit operators and the parallelograms of forces form an impossible combination.

The case against ectoplasm and psychic structures would be just as strong—which means that the argument for it would be just as flimsy and illogical—without as with a knowledge of the ectoplasmic artist's technique, but a moderately satiable curiosity regarding it may be satisfied.

The ways of rationalizing minds are more significant than the tricks that invite the rationalization. The chief trick is to evade detection. Like diplomacy, however apparently open and openly arrived at, psychic artistry operates behind screens. Tables, curtains, darkness, and, most of all, the *conditions imposed* are all screens. Another phase of the art is to give the appearance of permitting examination and control while stopping short of the critical point. The phenomena of ectoplasm and psychic structures were more effectively guarded by *prohibitions* than by a squad of policemen.

For ectoplasm *à la* Eva C., there is the possibility of regurgitation, as two Vienna physicians have amply shown. Some persons can swallow delicate tissues and bring them up at will; gynecological concealments are equally possible. There are many ways of producing ectoplasm; no *one* explanation applies to *all* the photographs. Father Heredia can produce ectoplasm from a hollow comb and a false finger, both of which objects appear in the Eva C. photographs; the finger itself is accepted as an ectoplasmic product, though the device may be bought in a conjuring shop. The thread on the picture connecting the ectoplasm on the medium's chest with her mouth is explained away as a "fluidic thread." The crinkled forms are obviously drawings on tissue, smuggled behind the cabinet when conditions are lax; pinholes were found on the curtains at the rear of the cabinet where the full figure phantoms had been attached. Even the heading of the newspaper, *Le Miroir*, from which the phantom illustrations were taken, is visible in the letters MIR; and among the recognizable but retouched portraits appear the King of the Belgians and President Wilson! It is hardly fair to ask the psychologist to include a course in sleuthing in his professional preparation.

An argument that must be met is that the phenomena have been *repeated*. No sooner had a French medium demonstrated ectoplasm than a Polish medium confirmed it; then a Galician, a Portuguese, a Dutch, and a German, thus establishing its international status. *Imitation is not confirmation.* We live in a rapidly communicating age. A successful trick is a challenge to others equally gifted to devise a more startling one. For versatility the palm may be awarded to the American entry in the person of "Margery," who began with ectoplasm and graduated to other psychic demonstrations.

Margery is original as well as imitative, her originality

proving her undoing. Margery is far more than an ectoplasmic artist; she is a miracle-producer extraordinary.
Her repertory, according to her sponsor, who is her husband, Dr. L. R. G. Crandon, includes breezes, raps, table-
tilting, long distance moving, teleplasmic rods, psychic
bell-ringing, reversing a chemical balance, matter penetrating matter, trance voice, automatic writing, supernormal sounds, perfumes, lights, materializations, apports,
paraffine hands, mind-reading, and fingerprints; but the
greatest of these is fingerprints!

To demonstrate a spirit by a fingerprint was a daring
innovation. Each sitter makes his thumb-print on dental
wax; one piece of wax is left blank and placed in hot
water near the medium. The spirit of Walter—Margery's
brother and spirit control—speaks: "There's my thumb-
print for you." The prints are all verified by an expert.
*There is a "psychic" thumb-print of a person not in the
room!* But the source of Walter's thumb-print has been
found. Mr. Carrington, a believer in at least some psychic
marvels, including Paladino, reports:

> For six years Walter has persistently claimed these as *his own
> thumb-prints* [there is even a photograph of Walter's teleplas-
> tic hand making a thumb-print], whereas painstaking investi-
> gation has shown them to belong to a living man—and the
> very man who supplied Margery with the original Kerr
> [dental wax] showed her how to make thumb-prints in it, and
> gave her three-dimensional impressions of his own thumb.[2]

Since apparently without Eva C.'s and Kathleen Gol-
lighers and Margerys there would be no ectoplasm, it is
in point to inquire what tempts them to embark upon this
uncertain career. Is it anything else than the hope of
having their exploits accepted as evidence of the super-

[2] The thumb-prints, like other "Margery" phenomena, have been and
still are the subject of sharp controversy. To any judicial mind, the evidence of deliberate fraud is convincing.

natural, and by that route captivating the public eye? Certainly their occupation would be gone were there not those prone to see ectoplasm in frothy gauze, telekinesis in levitating tables, spirits in thumb-prints and strange powers in everything; and the scientific demands of the day invite the rationalization of these extensions to knowledge.

It is not Eva C. but Charles Richet who created ectoplasm. She but made the substance, which would have commanded slight interest; he made the theory which arrested the world's attention. The theory was a challenge—a challenge of the rightness and adequacy of the laboratories and the concepts of science, which with all their apparatus, method and research, their analyzing, synthesizing, explaining, discovering, never found a trace of ectoplasm or of a psychic structure. Ectoplasm precipitates an issue. Either Eva C. and her ilk are frauds, or the physicists, biologists, and psychologists of our enlightened age have missed the unsuspected climax of their pursuits. In this instance, we must believe one way or the other—and in the other, madness lies.

Psychics, like politics, makes strange bedfellows. There are slum mediums and there are "Metapsychical Institutes." The case of "Margery" is presented in an elaborate, though specious discourse to an academic audience as an important subject of research. The process of naturalizing the supernatural has occupied the best minds for centuries. The urge to rationalize still finds a strong expression in the pursuit of the same interest, which from cave-man days peopled the world with spirits and found or demanded evidence of their presence. The scientist's rationalizing inagurated the ectoplasmic age, the *dernier cri* in rationalization, the ultimate formulation of an ancient wish as modernistic wisdom.

AFTERWORD

THIS ECLECTIC survey of the kingdom of unreason has been grouped around the dominant
tendencies that distort logic from its orderly
orbit. In content they follow the currents of history, but
equally the favored theorems that engage aberrant minds.
History and psychology combine. The whole forms as
authentic a record of the mind's occupation, is as much a
part of the panorama of cerebration, as are the useful
steps and stages of constructive science, which likewise has
its indirections and errors, its false leads and blind alleys.

The episodes of *Wish and Wisdom* and the errors in the
story of science are not of like temper, though naturally
they overlap. There is a difference between a scientist of
whatever period and a pseudologist, and that itself is one
of the significant demonstrations of this survey. The
pseudologies—the word is my own—are specifically the false
systems like astrology and alchemy, falsely formulated from
the start; but the term may be extended to the whole
range of 'ologies which, however they originate, promptly
embark upon the same order of illogical career. Cheirognomy and palmistry are typical pseudologies, and most
flagrantly so is numerology. It is true that what is near
of kin to legitimate science in one period becomes an
outcast in the next; it is also true that what is falsely interpreted or un-understood in one age is brought within the
range of effective science in another. As it is quaintly put
by a seventeenth-century commentator: "What was conjuring in the last age is Mathematiques in this." Movements in science consist of growth and outgrowth; but

381

through it all there runs a logical temper which is both an intention and a discipline, well developed in one master and weakly in another, that is typically absent in a pseudologist, and is replaced by a devotion that belongs in a different psychological camp. As history and personality are not matters of black and white, there are all sorts of combinations of both adherences; inconsistency and compartmental divisions of mind appear. But that, too, belongs to the ways of mind.

Living but once and in the setting of their time, driven to belief by the pragmatic urge, men must act upon what knowledge they have or upon what they regard as such; they cannot await its completion. The two pictures—of the sciences and of the pseudologies—are needed to project the disciplined and the native tendencies of mind, the wiser attempts and the deluded failures.

While the errors of science do not fall within my theme, the mind on science bent, in whatever degree of enlightenment—from primitive thinker to professional scientist—is subject to the mental temper of his day and generation. Through all their thinking runs a common liability to error, but in different manners and measures. The procession of error in the march of time is impressive. There are the crass and crude folklore beliefs, the early and noble but feebly equipped theories, the erratic projects of would-be scientists, the pseudologies proper and improper, the strayings and misleads within the guild employing scientific techniques. What they have in common may be presented, from our retrospective mount of vision, as a variety of intrusions into what was to become, when established, the matured, formulated scientific spirit.

The logical occupation is beset by intrusions from other human interests. Among these intrusions, spreading even more characteristically over the sciences than over the pseudo-sciences, is the moral intrusion, developing into the theological and in turn into the dogmatic intrusion. For this Galileo's mumbled retraction, *E pur si muove!*—"and still the world moves" as science and not dogma decrees—stands as the dramatic summary. Similarly, congeniality is an intrusion. It appears in many guises, from the harmony of the spheres of Pythagoras to the benevolent intentions read by Lavater in human physiognomies. Such intrusions in later stages divert science from its profitable orbit. Persisting in tradition, they may take form from the prestige and power of constituted authority. These reflections from the history of science illuminate the selected panorama of *Wish and Wisdom.*

The difficulty of attaining a logical discipline emerges conspicuously from this survey of how minds go wrong. The straight path of reason is narrow, the tempting byways many and easier of access. It takes a vigorous, a clear-sighted mind to follow the one; the appeal of the other is as various as the sorts and conditions of men. Logic has never been a popular guest at the feast of reason and the flow of soul. Yet sanity is prized among the supreme virtues. It is in its interests that this excursion was undertaken.

The map of the excursion itself, the sign-posting of the route, followed upon the blazing of the trail and the reconnoitering of the territory. The divisions of the fauna and flora fell into a convenient and consistent arrangement; they were empirically derived and present in part a philosophy, but much more a clinical record. With the case histories before him, the reflective reader may well put the question: What are the major causes for the popularity of wish-wisdom? What the major temptations that beset the logical pilgrim's progress on the persistent quest for truth? What, by the same token, are the frailties of the mind as a logical instrument, which the enthusiast or

the exploiter utilizes, or to which—so far as he is sincere—
he himself succumbs?

The answer can be only my individual impression presented somewhat in the order of a scale of practical consequence. I place first *vagueness,* with its symbol, the cloud.
If you would impose, be cloudy, vaporous, misty; soar
under conditions of low visibility, trailing a smoke-screen
in your wake. Erratic beliefs like wraiths shun daylight;
clarity is their vital enemy. And man, by the very necessities of his mental existence—by the urgencies of expression
and communication—has, in the supreme invention of
language, forged the very instrument of his undoing.
Words make effective cloud-screens. As indispensably as
they express thought when used lucidly they may as effectively mask it, obscure it, conceal its absence. In all ages,
cultists and propagandists of a hollow or a shaky cause
resort to verbal screenery. The more successful become
adept in linguistic obfuscation. My reference is not to the
most common employment, the political appeal, nor to
rhetoric, which Huxley called the pestilent cosmetic
smearing the fair face of truth. My theme is limited to
beliefs and faiths which in intent make an appeal to fact.
In another reference, I have called this trend the lure of
the obscure, accounting for the wide prevalence of the cult
of the occult.

I place vagueness first not because it is "enemy number
one" to good order in the logical household, but because
when not itself the chief culprit, it is ever an accessory in
the crime. Nebulous thinking rears a large family. The
rape of reason is accomplished by the lure of *analogy* and
the decoy of the *symbol.* Their trail is evident in marvels
and miracles, in cultist philosophies, in congenial conclusions, in vagaries and attempted rationalization. On many
a tombstone of a defunct cult might be inscribed: Died of
persistently anemic analogy, or done to death by an over-

dose of symbols—which diagnoses apply equally to still active theories and practices. The same *mésalliance,* the same temper of mind, intensified and extended, leads directly to the mystic.

Mysticism has many aspects—notably in pursuit of religious inspiration—which fall outside my theme. Whatever the grounds for assuming knowledge which cannot be confined within the ordinary forms of apprehension and statement, it is evident that the assumption of a cloudy esoteric *mise en scène* is no ground whatever for supposing that what is thus beclouded has any value. There is the legitimately abstruse and the abstrusely illegitimate—more plainly, mysticism and pseudo-mysticism. Transplanted in time and space, the modern occult promotes "factories of fake thought." It is far too late in the mind's history to claim a private revelation, an esoteric perquisite, a secret value for any one's thought. One might as well make a mystery of the value of pi.

All this obscuration enthrones vagueness in an incense-cloud of cryptic words, many of them strayed or stolen from alien oriental cults. The cult of vocabulary ministers to whatever vague philosophy pleases one's taste or caters to one's vanity. Once the name is accepted, the suspicion that it may have a spurious reality never occurs to the convinced mind; or if it does, it knocks at a closed door. Like the certificates of mining stocks, they are so beautifully engraved that they must represent rare values! Of such is the family of vagueness.

The urge to vagueness or the lure of succumbing to it does not proceed without protest or resistance. The conflict, whether or not it has a Freudian setting, is between that urge and the opposing one to seek foundation in fact. There is among our packet of prides the conceit of intellect, the dignity of the support of reason; the pride of rationality must also be satisfied. The esoteric soarer insists that his locomotion proceeds upon the *terra firma* of fact. Here is the second great divide which sets apart those who roam within and those who wander away from the straight logical path. Their defection results from a *feeble sense for fact*. In pronounced cases the diagnosis might read: fairly normal otherwise but feeble-minded for fact. That species belongs to a large family; their party affiliation is with wish when it opposes wisdom. The occultist, and the erratic thinker of other stripe, wants to have his cake of superior understanding and to eat that of accredited fact too.

In one mood the visionary may insist that the half-lights of his cloudland are adequate for realistic vision; in another, that his loyalty to fact is in no wise impaired by his ability to rise above it. That the visionary has his "facts" admits of no doubt. But their validity is another matter. To discuss it, we must bring to the footlights a most widespread fallacy commonly disregarded: that facts, like the rock of ages, are there by original dispensation—obvious, immutable, unshakeable! Some facts are; but even brutal ones, such as tumors and broken bones, may, by ardent cultists, become subjects for denial. Between facts ignored and facts fabricated, the realm of fact must itself steer a careful course.

The senses are indeed sentinels, but they are also sirens. When off guard, or in compliant mood, we see what we wish to see or are told is there to behold. Influential as is that distortion of vision, in the statistical mass of misleads, prepossession and faith-yielding are exceeded by the faulty sense of proof. There is no proposition in theory or practice for which its defenders cannot accumulate evidence with a vengeance. You can do so for any thesis, if you are impressed by quantity and disregard quality. To put it with didactic clarity: it is the *quality* of a fact that counts

—its assay and hall-mark under rigid examination. One fact critically established is worth a thousand loosely arrived at. All theories find confirmation, all cures work; and the theorist and the panaceist obtain the firm sense of security and loyalty to reality. They are buttressed by testimonials and hand-picked instances of corroboration. It is still pertinent to recall the words of Oliver Wendell Holmes: "Stretched like an impenetrable shield to protect the weakest advocate . . . against the weapons of the adversary, was that omnipotent monosyllable which has always been the patrimony of cheats and the currency of dupes from time immemorial—Facts! Facts! Facts!"

It is an old but still needed lesson that the determination of fact is as difficult a procedure as its interpretation; that most "facts" arrive with their interpretations so tightly wrapped around them that the separation of the fact from its envelope is precisely the expert's art.

There is hardly a story in my collection that fails to illustrate the point; the misleading envelope is in some instances derived from a prepossession set in a cloud, but not in all cases. Some vagaries are definite enough to be called specific, but are groundless. Examine the supposed ground for their support and you may again encounter a theory in the background of the vagarist's mind. There is, however, a different type of misfact which is not a mistake, but may be briefly disposed of as a varnished or an unvarnished lie. The fakir and the enthusiast and the fanatic indulge in an abundance of statements which are just not so. They would be so convincing if true that they are cited irresponsibly; naturally many of them do not merit disproof, or in their very nature cannot be disproved, since they are out of line of any rational experiment. Yet latterly the very sanctum of science has been invaded by the more pretentious thought-fakirs who apply the word "research" to their strange occupations. There is no god

whose name is so commonly taken in vain as that of
science, and the "fact" is his prophet.

A further item in the inventory of errors is the general
supposition—when strong a conviction, when moderate a
hospitality shading to an inclination—to posit or entertain
the reality of another world than that of physics and
chemistry and physiology, a world exempt from their laws
and subject to laws of its own, which those adept feel competent to deduce or somehow ascertain. Were it not for
this universal predilection, my harvest would have been
leaner. Anent the rationale of this urge there is much to
be said. Stated broadly, it sets forth that the bread of
reason—least of all the crust of logic—does not satisfy the
emotional cravings for the life abundant. Stated more narrowly, it reminds us that today the traditional faiths have
failed, leaving the emancipated multitudes at once dis-
illusioned and deprived of any measure of devotional thrill
under the new rationalistic dispensation. They find crumbs
of comfort in the pseudologies and the vaporous uplift
movements, which give them a warm, even superheated,
sense of their personal significance. This cannot be gain-
said; and it is left to each thinker to decide what price he
will pay for cherishing a reserved area for that indulgence.
Private worlds, even when shared by others of like tendencies, carry their hazard even as they confer their boon.
Everyone believes, as James emphasized, at his own risk.

Those more loyal to logical standards appeal to the very
triumphs of science to defend their extra-logical excursions. If X-rays, why not cryptesthesia? If cosmic waves,
why not mental waves? If potent radio-activity, why not
equally potent super-psychic powers? All of which brings
us again to seductive analogies remodeled to twentieth-
century patterns. The rebuttal I have already indicated:
the entire habits of thought out of which these physical

discoveries have come is of other fabric than that which entertains their alien analogies.

Scientific thought has established certain definite boundary lines, where, despite proximity, there is a deep chasm of separation. Walking on the earth's surface is a commonplace; walking on a cushion of air just one inch above the earth would be a miracle. Admittedly in the domain of psychic powers, such great divides are not readily located. Yet the appeal to the "more things in heaven and earth than are dreamt of in our philosophies" is often a resort of those with slight understanding of what "our philosophies" quite adequately explain. The psychologist particularly should recognize the claims of the unexplored frontiers of our being.

Where the personal factor dominates, complete objectivity becomes a counsel of perfection. It is our own revelations and coincidences which seem providential, our own "phantasms of the living," our own strange communions and premonitions, that carry a conviction which makes those of others seem distant and cold. Overestimating personal experience is itself a temptation; through our temperamental divides, experience affects us differently. Sir Walter Scott said that he did not believe in ghosts— he had seen too many of them; others believe because they have seen just one.

Yet I may properly offer the comparative study of the erratic, in which each theory, vision, or faith so flatly contradicts all others, or is so completely out of relation with them, as a reciprocal and manifold refutation. The implausibility of the whole weakens the plausibility of any portion. No mind that remained hospitable to a large selection of these philosophies could keep sane. And this is our final criterion: the sanity of belief. It is only a loyalty to a world in which wish and wisdom are rightly proportioned that can further the higher sanity.

INDEX

There has been no attempt to make this index exhaustive in small details, particularly under the main titles and names indicated in the table of contents. Subtitles within chapters are included when distinctive. With some exceptions, the general concepts around which the thesis turns—such as belief, error, doctrine, fallacy, prepossession, vagary, superstition, wisdom, wish—likewise do not appear in the index. These are considered in their logical and psychological aspects in the introductory essay, in the arguments, and in the afterword. For the rest, as illustrations of principles and summaries of conclusions, they find their place in the appropriate episodes where the reader acquainted with the work will readily find them.

391